KU-183-630

Food and Drink sections. He also added the final chapter on sights around Prague and the new sections on Language and Further Reading.

Maria Lord updated and rewrote the chapters on Music, Art and Architecture, and thoroughly overhauled the Places section. She wrote the new chapters on Holešovice to Bílá Hora, Smíchov and Barrandov, and Vinohrady and Žižkov, as well as the Photo Features on the National Gallery, Communist Prague and Czech Modernism, and the box on Czech Film. She also added to and updated the final sections on Transport, Accommodation, Activities and Practical Information.

This book builds on the earlier editions, which were edited by **Cameron Duffy**, **Zoë Ross**, **Joachim Chwaszcza** and **Pam Barrett**. Previous updaters who worked on the book include **Jennifer Anne Perez**, **Andrew Steven Harris**, **Martha Lagace** and **Mimi Fronczak Rogers**. The original contributors were **Joachim and Christine Chwaszcza, Eva Meschede, Ota Filip, Vilem Wagner, Johanna von Herzongenberg, Frantisek Kafka** and **Franz Peter Künzel**.

Many of the photographs are the work of **Glyn Genin** and **Pete Bennett**, regular photographers for both Insight Guides and Berlitz Pocket Guides, as well as the Prague-based photographer **Richard Nebesky**. Picture research was carried out by **Jenny Kraus**, the book was proofread by **Neil Titman** and the index was compiled by **Elizabeth Cook**.

The contributors

This thoroughly revised edition of *Insight City Guide: Prague* has been updated by **Maria Lord** and **Mike Ivory**. Much of the text has been rewritten and a number of new chapters added to reflect the changing face of this beautiful city.

Prague has been at the forefront of European history for centuries, from the Middle Ages when it was the residence of the Holy Roman Emperor, to the political upheavals of 1989. Emerging from this at the beginning of the 1990s, Prague found itself the most popular destination for visitors in Central Europe, and this guide looks at both the turmoil of its history and the contemporary city.

For this latest edition, Mike Ivory rewrote the History, Literature, and

CONTACTING THE EDITORS

We would appreciate it if readers would alert us to errors or outdated information by writing to:

Insight Guides, P.O. Box 7910, London SE1 1WE, England.
Fax: (44) 20 7403-0290.
insight@apaguide.co.uk

www.insightguides.com

Discovery
CHANNEL

Maps

Travel Tips

THE BEST OF PRAGUE

Unique attractions, eating and drinking, music and galleries... here, at a glance, are our recommendations for a stay in the city

ONLY IN PRAGUE

- **Old Town Square.** One of the most beautiful urban spaces in Central Europe. *See page 121.*
- **Astronomical Clock.** Prague's medieval timepiece, complete with animated models is a favourite sight. *See page 124.*
- **The Charles Bridge.** This beautful Gothic crossing is decorated with numerous Baroque statues. *See pages 116–7.*

- **Prague Castle.** The seat of power, and with an unmistakable silhouette, it has been pivotal in the city's history for centuries. *See page 77.*
- **The Vltava** The river runs though the heart of the city, providing inspiration to many Czech artists.
- **Wenceslas Square.** Heart of the New Town and scene of dramatic political events. *See page 147.*

RIGHT: the lovely Baroque pilgrimage church of the Loreta.

LEFT: the astrological face of the Old Town Hall clock, designed by the 19th-century artist Josef Mánes.

CHURCHES AND MONASTERIES

- **The Týn.** The Týn's distinctive towers dominate Old Town Square. *See page 122.*
- **St Vitus's.** Prague's cathedral is a masterpiece of Gothic architecture. *See page 81.*
- **St Nicholas's.** This glorious Baroque building is one of the city's highlights. *See page 102.*
- **The Strahov.** A monastery complex

with two exquisite Baroque libraries. *See page 96.*
- **The Loreta.** The replica of the *Casa Santa* here draws many pilgrims. *See page 94.*
- **Church of the Holy Heart.** Josip Plečnik's extraordinary Modernist fantasy. *See page 190.*
- **St George's Basilica.** The city's finest surviving Romanesque structure. *See page 86.*

WALKS

- **The Royal Way**. Walking from the Powder Tower by náměstí Republiky, along Celetná, across Old Town Square, down Karlova, across the Charles Bridge and up Nerudova to the castle takes you past many of the city's finest sights and also retraces the coronation route of the Bohemian kings.

- **Across Petřín Hill**. Start by the Kinsky Villa, climb up through the park and follow the hill round, ending up in the beautiful castle gardens.
- **Along the Vltava**. Walking along the river embankments from the Čechův most to Vyšehrad gives you wonderful views and a fascinating slice of city life.

RIGHT: looking down from Petřín Hill to the Church of St Nicholas and Malá Strana.
BELOW: Stromovka in the north of the city is a lovely place to play and relax.

PRAGUE FOR CHILDREN

- **The Story of Prague Castle**. A new exhibition with games and interactive screens. *See page 86.*
- **Zrcadlové bludiště**. A distorting mirror maze on Petřín Hill. *See page 113.*
- **Fata Morgana Greenhouse**. This new glasshouse is steamy and verdant, with a walk-through tropical aquarium. *See page 178.*

- **The National Technical Museum**. A treasure house of steam engines, planes and models. *See page 169.*
- **Historic Tram Ride**. Old tram 91 takes you around the city centre. *See page 179.*
- **Parks**. Prague's many green spaces provide great scope for outdoor play and adventure. *See page 8.*

CLASSICAL MUSIC VENUES

- **The Rudolfinum**. This splendid concert hall is home to the Czech Philharmonic, one of the world's greatest orchestras. *See page 129.*
- **Obecní dům**. A glorious Art-Nouveau building with a stunning concert hall. The Prague Symphony Orchestra are resident here. *See page 126.*
- **Statní opera**. A lovely auditorium; the company are noted for their adventurous productions of opera and ballet. *See page 149.*
- **Národní divadlo**. The National Theatre is the place to see performances of Czech classics like *The Bartered Bride*. *See page 153.*
- **The Estates Theatre**. A beautiful opera house; Mozart's *Don Giovanni* was first performed here. *See page 132.*

RIGHT: one of Bohemia's greatest composers, Antonín Dvořák.

OPEN SPACES

- **Stromovka.**
  A large wooded park, once a royal hunting ground. *See page 176.*
- **Letná Park.**
  Set above the river with great views over the city. *See page 169.*
- **Petřín Hill.**
  Above Malá Strana is central Prague's largest stretch of green. *See page 112.*
- **University Botanical Gardens.**
  A haven of peace in Nové Město. *See page 156.*
- **Prague Botanical Gardens.**
  Extensive gardens and a superb glasshouse. *See page 178.*

- **Kinsky Gardens.**
  Above the deep, green lawns is a delightful wooded hillside. *See page 183.*
- **Kampa Park.**
  A small, civilised patch of green beside the river. *See page 110.*
- **Waldstein Gardens.**
  A delightful pool and fake grotto in Malá Strana. *See page 106.*
- **Prague Castle Gardens.**
  Beautiful formal gardens spread over the castle ramparts. *See page 88.*
- **Vrtba Gardens.**
  An exquisite Baroque garden with lovely views. *See page 107.*

ABOVE: the Japanese Garden, just one of the delightful landscaped sections of the Prague Botanical Gardens; further up the hill is the new Fata Morgana glasshouse.
BELOW: the beautifully restored Museum Kampa is one of Prague's best showcases for contemporary art.

MUSEUMS AND GALLERIES

- **The National Gallery.**
  The many parts of the national collections have some outstanding works of art, from medieval to contemporary works. *See pages 90–1.*
- **Lapidarium.**
  The city's collection of public sculpture, including the orginals from the Charles Bridge. *See page 175.*
- **Náprstek Museum.**
  A stunning collection of ethnographic material from Africa, Asia and Oceania. *See page 131.*
- **Jewish Museum.**
  The synagogues of Prague make up this museum of Jewish history and culture. *See page 139.*

- **City of Prague Museum.**
  A fascinating tour through the city's history. *See page 151.*
- **Decorative Arts Museum.**
  A great collection beautifully displayed; one of the best in the city. *See page 128.*
- **City Transport Museum.**
  Trams and buses galore. *See page 179.*
- **Dvořák Museum.**
  Dedicated to the life of the famous composer. *See page 157.*
- **National Museum.**
  A huge, if idiosyncratic, collection. *See page 149.*
- **Museum Kampa.**
  A chic space for contemporary art. *See page 110.*

PLACES TO EAT

- **Allegro**.
  Consistently voted the best in the city. *See page 133.*
- **Arzenal**.
  Designer glass and hot Thai cusine. *See page 133.*
- **Cicala**.
  Delicious and authentic Italian cooking. *See page 158.*
- **David**.
  Stylish food and delightful service. *See page 114.*
- **Flambée**.
  Rich and delicious French dishes. *See page 134.*

- **Kampa Park**.
  Beautiful fish, views and people. *See page 114.*
- **Pálffy Palác**.
  Classy dining in aristocratic surroundings. *See page 114.*
- **U Maltézských rytířů**. A lovely Malá Strana cellar restaurant. *See page 115.*
- **U patrona**.
  Classic Bohemian dishes and polished service. *See page 115.*
- **V zátiší**.
  Beautifully cooked food and welcoming staff. *See page 135.*

ABOVE: many of Prague's bars and restaurants are set in atmospheric cellars.
BELOW: Frank Gehry and Vlado Milunič's astonishing and controversial "Fred and Ginger" building.

CAFÉS, PUBS AND BARS

- **Café Slavia**.
  A Prague institution overlooking the river and National Theatre. *See page 134.*
- **Cukrkávalimonáda**.
  Small and sweet, with great breakfasts. *See page 114.*
- **Pivovarský dům**.
  A micro-brewery with great, and unusual, beers. *See page 159.*
- **Square**.
  Chic and slick on Malostranské náměstí. *See page 115.*

- **St Nicholas Café**.
  While away the evening in this relaxed cellar bar. *See page 115.*
- **Tretter's**.
  Prague's best cocktails; delicious drinks with class. *See page 143.*
- **U černého vola**.
  Widely held to be best the best pub in the city, with superb beer. *See page 99.*
- **U medvídků**.
  A classic Prague beer hall with decent food. *See page 135.*

PRAGUE'S ARCHITECTURE

Much of Prague's glory lies in the fabric of the city and its wonderfully preserved architecture, which ranges from early Romanesque basilicas, to Gothic and Baroque churches, to iconic examples of Modernist housing.

Romanesque The earliest buildings in Prague date back to the 11th century, of which the **Basilica of St George** is the best preserved.

Gothic the most glorious example of Gothic architecture in Prague is undoubtedly **St Vitus's Cathedral**, but other wonderful Gothic constructions include the **Charles Bridge** and the **Vladislav Hall**.

Renaissance In the gardens of Prague Castle are two charming buildings, the sgraffitoed **Ball Court** and the elegant **Belvedér**.

Baroque The twin churches of **St Nicholas**, one in Malá Strana the other just off Old Town Square, are perhaps the most wonderful examples of Baroque architecture in a city with many fine, ornate buildings.

Art Nouveau The glorious **Obecní dům** is Prague's most celebrated example of Art Nouveau, but other fine buildings can be found along Wenceslas Square, in particular the **Hotel Evropa**.

Modernist and Contemporary Prague's hidden treasures are its revolutionary Cubist and Functionalist houses. The cluster of three **Cubist buildings** in Vyšehrad and the boldly Modernist **Baba Estate** are among the finest examples. Newer additions to Prague's skyline include **Danube House** and the **Tančící dům**.

THE HEART OF EUROPE

Beautiful and mysterious, charming and seedy,
boisterous and withdrawn... Prague is an intriguing
paradox, and its inhabitants make this one of
Europe's most fascinating destinations

Prague is a paradox; at least that is the view of Czech writer Ivan Klíma in his short essay *The Spirit of Prague*. On the one hand it is the mystical, alchemical city of popular imagination, on the other a prosaic world of beerhalls and dumplings. Is it the city of Old Town winding alleys or the bold vista of Wenceslas Square? A city of revolution, from the 15th century Hussites to the grand gestures of 1968 and 1989, or one which has quietly retreated into itself under autocratic regimes, from the Habsburgs to the period of "normalisation" following the Prague Spring?

The truth is, of course, that Prague is all of this and more. This endless dichotomy is summed up in the writers – almost exact contemporaries – Franz Kafka and Jaroslav Hašek. One German-speaking and Jewish, the other Czech and Catholic (though neither had much time for organised religion, seemingly a characteristic of the city's inhabitants). And Kafka's Joseph K. of *The Trial* and Hašek's Josef Švejk could not, it appears, be more different, yet both defy authority through subversive inaction (a tactic sometimes bemoaned by the Czechs of themselves). It might also be argued that the city's position at the heart of Europe – literally and metaphorically, at the crossroads of Catholic and Protestant, Germanic and Slav, Gothic and Baroque – makes Prague a unique summation of, and gives it a unique perspective on, the European human condition.

Although the charmingly naive optimism that followed the Velvet Revolution has now died down – not least as the Czechs face up to life under capitalism, membership of the EU and NATO, and a string of corruption scandals – there is still a sense that this is a city rediscovering and reinventing its past, and Prague remains a delightful, and not least beautiful, place to visit. All year round hordes of tourists descend on the city, yet Prague remains essentially Bohemian. And while its days as a European centre of writers and artists have all but vanished, much has been preserved. There are magical squares, with their mysterious play of light and shadow, and music on every corner. And in its narrow streets it is almost possible to imagine that Rabbi Löw's Golem, the clay monster which came to life, might still be lurking somewhere, out of sight. ❑

PRECEDING PAGES: golden light on the Charles Bridge; the Klementinum's fabulous Baroque library. **LEFT:** Hradčany's atmospheric back streets.

FROM LIBUŠE TO THE HABSBURGS

From the first romantic and mythical dynasty to the
first dukes and kings, Prague began to develop
into an important hub of European trade

The foundation of Prague is surrounded by myth. According to legend, Princess Libuše, ruler of a Slav tribe which had always been led by women, chose a humble ploughman, Přemysl, as her husband. She instructed him to seek out a village on the banks of the Vltava and to found a city there, for which she prophesied great things. According to the legend, Přemysl led a group of followers to the place Libuše described and there founded the Golden City of Prague.

The rise of the Přemyslid dynasty

Legend apart, archaeologists confirm that the Prague area has been inhabited since Neolithic times. Celts settled here around 400 BC, Germanic tribes joined them some four centuries later, and Slavs arrived in the 6th century AD. Power struggles were waged for several centuries, and it is probably the emergence of the Přemyslids as the ruling dynasty that engendered the myth of Princess Libuše and the ploughman. The evolution of the city as the political and cultural centre of Bohemia is tied with the rise to power of this dynasty. The battle for supremacy in the Bohemian and Moravian regions between the Slavníkovci and the Přemyslids was won by the latter towards the end of the 9th century. Their rulers moved to a strategic rocky outcrop on the right bank of the Vltava, and built their first stronghold.

Settlements developed in the area below, at first inhabited by people directly supplying the

castle, but later by craftsmen. In the early 10th century the Vyšehrad was built, on the same bank of the Vltava *(see pages 160–3)*, but some distance south of the old castle. The Hradčany was founded later, on an equally commanding left-bank site *(see page 77)*. The Přemyslids consolidated a political base as the nucleus of the Bohemian state. Prague quickly became an important centre for trade.

The founding of the bishopric

A decisive point in the development of Prague was the success of Boleslav II (967–1035) in obtaining the consent of the Holy Roman Emperor for the founding of a bishopric in

---

LEFT: Charles IV, from a votive tablet by Johann Ocko.
RIGHT: Libuše, founder of Prague.

AD 973. The first bishop was the monk Vojtěch (or Adalbert), appointed in AD 982. Vojtěch was forced to flee Prague on several occasions and died a martyr's death on the shores of the Baltic. His relics were seized by Boleslav's successor, Břetislav I (1035–55), and brought back to the city. The plan to use the relics to raise the status of Prague's cathedral failed, but Prague greatly increased in international importance during Břetislav's reign. His greatest achievement was the union of Moravia and Bohemia, although he was forced to recognise his dependence on the German Empire.

Břetislav's successor Spytihněv II (1055–61) expelled German merchants from Prague

and built St Vitus's Basilica. His successor, Duke Vratislav I (1061–92), proved an ally of Henry IV, who made him King of Bohemia.

The market place of Prague

Prague market place is first documented in the late 11th century. It was situated in the area of the Old Town Square (Staroměstské náměstí). In the early 12th century this began to develop into a settlement, becoming known as the Old Town (Staré Město). In the ensuing construction boom, the Romanesque style spread, as the churches dating from this time show.

Soběslav I (1125–40) completed the alterations to the Vyšehrad, begun by Vratislav II. The Romanesque churches and the castle citadel were completed and the clay walls replaced with stone fortifications. Soběslav also encouraged the expansion of trade. Under his patronage, the Vyšehrad Cathedral Chapter produced the Vyšehrad Codex, a richly decorated manuscript.

King Vladislav I (1140–72) moved the ruler's residence to Hradčany, founded Strahov Monastery, built a royal palace, extended St Vitus's, and started construction of the stone Judith Bridge.

In 1170, in about the same place as today's Charles Bridge, King Přemysl Otakar I (1198–1230) completed the building of the Judith Bridge, creating a permanent link between the castle and the Old Town. On the opposite bank he also founded the community known as Malá Strana, which became the home of skilled workers, carters and fishermen. Bohemia rose to become an important Central European power and Prague an international meeting place.

Extraordinary privilege

By 1230 the Old Town had been given borough status and, in 1231, King Wenceslas I (1230–53) defended it with a system of walls and fortifications. The building of a city wall was a sign of extraordinary privilege: it protected the city from outside attack and bestowed freedom on its citizens, encouraging people to settle here. The Old Town was administered by a judge appointed by the king, and by councillors elected by patrician families. A Jewish quarter was established, ruled directly by the king. In 1257 the Malá Strana was granted the privileges of a city, and Hradčany followed, developing as the district of the aristocracy and clergy. Thus at the beginning of the 14th century, Prague consisted of three towns, each administratively independent and socially and demographically distinct.

The Imperial capital

In the middle of the 13th century the fortunes of Bohemia and therefore of Prague were determined by the political and military successes of King Přemysl Otakar II (1253–78). His power, which rested on the vast wealth derived from the silver mines of Bohemia, rose steadily until he reached a position of

Rudolf of Habsburg, then Henry again. The Přemyslid dynasty finally came to an end when the young Wenceslas III, the last of the line, was assassinated in 1306 during a campaign in Poland.

The times were marked by political power struggles, in which the patrician families of Prague took part with varied success. The city was besieged, laid waste and plundered several times. In 1310, the Bohemian Estates chose John of Luxembourg (1296–1346) as their new king. John was intensely – and expensively – involved in imperial politics and spent most of his time out of the country. Prague Castle gradually fell into decay.

hegemony in Central Europe. He advanced into Hungary and Slovakia and pushed the frontiers of Bohemia as far as the Adriatic. He won the respect of both Pope and Holy Roman Emperor, but then died at the Battle of Dürnkrut fighting Rudolf of Habsburg, who considered the Czech king his greatest rival. The crisis concerning succession was partially alleviated when the claims of King Wenceslas II to the Polish throne were recognised. For a while Henry of Carinthia, Wenceslas II's brother-in-law, ruled, then

Emperor Charles IV

John's son, who was to become Charles IV, was born in Prague in 1316 and spent his early years there. But in 1323 he was sent to Paris to the court of his uncle, the King of France, where his education was entrusted to the future Pope Clement VI. Young Charles fell in love with all things French and abandoned his baptismal name of Wenceslas, adopting that of Charlemagne ("Charles the Great"), after his role model and personal patron. He studied at the University of Paris and travelled through Europe, absorbing the languages and cultures of the various nations. He later married the equally cultured Blanche of Valois. In 1333,

LEFT: statue on the tomb of Ottokar I, Sv. Vitus.
ABOVE: Charles IV with the imperial regalia.

still aged only 17, he was made governor of Bohemia and Moravia. Despite his youth, Charles had gained invaluable experience from his travels and education, and sought to bring prosperity to the country. One of his first acts was to rebuild Prague Castle, remodelling it on buildings he had admired in France.

When John was killed fighting the English on the battlefield of Crécy in 1346, Charles was elected King of the Germans and, one year later, King of Bohemia. In 1355 he was crowned Holy Roman Emperor. He chose Prague as his permanent residence and set about making the city the political and cultural hub of Central Europe.

PREACHER OF THE PEOPLE

Jan Hus (John Huss in English) was born around 1370 in Husinec, southern Bohemia. He became a priest in 1400 and was influenced by the English theologian John Wyclif (1324–84). Like Wyclif, Hus urged a return to the Bible and greater involvement of the clergy with the common people. He made fiery speeches against the worldliness of the Church and the immorality of clerics. Forbidden to preach by the Archbishop of Prague, he refused to obey. He was expelled from Prague, then in 1415 summoned to appear before a grand council at Constance. He was tried, found guilty of heresy, and burnt at the stake.

Charles University

Prague gained considerably in cultural importance when the university – the first in Central Europe – was built. Charles IV granted the official founding charter on 7 April 1348. The Charles University was intended to draw together scholars from all regions of the empire, and had a similar constitution to that of Charles's Alma Mater, the University of Paris. It was divided into four "nations": Bohemian, Bavarian, Saxon and Polish. These did not represent national groupings, but symbolised the four points of the compass by giving them the name of the nearest neighbour in that direction. Each "nation" had a vote in the university's decision-making, and the posts of rector and chancellor were filled by each "nation" in turn.

To begin with, lectures were held in churches and in the Lazarus House in the Jewish Quarter. The move to the Carolinum, today one of the oldest university buildings in the world, did not take place until 1356. Charles, who was a writer himself and one of the few educated medieval rulers, was able to gather leading thinkers and scholars of his time around him, including such luminaries as Cola di Rienzi and Ernest of Pardubice, who later became Archbishop of Prague.

A masterpiece of civic planning

Charles made his most noticeable mark on the development of Prague, however, by founding the New Town (Nové Město) and thereby almost doubling the city's area.

Laid out beyond the walls enclosing the Old Town, this extraordinary urban project incorporated small settlements and several monasteries, among them the convent of Our Lady of the Snows and the Emmaus Monastery, which were founded in 1347 and planned to fit in with the designs for the New Town. Also in 1347, the foundation stone of the Charles Church was laid.

Neither the plans nor the name of the architect have survived, but an analysis of the basic town plan, which remained almost unaltered until well into the 19th century, shows clear evidence of creative and far-sighted planning. The official founding charter was granted by Charles on 3 March 1348 – probably the day on which the foundation stone for the city wall was laid. Settlers who wanted to live in the New Town were assigned plots of land and, in return for tax concessions, had to complete their houses within 18 months.

The New Town consisted of four large sections: the central section was laid out around the Horse Market (now Wenceslas Square), the southern section around the Cattle Market (now Charles Square), while the north was dominated by the merchant street of Hybernská and the Hay Market (which has kept its name – Senovážné náměstí). The lower area, the former settlement of Slup, planted with orchards and vineyards, was hardly built up at all, and much of it remained free of development until well into the 19th century.

The scale of the plan is remarkable. Ječná (Barley Street) is nearly 27 metres (89 ft) wide, and Charles Square, with a length of 520 metres (1,706 ft) and an area of 8 hectares (20 acres), is the largest square in Europe. Nor were Charles's building schemes confined to the castle and the New Town. On the left bank of the Vltava a new wall was built and the area of the Malá Strana increased considerably. At the same time, building began on Petřín Hill.

The Hradčany settlement was also fortified. Part of this fortification is known as the "Hunger Wall" because Charles ordered its construction during a time of widespread poverty in order to provide employment. In the Old Town, too, the monastery and St James's Church were rebuilt, alterations made to the churches of St Aegidius, St Martin, St Castullus, St Gall and St Nicholas, and the Church of the Holy Ghost was constructed.

After the boom time of Charles's rule, Prague, at the end of the 14th century, consisted of two castles and four towns with an area of 800 hectares (2,000 acres) and a population of over 50,000, making it one of Europe's largest cities. Within its walls were around 100 monasteries, churches and chapels and several dozen markets. Prague had been promoted to an Imperial residence, an archdiocese, the seat of a papal legate, and a university town. The money minted at Kutná Hora *(see pages 206–7)* served as the currency for the entire region. In alliance

with the kings, foreign merchants, notably Germans and Italians, became economically and politically powerful.

First signs of unrest

But social stability was undermined by the emergence of guilds of craftsmen which were often torn by internal conflicts. Poor inhabitants provided a further volatile element, as the taxes necessary to fund the Emperor's expensive projects placed a disproportionate burden on the poor. When Charles IV died on 29 November 1378, he left Prague with a lot of building sites and a lot of problems smouldering under the surface. Nevertheless, he was one of Europe's

outstanding figures, and his country undoubtedly flourished during his reign.

Wenceslas IV

Charles's son, Wenceslas IV, faced strong political opposition within the Empire and had to accept a considerable loss of authority. Prague decreased in importance; building work slowed down, and economic difficulties led to a depression that brought social unrest. The dissatisfaction of large sections of the population, especially the poverty-stricken (mostly Czech) inhabitants of the New Town, was focused on the rich (mostly foreign) patrician families and on the clergy.

LEFT: Jan Hus, who attacked the church's worldliness.
RIGHT: Wenceslas IV, who faced economic problems.

In 14th-century Europe, opposition to the luxurious and often immoral lifestyle of the monastic orders was growing. In Prague they had already come under critical fire during the reign of Charles IV. In the mid-14th century, Konrad Waldhauser (d. 1369) and Jan Milič of Kroměříž (d. 1374) were prominent preachers who attacked lax monastic lifestyles.

In 1391, the Bethlehem Chapel was founded *(see page 131)*. The simplicity of its exterior (the chapel was rebuilt to original plans in 1950–3) marks it as a response to criticisms of decadence. In 1402, the religious reformer Jan Hus (*circa* 1370–1415) began to preach here against the worldliness and corruption of the church.

were outraged; many of them, together with their students, moved out of Prague and began an Empire-wide campaign against the university. Prague's clergy reacted with a series of arrests and repressive measures. Hus himself was tried and executed in 1415 *(see panel, page 20)*, but trouble continued, fomented by another radical preacher, Jan Želivský.

The first defenestration

Escalation of the conflict came on 30 July 1419, when an angry mob led by Želivský marched to the Town Hall in the New Town and demanded the release of a group of Hussite prisoners. The councillors refused, and the

The Hussite Wars

Hus's ideas for reform were very popular among Prague's citizens, and even with Wenceslas IV, but the Church hierarchy, not without reason, regarded him as their enemy.

In 1398, Hus was appointed to the university as professor of philosophy. Here he continued to expound his ideas, but he was defeated in a vote by the "nations" – most academics condemned his thinking. In 1409, the dispute reached a crisis: it was no longer purely a theological quarrel, but had nationalist overtones. When Hus's supporters obtained a decree granting the "Bohemian nation" in the university a majority of votes, German academics

enraged citizens stormed the building, hurling the councillors and seven other citizens from the window to their deaths. This initiated the peculiar Prague tradition of dealing with one's opponents by "defenestrating" them. Unrest spread rapidly. The Hussites occupied the Town Hall and elected their own councillors. Wenceslas made no effort to suppress them and, in August, approved the new appointments. Perhaps he hoped to calm the conflict, but the signal came too late. Wenceslas IV died on 16 August 1419. The next day, the Hussites stormed the Carthusian monastery in Ujezd and continued the revolution.

For a decade and a half, much of Central

Europe experienced terror and destruction, as fanatical Hussite troops rampaged across the region, initially under the inspired military leadership of a blind squire from southern Bohemia named Jan Žižka. In 1420, the Hussites won a notable victory on Prague's Vítkov Hill, when their plebeian soldiery massacred the heavily armoured knights of the Imperial army. Eventually the storm blew itself out. The Hussites split into two factions, the more moderate calling themselves Utraquists. In 1434, the Utraquists allied themselves with Catholic forces and routed their radical opponents at the Battle of Lipany. In 1458, the people of Prague acclaimed an Utraquist nobleman, George of Poděbrady, as their king. George ruled Bohemia for 13 years, and Prague, laid waste by the revolution, blossomed once more. George had the towers of the Týn Church and the Bridge Tower in the Malá Strana built. But he had little more to do before Rome incited the people against the "heretic king".

During the rule of George's successor, Prince Vladislav II of the Polish Jagiellon dynasty (1471–1516), another defenestration occurred. Vladislav had let the Catholics back in. They occupied the Old Town Hall, arming themselves against the Utraquists. But their dark plots were made public, and on 26 September 1483 an angry group of people stormed the Town Hall and threw the spokesman and the mayor of the Old Town out of the window.

In 1484, Catholics and Utraquists made peace once more, with the Treaty of Kutná Hora. The unrest had badly upset Vladislav, whose residence was in the royal palace in the Old Town. He decided to move out of the restless city to the castle, which he then had renovated. The masterpiece of the renovation is the late-Gothic Vladislav Hall, designed by Benedikt Ried (1454–1534).

In the early 16th century, the teachings of Martin Luther led to a split among the Utraquists. The Old Utraquists were against the Reformation; the New Utraquists supported it. Catholicism also found support in the reign of Vladislav's son Louis (1516–26). Following Louis's death while fighting the

Turks in Hungary, another ruler had to be elected; the choice – the Austrian Archduke Ferdinand I of Habsburg (1526–64) – turned out to be a fatal one.

Habsburg rule

During Ferdinand's reign Prague became the most important prop of Habsburg rule, and Rome found more support for its fight against the Utraquists. The Hussite era now moved to its end. Ferdinand soon quarrelled with representatives of the Bohemian nobility and relieved them of political power.

Ferdinand left his mark on the city with the construction of the Summer Palace or

Belvedér, which finally helped the Renaissance to establish itself in Prague. The Belvedér, on a hill opposite the Hradčany, made the Bohemian nobility aware of the architectural innovations begun in Italy, and many of them built or rebuilt their palaces in the latest Italian style. The Schwarzenberg Palace in Hradčany (originally built by the Lobkowicz family and previously the home of the Military Museum) is a fine example *(see page 78)*. Before this, however, there was more fighting to be done.

In 1546 open conflict broke out once more. Ferdinand went to war against the Protestant German princes, although the Bohemian

LEFT: a paneful death – *The Defenestration of 1618* by Wenzel von Broznik (1851–1901).
RIGHT: Rudolf II, who was obsessed by the occult.

nobility refused to support him in a war against their religious brethren. However, the king returned victorious, with one thought clearly in mind: revenge. All the privileges won in Hussite times were taken away, all public property was surrendered to the crown, and the way made open for the return to power of the Catholic Church. In 1561, Ferdinand appointed a new Bishop of Prague – a post which had not been filled since the Hussite revolution.

A cultural rebirth

Despite its loss of political independence, Prague acquired new prominence in 1583,

when it became the residence of a new ruler, Emperor Rudolf II. Many historians compare the Rudolfine era with the glorious reign of Charles IV, though there could hardly be a greater contrast than that between the visionary, dynamic Charles and the reclusive, eccentric Rudolf. Obsessed with astrology, alchemy, the occult, and other strange byways of science, the Emperor was also a passionate collector and patron of the arts. Life came back to the city, as scholars, scientists, painters, sculptors and craftsmen of all kinds were attracted to Rudolf's cosmopolitan court, among them a not inconsiderable number of quacks, charlatans and adventurers. Among

the treasures amassed by the Emperor were paintings by his favourites, Dürer and Pieter Brueghel the Elder. If unable to get hold of the original, he had it copied by Jan Brueghel or Pieter the Younger. Rudolf also acquired paintings by other leading artists of the Renaissance: Titian, Leonardo, Michelangelo, Raphael, Bosch and Correggio. Meanwhile, alchemists like the earless Englishman Edward Kelley toiled in the castle laboratories attempting vainly to turn base metal into gold, while more reputable savants such as astronomers Tycho Brahe and Johannes Kepler investigated the secrets of the skies and stars. Rudolf is even supposed to have summoned the famous Rabbi Löw from the Ghetto to the castle, though the content of their consultations remains unknown.

As Rudolf attended to his arcane interests, social and political conflicts continued to seethe. Tension grew between the Emperor and his ambitious brother, Archduke Matthias, who took control of the army during a war with the Turks between 1593 and 1609. This family quarrel was a long-awaited trump card for the Protestants. Rudolf, under pressure from Matthias, had to make concessions. In 1609, the Bohemian nobility forced the king to issue the Majestát (Letter of Majesty) guaranteeing religious freedom throughout the country. But in 1611 Rudolf was forced to surrender the crown to his brother. He died barely a year later, defeated and, some say, mentally ill.

The Thirty Years War

In all ages there have been places in the world where political observers can feel the pulse of the times beating, places where a Zeitgeist is created. Prague in the early 17th century must have been such a place. The gulf between the House of Habsburg and the Bohemian nobility, between Catholic and Protestant, was a reflection of the political situation throughout Europe, though the conflict here had a long tradition unparalleled anywhere else. It was no surprise, then, that Prague was the place over which the storm clouds of war, which had been hovering threateningly all over Europe, broke first.

In 1617, Archduke Ferdinand of Styria was crowned King of Bohemia. In order to consolidate his power, he had agreed to the terms of Rudolf II's Letter of Majesty guaranteeing religious freedom and the unrestricted building of churches. But Catholic Ferdinand soon showed himself to be a staunch supporter of the Counter-Reformation. Protestant churches were closed, some even burnt down. Such harsh and merciless actions led to open revolt. On 23 May 1618, having hatched their conspiracy in a Malá Strana palace, Protestant noblemen led by Count Thurn stormed up the slope to the castle and burst into the Court Chancellery where Ferdinand's representatives were gathered. "Follow the old Prague custom – throw them out of the window!" a voice from the crowd is said to have shouted. Little encouragement was needed. Count Martinic, Governor Slavata and their secretary Philipp Fabricius were thrown 15 metres (50 ft) to the ground, landing in a dung heap, which saved their lives.

This, the most famous of all Prague defenestrations, had far-reaching consequences, and is generally regarded as the starting signal for the horrors and miseries of the Thirty Years War. Ferdinand was deposed and Frederick V, the Elector of the Palatinate in Germany, was made King of Bohemia. His queen was the Stuart Princess Elisabeth. From his base in Vienna, Ferdinand resolved to pay them back.

On 8 November 1620, the combined armies of the Emperor and the Catholic League were drawn up on White Mountain outside Prague, facing Frederick's Bohemian Protestant army. The outcome of the battle was decided within hours. The Protestant soldiery fled back behind the city walls, and Frederick retreated to the Netherlands, earning himself the humiliating title of "Winter King" since he had only reigned for one season. The Catholic troops, many of them mercenaries, plundered the city, the damage running to millions of guilders.

Revenge was savage. On 21 June 1621, some 27 of the most prominent rebels were ceremonially executed in the Old Town Square and the severed heads of 12 of them impaled on the Bridge Tower in the Old Town as a permanent warning. Even before the executions were carried out, Emperor Ferdinand had reinstated the Catholic clergy. In the same year all non-Catholic clergy, including the eminent philosopher and teacher Jan Amos Comenius, were forced to leave Prague. The Emperor had torn up Rudolf's Letter of Majesty with his own hands. In the years that followed, given the choice of conversion or emigration, tens of thousands of Protestants left the land, among them many members of the native aristocracy.

Wallenstein's palace

The Thirty Years War devastated much of Central Europe, but as in all wars, there were those

who profited. Foremost among them in Bohemia was Albrecht von Wallenstein (Valdštejn in Czech), the military commander who was to meet an ignominious end at the hands of assassins in 1634 (see page 105). Before his demise, the immensely wealthy Wallenstein was one of the few who could afford to build amid the confusions of wartime. Demolishing a large part of Malá Strana, he constructed a vast and splendid palace set in an equally extravagant walled garden with an aviary, grottoes, statuary and fountains. Wallenstein's palace set the scene for a post-war wave of Baroque building which was to add immensely to the city's beauty. ❑

LEFT: Van Dyck's portrait of General Wallenstein.
RIGHT: Maria Theresa, Empress of Austria.

NATIONALISM AND THE REPUBLIC

By the 19th century, the Czech people, having grown
tired of battles and strife, began to campaign for
independence from their increasingly troubled rulers

I n the two centuries which followed defeat at
the Battle of White Mountain in 1620, Czech
national consciousness and culture virtually
disappeared. This period is known to Czech
historians as the *temno*, a kind of dark age in
which a foreign nobility was installed in the
Czech lands, owing its loyalty not to the country but to the Habsburg regime in Vienna. The
aristocracy and upper classes spoke only German, with Czech downgraded to the language
of peasants, craftsmen and the urban poor. The
darkness was, however, tempered by much
architectural and artistic brilliance, with Prague
owing much of its present allure to the glories
of baroque building, painting and sculpture.
Most of this aesthetic endeavour was carried
out in the service of the Counter-Reformation
which vigorously re-Catholicised the Czech
lands, once such a stronghold of Protestantism.

The Czech Revival

The late 18th century was a great period for
theatre in Prague. In 1781, the Nostitz Theatre
(today the Estates Theatre) was opened,
attracting the German-speaking upper classes
to plays such as Lessing's *Emilia Galotti* and
operas including Mozart's *Don Giovanni*.
Czechs struggled to stage performances in
their own language. In 1785 they gained per-
mission to do so, but only for a time.

Czech players moved to the Bouda (Shack),
a little wooden theatre in the Horse Market
(now Wenceslas Square). The Czech language

could no longer be suppressed. Czech books
and newspapers returned, and the language
was again taught at the university.

In 1833, the Englishman Edward Thomas
started the production of steam engines in Karlín. Prague began to develop as an industrial
centre; the city's growth drew in a Czech-
speaking proletariat from Bohemia and beyond
and a Czech middle class emerged, diluting the
city's previous German character. Tension
increased between Germans and Czechs,
although at first they had a common enemy:
the all-powerful Viennese State Chancellor
Metternich, the representative of a reactionary
and repressive regime. But while German

LEFT: Václav Havel with shades of Jan Nepomuk.
RIGHT: *fin de siècle* Wenceslas Square.

nationalists desired Bohemia to form part of a liberal, united Germany, Czechs wanted a federal Austrian Empire in which they would dominate an autonomous Bohemia.

Violence at the Pan-Slav Congress

As the tide of revolt swept over Europe in 1848, the "Year of Revolutions", a Pan-Slav Congress met on 2 June in the museum building of Prague. One of its main demands was equal rights for all nationalities. The leader of the movement was the Czech František Palacký: "Either we achieve a situation where we can say with pride: 'I am a Slav', or we shall stop being Slavs," he pronounced. The

TOMÁŠ GARRIGUE MASARYK

The first president of Czechoslovakia was a philosophy professor. Born in Moravia, Masaryk (1850–1937) seemed destined to be a blacksmith. But his high intelligence was recognised by a village priest, and he was sent to study in Vienna, where he received a doctorate. In exile during World War I, he gained Allied support for a state of Czechoslovakia. In 1918 he became president of the new country. During his term of office, Czechoslovakia flourished as a centre of culture, industry and freedom. Masaryk did not live to see his country crushed by Nazi Germany, but his legacy lives on in the ideal of an ethnically diverse society based on democracy.

congress came to a violent end. After a Slavonic mass, rioting broke out, the militia fired into the crowd, and the nationalist movement was crushed in bloody fighting.

Following the revolutions of 1848, all the nations of the Austrian Empire came under the rod of absolutism; the Czech language was even forced out of civil service departments. But after the Austrians were driven out of northern Italy in 1859, their power weakened. On 5 March 1860 an "extended Imperial council" was called. Representatives from different lands sat with councillors appointed by the Emperor. In 1861, a Czech could become mayor of Prague, but nationally the Emperor favoured German-speaking Bohemians. The Czechs remained loyal to the Emperor when war broke out with Prussia in 1866, but were not rewarded with equality or autonomy.

The Czechs did win minor battles. Their long-awaited national theatre was completed by 1881 but destroyed in a fire just before it was due to open. It was quickly rebuilt and opened in 1883 with a performance of Smetana's *Libuše*. It remains a symbol of Czech nationalism today. Work began on the Rudolfinum in 1876, in 1893 the National Museum was built and in 1882 the university was split into separate Czech and German institutions.

World War I and independence

By the start of World War I, Czechs were still struggling for equal rights with the Germans of Austria. The war increased the estrangement: Austrian Germans fully supported the war effort of the Central Powers, while most Czechs opposed it.

Tomáš Garrigue Masaryk, who represented Czech causes in Vienna, where he led the People's Party in the Imperial parliament, headed the campaign for independence. Together with his former student Edvard Beneš and Slovak astronomer Milan Štefánik, he devised a union between Czechs and Slovaks. He contacted his exiles in Allied nations and organised Czechoslovak legions to fight on the side of the Allies. He convinced Allied leaders including US President Woodrow Wilson of the importance of "autonomous development" for all the nations of the Habsburg Empire. A declaration favouring a union of the Czechs and Slovaks was issued in Pittsburgh on 31 May 1918.

After the recognition of the Czechoslovak National Council by France, other Allies followed suit, and on 18 October simultaneous declarations of independence were issued by Masaryk and Beneš in Washington and Paris. The Habsburg monarchy, on the point of collapse, had to accept the terms. The Czechoslovak Republic was proclaimed by the Prague National Committee on 28 October 1918, a move that was repeated by the Slovak National Council two days later.

But the borders of the new state were still not confirmed: the Germans of Bohemia wanted to join with German-speaking Austria, the inclusion of Slovakia in the Czech Republic had not

should look, and it was relatively easy for Beneš to get them to agree to the incorporation of Slovakia into the new state, against the passionate opposition of Hungary, which had ruled Slovaks for a thousand years. Most Slovaks were happy with this union with their brother Slavs, but the autonomy they expected never materialised, a source of much subsequent unrest.

The incorporation of the German-speaking areas of Bohemia and Moravia into Czechoslovakia had even worse consequences, fatal to the country's long-term survival. Following the formula of US President Woodrow Wilson, representatives of the Bohemian Ger-

yet been decided, and Poland was claiming the coal mines in the former duchy of Těšín.

On 14 November, Tomáš Masaryk was elected president of the Republic and was welcomed back by the enthusiastic people of Prague after four years of exile. Foreign Minister Edvard Beneš – who would be Masaryk's successor in presidential office – made skilful use of the last weeks of the war and the time after Germany's surrender. The Western Allies had no clear idea of how post-war Europe

LEFT: Tomáš Garrigue Masaryk.
ABOVE: Adolf Hitler, on a stamp and in reality, surveys his Bohemian "Protectorate" from Prague Castle.

mans had declared an "autonomous province of the state of German Austria", to which Czech troops retaliated by occupying German-settled areas. The Peace Conference decided in favour of Czechoslovakia. Without a plebiscite being held, the German areas went to Czechoslovakia. Parts of Těšín were also given to the new state despite the unwillingness of their German and Polish inhabitants.

A Trojan horse

From the start, the Germans of Czechoslovakia saw themselves as an oppressed minority, disadvantaged by language rulings, land reform, and the unfavourable position of the German education system and industry. The economic effects of the Great Depression affected the German-speaking areas of the country particularly badly, and in the winter of 1932–3 some two-thirds of the 920,000 unemployed in Czechoslovakia were Germans. In 1933, Konrad Henlein, a gymnastics teacher, founded the nationalistic Sudetendeutsche Heimatfront (SHF), the Sudeten German Home Front. In 1935 the party, now known as the Sudetendeutsche Partei (SDP) – the Sudeten German Party – took part in elections. They won 68 per cent of German votes, making them the strongest group in parliament, and they began to demand autonomy for German areas.

It did not take long for Henlein to make contact with Hitler, and soon he and his party became puppets of their mighty patron. The SDP's demands became more and more radical over the years, and their goals shifted from equal rights to inclusion in the German Reich.

Nazi occupation

Afraid of war, France and Britain finally gave in to pressure from Hitler. On 30 September 1938, Chamberlain, Daladier, Mussolini and Hitler signed the Munich Agreement which severed the Sudetenland from Czechoslovakia and gave it to the Third Reich. Despite an Anglo-French guarantee to protect what

remained of the country, they failed to act when, on 15 March 1939, Hitler's troops marched into Prague and the dictator declared Czechoslovakia dead. The Czech lands became part of the Third Reich, the "Protectorate of Bohemia-Moravia", while the Slovaks were pressured into declaring the "Slovak State", nominally independent but in fact the most servile of Nazi puppets.

Despite guarantees that Czech national life should be safeguarded, the Nazis set out to dominate their new subjects. The intelligentsia were harassed, universities closed and newspapers banned. The Barrandov Studios were forced to make propaganda films. Thousands of people were imprisoned in the concentration camps of Dachau and Oranienburg. (For the treatment of Prague's Jews, *see page 138*.) Pressure intensified when the ruthless head of the *Sicherheitsdienst*, Reinhard Heydrich, replaced the relatively lenient Von Neurath as *Reichsprotektor* in 1941. Deservedly known as "The Hangman", Heydrich was targeted by the Czechoslovak government in exile in Britain; parachutists sent to assassinate him finally succeeded in doing so in May 1942. Terrible reprisals were exacted for Heydrich's death; as well as the destruction of the village of Lidice *(see page 202)*, many hostages were executed and the population was cowed into utter submission. Until the very last days of the war, there was no chance of meaningful resistance in the Czech lands, though the Slovaks, in the National Uprising of 1944, made a gallant but unsuccessful attempt to break free from their alliance with Germany. Otherwise, Czechoslovak honour was upheld by thousands of exiled soldiers and airmen fighting alongside the Western Allies and the Soviet Union.

On 5 May 1945, three days before the war ended, the people of Prague rose up against the Germans, calling for help from the US, whose soldiers had reached Plzeň in western Bohemia, and from the Red Army to the north. Eager to claim this rich prize, the Russians marched into the city, where they were greeted as liberators, immensely enhancing the prestige of the Soviet Union and of Communism.

The rise of Communism

In post-war Czechoslovakia the path to socialism had been smoothed as in no other country. Before World War II, the country was one of Europe's highly developed nations, with modern light and heavy industries, and efficient agriculture. Above all, it had a confident, highly qualified proletariat and a class of educated intellectuals and artists, who were, if not actually members of the Communist Party, nonetheless mainly left or liberal-left in their views. The Czechs' perception of the Soviet Union and socialism was positive. Following the rebirth of nationalism in the early 19th century, the Czechs viewed Russia as a Slav older brother.

In the last free elections for more than 50 years, the Communists won 38 percent of the

The Stalin years

The cause of this disillusionment was Josef Stalin, who mercilessly forced the Czechoslovaks to accept his version of Communism. From 1948 onwards, the Czechoslovak Communist Party, by now Stalinist in orientation, succeeded in destroying any idea of a specifically Czechoslovak road to socialism.

The rule of the Stalinists, first under Gottwald and then under Antonín Novotný, had dire consequences for Czechs and Slovaks. In the late 1950s and early 1960s scepticism and cynicism spread throughout the country. Hardly anyone still believed in Marxism or Leninism, or even in the idea of just

votes, and Klement Gottwald became leader of a coalition government. However, this was not enough for the Soviet Union, and in February 1948, the Communists gained total control of Czechoslovakia in a bloodless coup. A month later, Foreign Minister Jan Masaryk, the only non-Communist still in government, was found dead in the courtyard below his office. The Communists could still count on the support of the majority of Czechoslovaks, but disillusionment was just around the corner.

LEFT: design from a Czechoslovak Communist poster.
ABOVE: the Ninth Congress of the Czech Communist Party, held in Prague in 1949.

and fair socialism. What is more, the economy, subject to a series of Five-Year Plans, was at rock bottom by 1963. The failure of the latest plan and the near collapse of the national economy led to a reappraisal of the direction in which society was heading, both within the Communist Party and outside it, a reappraisal which was eventually to lead to the "Prague Spring" of 1968.

Literature and politics

Ever since the rebirth of Czech national consciousness in the early 19th century, writers had played a vital role in both shaping and responding to nationalist aspirations. In the years before the Prague Spring of 1968, a literature independent of the Communist Party censorship machine was able to develop, despite the existence of watchful censors.

When the crisis of Czechoslovak Communism eventually came, in the early 1960s, it was authors such as the future Nobel Prize-winner for Literature, Jaroslav Seifert, the lyric poets Vladimír Holan, František Halas and others, who replaced the party functionaries as spokesmen for political and moral values. By 1965 at the latest, Czechs and Slovaks had realised that this form of "existing socialism" could not continue, and, searching for something to cling to, they rediscovered

their poets, authors and filmmakers. The term "socialism with a human face" is usually associated with Alexander Dubček, who became an internationally known figure in 1968. It was, indeed, an ideal which Dubček wished to realise, but its programme was developed not by the Communist Party and its exhausted and insecure ideologists, but by the writers and artists of the Prague Spring.

End of a dream

"Socialism with a human face" was not Utopia but, had it been realised, it would have been a great step forward, laying the foundations for a more equitable society. Ideas put

forward in the course of 1968 included federal autonomy for the Slovaks, long overdue industrial and agricultural reforms, a revised constitution that would guarantee civil rights and liberties, and democratisation of the country and the party. Behind these proposals lay a bitter admission and an undertone of despair: up until the spring of 1968 the face of socialism in Czechoslovakia had obviously not looked very human at all. The dream of an efficient, just and happy socialist society came to an abrupt end on 21 August 1968, when the armies of the Soviet Union and several of its Warsaw Pact allies marched in and destroyed the Czechoslovak hope of national independence. They left behind them the power structure of a totalitarian, neo-Stalinist state, which, although it called itself socialist, had very little to do with the ideals of true socialism that Prague reformers under Dubček had believed they could achieve.

Under the "normalisation" regime of Dubček's successor, the hard-liner Gustav Husák, many writers, composers, journalists and historians, as well as scientists, found themselves unemployed and forced to accept menial jobs to earn a living. Some left the country, and those who stayed and tried to continue the struggle were silenced. But despite the indifference of the mass of the population, discontent continued to smoulder.

It erupted again in January 1977, when a group of intellectuals signed a petition, known as Charter 77, in which they aired their grievances against the Husák regime. The spokesman of the group, Václav Havel, had already written, in an open letter to President Husák two years before: "You have chosen the path that is the most convenient for you and the most dangerous for the country: the path of maintaining external appearances at the cost of internal collapse… the path of merely defending your power, at the cost of deepening the spiritual and moral crisis of this society and the systematic erosion of human values."

A political earthquake

After the massive changes in other Eastern Bloc countries in the late 1980s, the Czechoslovak Communist regime could not hope to save itself. The citizens of Prague demonstrated in Wenceslas Square in their thousands and, despite the obstinate stance of the authorities and the contingents of police and security forces, their voices could no longer be silenced. Remarkable though it would have seemed just a few months before, one of the last Communist governments in the world was about to come toppling down. After the peaceful revolution in East Germany, a "Velvet Revolution" now took place in Prague in November 1989.

Václav Havel was a central figure in the protests. On 29 December 1989, he was elected president by the parliament in Prague. Dubček, veteran leader of the Prague Spring, was voted leader of the Federal Assembly.

cleansing, an atonement by a handful for the rest of society, and a practical measure to bar tainted officials from public office.

Dividing the country

A key question for Czechoslovakia was how to achieve the economic reforms that would lead to a free market. When the economy began its shift away from socialist planning after the revolution, the Slovaks were on the receiving end, suffering disproportionately from the effects of transition to a market economy. Economically irrational but emotionally understandable, Slovak separatism was a symptom of uncertainty, a force liberated by

In the summer of 1990, in the first free elections for two generations, the Civic Forum Party received the endorsement of most of the electorate. But as in most revolutions, even velvet ones, its leaders gradually drifted apart as the common enemy disappeared. The differences of opinion surfaced, for example, during debates on the "outing" of those who had held any high office in the Communist Party or who had had any connection with the secret police. Known as *lustrace*, the controversial process was meant to be a spiritual

changed circumstances at a time when the state's institutions were not strong enough to contain it. Despite President Havel's opposition, a "Velvet Divorce" took place on 31 December 1992, and two new countries emerged on 1 January 1993: the Czech Republic and Slovakia.

An "economic miracle"?

In the new Czech Republic, market reforms in the early to mid-1990s soon reached breakneck speed under the abrasive but dynamic new prime minister, Václav Klaus (frequently in conflict with Havel, now president of the Czech Republic). An ambitious privatisation

LEFT AND ABOVE: local resistance and the distribution of *samizdat* literature during the "Prague Spring".

programme – including a coupon scheme that gave every adult the chance to buy shares in the state firms being privatised – was accompanied by an apparently successful balancing of the budget, with an increase in exports, reduced inflation, low unemployment and impressive growth rates. Such a consistently upbeat picture could hardly fail to attract foreign investment and commentators began talking openly about an "economic miracle" emerging in the Czech Republic.

The high point was reached in 1995, when the Czech Republic became the first post-Communist state to join the Organisation for Economic Cooperation and Development

Into the 21st century

As the Czech Republic adjusted to the economic realities of the new millennium, it began to transform itself from a post-Communist success story into a fully-fledged Western nation, aspiring to the same European stature as countries like France, Spain, the UK or Italy. In November 2002, it became the first former Soviet satellite state to host a NATO summit, a milestone event for a nation that previously stood on the opposite side of the Iron Curtain. Czech leaders wasted no opportunity in using the conference to prove their worth on the world stage. But the summit served only as a precursor to an even more profound step

(OECD), an important step on the road to the country's long-term goal of full membership of the European Union. The country, along with Hungary and Poland, joined NATO in March 1999, and the Czech Republic became a member state of the European Union on 1 May 2004.

The consumer boom created a huge demand for Western goods and services at the expense of domestic suppliers, leading to a ballooning trade deficit. But by the late 1990s, as inflation rose and then rose again, the coupon-privatisation scheme floundered, and ordinary Czech savers were hit by a spectacular wave of banking collapses, amid worrying allegations of fraud and corruption.

towards Westernisation. Following in the footsteps of fellow former Soviet Bloc states like Poland and Hungary, the Czech Republic voted by an overwhelming margin in June 2003 to join the European Union.

Viewed as a model candidate among former Communist satellite states, the Czech government initiated drastic changes to its financial and regulatory systems to conform with EU standards on everything from sales tax to labour laws. Along with nine other states (including Slovakia), the country has been formally welcomed into the EU and it seems likely that the Czech crown will be replaced by the euro in several years time.

After decades of living under a totalitarian regime, however, it will probably be many years before Czechs adapt culturally to the western European mindset and lifestyle.

Havel steps down

No greater a symbol can be found of the Czech Republic completing its transformation from a former Soviet state than the departure of Václav Havel from public life. Havel had served as the nation's leader, with only a slight interruption, since the Velvet Revolution. But in February 2003, with his health uncertain and the Czech constitution preventing him from seeking additional terms, he stepped down.

Similar political dramas to those of the presidency have also been played out in the ruling Social Democrats. They had won elections in 1998 and, with a greatly reduced number of seats, in 2002; although in the process prime minister Miloš Zeman had been replaced by Vladimir Spidla following large public demonstrations. The party was then trounced in the 2004 European election, and Spidla stood down to be replaced by the youthful Stanislav Gross, who has since been replaced by Jiří Paroubek.

The opening years of the 21st century, however, provided non-political storms as well. In August 2002, several weeks of torrential rains pounded Central Europe, swelling the rivers

The battle to replace Havel, however, very nearly plunged the government into unprecedented crisis. Though in other countries the president often serves as a figurehead with the prime minister the seat of authority, the Czech system affords the president's post some real power, and the deadlocked contest for the office left the government in a dangerous political impasse. But after several stalemated ballots, and without an acting president for several weeks, a coalition finally elected former Prime Minister Václav Klaus to replace Havel.

to capacity and beyond. The Czech Republic's infrastructure was unable to cope. The waters rose up through the sewers, crested flood barriers and submerged entire streets and neighbourhoods beneath the muck. Streets buckled and buildings collapsed; the Prague Metro system was nearly devastated, as waters broke through the walls between tunnels and flooded underground stations to street level.

The disaster devastated the lower parts of the city but the rebuilding effort went surprisingly smoothly, and with the exception of markers showing the level reached by the waters, there are few remaining signs that the flooding ever took place. ❑

LEFT: crowds in Wenceslas Square, 1989.
ABOVE: Stanislav Gross and Václav Klaus.

Decisive Dates

Early History and Přemyslids

*c.***400 BC** A Celtic tribe, the Boii, invade the area and give it the name Bohemia.
6th century AD The Slavs come to the area.
*c.***620** A Frankish merchant named Samo establishes the first state in the area.
Late 9th century Prince Bořivoj, of the Přemyslid dynasty, builds the first castle in Prague.
*c.***935** Prince Wenceslas, patron saint of Bohemia, is murdered by his brother Boleslav I.
973 The bishopric of Prague is founded.
1085 Prince Vratislav is proclaimed the first

King of Bohemia by Emperor Henry IV.
1158 King Vladislav I founds the Strahov Monastery and commissions the first stone bridge, the Judith Bridge, across the Vltava.
1173–8 Prince Soběslav II gives equal rights to German settlers and awards special privileges to German merchants.
1253–78 Přemsyl Otakar II extends the Bohemian kingdom to the Adriatic, but it is lost when he is killed at the Battle of Dürnkrut.
1306 Young King Wenceslas II is murdered, ending the Přemyslid dynasty.

The Golden Age and Hussite Wars

1310 King John of Luxembourg marries the Přemyslid princess Elizabeth and founds the Luxembourg dynasty.
1344 Prague becomes the seat of an archbishopric.
1348 King Charles I (later Emperor Charles IV) founds the university and makes the city the Imperial capital, laying out the New Town, employing Peter Parler to work on St Vitus's Basilica and the Karlův most.
1393 King Wenceslas IV has John of Nepomuk thrown into the Vltava from Charles Bridge.
1402 Jan Hus begins preaching reform of the Church at the Bethlehem Chapel.
1409 German professors dispute the teachings of Jan Hus and move to Leipzig to found a new university.
1415 Jan Hus is burned at the stake.
1419 Hussites, led by Jan Želivský, throw Catholic councillors from a window in the New Town Hall (the first defenestration) and begin the Hussite Wars.
1420 At the Battle of Vítkov the Hussites, led by Jan Žižka, repel Emperor Sigismund's army.
1434 Two Hussite factions – moderate Utraquists and radical Taborites – meet at the Battle of Lipany, which the Utraquists win.
1458 The leader of the Utraquists, George of Poděbrady, becomes King of Bohemia.
1471 The Polish Jagiellon dynasty takes over the rule of Bohemia.
1526 Jagellion King Louis is killed at the Battle of Mohács in Hungary and the Bohemian throne passes to the Habsburg dynasty.

Habsburg rule

1576 Under Emperor Rudolf II, Prague becomes the Imperial residence and is a magnet for artists and scientists from all over Europe.
1609 Rudolf's Letter of Majesty grants freedom of religious worship.
1618 Archduke Ferdinand tears up the Letter of Majesty. Two Imperial councillors and their secretary are thrown out of a window in Hradčany (the second defenestration), the starting signal for the Thirty Years War.
1620 At the Battle of White Mountain the Bohemian army is defeated by the Catholic forces of Emperor Ferdinand. The Protestant "Winter King", Frederick of the Palatinate, flees, the leaders of the uprising are executed, and Protestants go into exile. The Counter-Reformation enforces Catholic orthodoxy and

enriches the townscape with baroque churches and monasteries.

1680 Bohemian peasants revolt against the feudal government.

1740 In the War of the Austrian Succession, the armies of Bavaria, Saxony and France capture Prague. Maria Theresa becomes Empress.

1757 Prussian forces bombard Prague. Maria Theresa repairs the damage to the city and has Prague Castle extended.

1781 Under Josef II, serfdom is abolished, and Prague's Jewish citizens are awarded civic rights. The ghetto is renamed Josefov.

1784 The previously independent towns of Prague are amalgamated.

1845 Arrival of the railway. The Industrial Revolution draws in Czechs from the countryside, diluting the German character of the city.

1848 A Pan-Slav Congress meets in Prague, led by František Palacký. An uprising is crushed by Austrian forces, and reactionary rule from Vienna is reimposed.

1880s The Czech National Theatre opens with a performance of Smetana's *Libuše*. Dvořák and Janáček gain international recognition.

1914 Tomáš Garrigue Masaryk goes into exile and gains Allied support for a new state uniting Czechs and Slovaks.

Czechoslovakia and after

1918 The Republic of Czechoslovakia is proclaimed on 28 October. Masaryk becomes the first president, Edvard Beneš Foreign Minister.

1935 Edvard Beneš succeeds the ailing Masaryk as the country's president.

1938 The Munich Agreement cedes the Sudetenland to Germany.

1939 Slovakia declares independence and what is left is incorporated into Germany as the Protectorate of Bohemia and Moravia.

1942 *Reichsprotektor* Heydrich is assassinated; the village of Lidice is obliterated in revenge.

1945 Prague rises against its German occupiers several days before the arrival of Soviet forces. Czechoslovakia's 3 million Germans are expelled, many dying in the process.

1948 *Coup d'état.* Beneš resigns as president and is succeeded by Communist leader Klement Gottwald.

1950s Stalinist show trials and execution of prominent Communists after forced confessions.

1968 The "Prague Spring", an attempt to introduce "socialism with a human face" under Party Secretary General Alexander Dubček. The attempt is crushed by Warsaw Pact invasion.

1969 Dubček dismissed and "normalisation" – a return to strict Stalinist orthodoxy – is overseen by party leader Gustav Husák.

1977 Charter 77 is founded.

1989 The Velvet Revolution, led by mass demonstrations and strikes, forces the Communist government to resign. Václav Havel becomes president. Communists are banned from participating in government.

1992 Czech and Slovak representatives fail to agree on a federal constitution, and decide – without a referendum – to split the country.

1993 Two new states, the Czech Republic and Slovakia. Havel is re-elected president. The country enters a period of commercial boom.

1994–8 Prague is politically turbulent following accusations of official corruption.

1999 The Czech Republic joins NATO.

2002 Prague suffers devastating floods.

2003 Václav Havel is succeeded as president by former prime minister Václav Klaus.

2004 The Czech Republic becomes a member of the European Union.

2005 Jiří Paroubek becomes prime minister. ❏

LEFT: defenestration leads to the Thirty Years War.
RIGHT: Alexander Dubček greets the crowds.

FOOD AND DRINK

International dishes of all kinds can readily be found in
Prague, but the rich and hearty traditional cuisine
of the Czech lands should not be missed

Bohemian cooking is based on the abundant produce of the country's fertile farmland, its orchards, rivers and ponds, and its vast forests teeming with game. It's unpretentious fare, intended to sustain body and soul rather than form the subject of sophisticated conversation or provide a balanced range of vitamins, but nonetheless delicious. It features meat, nourishing soups, potatoes and above all, dumplings, with fresh fruit and vegetables relegated to a secondary role. Bohemian cooks were once much in demand in establishments all over the Habsburg Empire, and were responsible for many good things now thought of as typically Viennese, particularly in the field of fine pastries.

Starting the day

Czechs begin the day in a frugal way, with a breakfast *(snídaně)* possibly consisting simply of a cup (or three) of coffee *(káva)* made in the time-honoured fashion by pouring boiling water onto finely ground beans in the cup and letting the mixture settle before attempting to drink it. Tourists in their international hotels are unlikely to be served coffee in this way, and the more or less sumptuous buffet provided will almost certainly fuel the morning's sightseeing. By contrast, once out on the street, the native inhabitant's appetite is likely to be kindled by the sight of one of the many sausage stands that stud the townscape. Czech

LEFT: Budvar, one of the sublime local brews.
RIGHT: ham and sausages form the centrepiece of this Christmas display.

sausages are among the best in the world. The favourite is the *párek*, often sold in pairs (as *párky*), a Frankfurter that should really be called a Praguer as it was here that it originated. A fatter version is called a *vuřt* (cf. German *Wurst*), while a *klobása* is an even bigger variety, coarse-textured, with a thick skin and plenty of fatty globules. Sausages are usually accompanied by a dollop of mild-tasting mustard. Marginally healthier snacks in the form of little open sandwiches *(obložené chlebíčky)* can be bought at delicatessens; the topping may include slivers of ham, salami, hard-boiled egg, fish roe, plus potato salad, a slice of tomato or a gherkin.

Lunch

If there are no plans for dining out in the evening, lunch *(oběd)* is likely to be the main meal of the day. It will normally begin with soup *(polévka)*, with choices ranging from simple meat broth *(vývar)* with dumplings to a thick potato cream soup *(bramborová)* or a bowl of tripe soup *(dršťková)* (reputed to be an excellent hangover cure). In pretentious restaurants, beware of the tray of hors d'oeuvres you may be offered; far from being complimentary, they may add substantially to the bill. The main course is referred to jokingly as *vepřo-knedlo-zelo* (pork-dumpling-cabbage), and pork *(vepřové maso)* it is indeed likely to

be; the pig is king in this country, his meat almost certainly tastier than anything you are likely to get at home. Most pigs are raised en masse, but many villagers keep a porker or two which is destined to be slaughtered in more or less ceremonial fashion in autumn or winter. Every part is made into some tasty comestible, much of it being consumed on the spot with friends and neighbours in what is known as the *zábíjačka* (slaughter) or *vepřové hody* (pork festival). In the restaurant, pork can be roasted *(pečené)*, fried *(smážené)* or come in the form of a schnitzel *(řízek)*. The roast will be served with a delicious sauce, soon soaked up by the accompanying

dumplings. In this country, the dumpling *(knedlík)* enjoys even more veneration than the pig. It can be made from flour, bread, potatoes or semolina, with added yeast, baking powder, eggs, milk or sugar. The best of course are those made by mother or grandmother, who will almost certainly have devised her own recipe. The *knedlík* is prepared in a loaf-like form, which is then cut with a wire, *never* with a knife. The least important of the famous *vepřo-knedlo-zelo* trio is the cabbage, invariably shredded. It might be the spicy red variety, or sharp-tasting sauerkraut flavoured with caraway seeds.

After pork, beef *(hovězí maso)* is the most popular meat, especially when served as *svíčková na smetaně*, fillet or sirloin topped with a slice of lemon and a spoonful of cranberries, and swimming in an abundant cream sauce. Tougher cuts of beef are made into goulash, less elaborate than in Hungary where it originated, but still with added flavour given by onion and paprika. Alternative main courses at lunchtime might feature veal *(telecí maso)* or chicken *(kuře)*. A request for vegetables other than cabbage is likely to be met with raised eyebrows. Salad *(salát)* is more common, probably not in the form of tossed green lettuce, but as a mixture consisting variously of cucumber, onion, red pepper and tomatoes wallowing in a sweetish, vinegary sauce. Potatoes *(brambory)* may be boiled *(vářené)*, mashed *(kaše)*, roast *(opekané)* or chipped *(hranolky)*.

Vegetarians will find specialist establishments catering to their needs, which is just as well since mainstream restaurants are unlikely to offer them much more than an omelette or fried cheese *(smážený sýr)*; the latter is better than it sounds, consisting of thick slice of semi-molten local cheese (usually *hermelín*) in a breadcrumb coating and enlivened by a dollop of tartare sauce. Vegetarians and carnivores alike should latch on to the local passion for fungi. The environment of the Czech Republic is particularly favourable for the growth of a bewildering array of mushrooms *(houby)*, a detailed knowledge of which seems part of everyone's heritage. Fungi in all shapes and sizes are hunted down and picked in favourite spots in the countryside, brought home, and fried or more likely dried, to be added later to all kinds of dishes, notably cabbage soup.

Most locals will finish their lunch at this point, perhaps rounding it off with a cup of coffee. The range of desserts offered will be quite limited. There might be thin crepes *(palačinky)*, wrapped around cottage cheese *(tvaroh)*, ice cream *(zmrzlina)*, fruit or nuts, and perhaps served with a chocolate sauce. The dumpling makes a triumphant reappearance, this time as an *ovocný knedlík*, filled with plums or apricots. This is really a meal in its own right, and indeed it is sometimes eaten as such, usually at home.

Cakes and pastries

Pleasant moments may be spent in a café *(kavárna)* or patisserie *(cukrárna)* sampling

uct *(ruská zmrzlina)* sandwiched between a couple of wafers.

Dinner

When taken at home, the evening meal is usually a less substantial fare than lunch. It might consist simply of a sausage or some sort of processed meat such as salami *(salám)* eaten with a couple of slices of the country's delectable rye bread *(chléb)*. Prague ham *(šunka)* is justly famous, though the local version of brawn *(tlačenka)*, made from leftover bits of the pig and certainly tasty enough, may not be to everyone's liking. Some members of the family will even be satisfied with just a

some of the delicious and often wonderfully light cakes and pastries that are the equal of anything offered in Vienna. Choose from tarts, strudels – especially apple strudels – sponge cakes, various elaborate creations featuring fruit, cream or nuts, or *koláčky*, buns with a filling of *tvaroh*, poppy seeds, or *povidla*, a delicious, dense dark plum jam. Czechs are as keen on ice cream as anyone and there are plenty of brands to choose from, including local ones. A traditional cheap and cheerful favourite is a slab of the creamy Russian prod-

dessert such as plum dumplings. But if eating out, this is the moment to move beyond *vepřo-knedlo-zelo* and sample some of the more prestigious creations of Czech cuisine. In a reputable establishment you should not miss the chance to try roast duck *(kachna)* or even better, roast goose *(husa)*. As well as making a celebratory meal for grand occasions, the geese which sometimes seem to outnumber the human population in the country's villages are also force-fed to provide *husí paštíka*, liver paté as good as the finest French foie gras. The goose's grossly distended liver *(játra)* is also roasted to make an utterly irresistible dish, irresistible that is if

---

LEFT: enjoying a beer outside.
ABOVE: dumplings, stew and cabbage.

you don't dwell on what the unfortunate bird has had to go through.

The fields and forests beyond Bohemia's villages harbour a great variety of game, which is perhaps best eaten in one of the capital's specialised restaurants. Wild boar (*kanec*) makes an interesting alternative to the ubiquitous pig, though it is less likely to appear on the menu than venison (*srnčí maso*), pheasant (*bažant*) or partridge (*koroptev*).

Prague is a long way from the ocean, and although seafood is more available than it used to be, it makes sense in this landlocked country to try its freshwater fish. Roasted or fried trout (*pstruh*) features on many a menu, but the

Where to eat and drink
Restaurants

Prague restaurants (*restaurace*) vary enormously in character and price, with some – but only some – indication of their quality given by the official rating of I (highest) to IV (lowest). Bargain meals are still to be had in some city-centre establishments; following office workers on their way to lunch is one way of discovering them. At the other end of the scale are establishments such as those in the international hotels, with a full complement of *maîtres d'*, wine waiters and cloakroom attendants.

Prague used to be notorious for the surliness and frequent dishonesty of restaurant

characteristic Czech fish is the carp (*kapr*). Carp are raised in their thousands in the fishponds which stud the country and which are particularly prominent in the landscape of southern Bohemia. Netted in their millions in December, carp are brought to town, sold live from barrels and kept in the family bathtub before being slaughtered and cut into steaks, breaded and fried to form the centrepiece of the traditional Christmas Eve dinner. In restaurants, carp is more likely to be served as *kapr na černo* in a black, sweet-and-sour sauce made mysteriously from such ingredients as nuts, raisins, sugar, beer and vinegar. Do try it, but beware the many little bones.

staff. The situation has improved enormously, but diners still need to keep a watchful eye on the bill; menu prices include value-added tax, but some waiters persist in adding it to the total, subsequently pocketing it for themselves. Opportunities for romantic dining abound in this city of ancient buildings, narrow lanes, secret gardens, and sudden vistas. Several establishments make the most of their riverside location.

A *vinárna* was traditionally an establishment serving wine rather than beer, often from a particular region or even vineyard, but nowadays is just another term for a restaurant with some pretensions to refinement.

Pubs and bars

The most basic establishment is the *hostinec* or *pivnice*, best translated as a beerhouse, where the atmosphere is likely to be smoky, the service unrefined, and the chance of getting something gastronomic to eat nil. Next up the ladder is the *hospoda*, the pub or beer hall, and a number of venerable Prague taverns have steadfastly held on to their traditional ambience and clientele. Most pubs are tied to a particular brewery, serving its product on draught in half-litre glasses. Some take great pride in the way in which they keep and serve their beer; the reputation of *U zlatého Tygra* (The Golden Tiger), a pub in the Old Town, is

when empty. Before drinking, toast your companions with a call of *Na zdraví!* ("To health!"). A tally of the glasses drunk is kept on a scrap of paper on the table. When you've had enough, ask for the bill *(zaplatím, prosím)* and pay up, making the sum up to the nearest round figure rather than leaving a large tip.

Note that many *hospody* serve perfectly good meals (though the choice may be limited) and that those at the top end of the scale may be little different from *restaurace*.

While historic establishments such as the Golden Tiger are a feature of the historic districts of central Prague, some of the best areas to find other versions of the authentic Czech

largely based on the temperature of its ancient cellars, ideal for the perfect preservation of Pilsner. On entering a *hospoda*, you may well find that there are no unoccupied tables. This doesn't matter in the least. Just ask whether a chair or a space on a bench is free *(Je tu volno?)* and if the answer is positive take your seat. The form with overcoat or jacket is to hang it on the stand provided rather than drape it over the back of your chair. There's no need to signal for service; the waiter will sooner or later dump a beer in front of you and replace it

LEFT: posh dining in Barock.
ABOVE: the more traditional night out.

pub experience are slightly further afield. Easily accessible is Žižkov, a suburb in Prague III, a former working-class neighbourhood, still unpolished in places, which proudly claims the largest number of pubs per capita in the whole of the city. Mixed in with plenty of authentic smoke-filled establishments full of people playing card games is a newer crop of equally smoky places patronised by a younger crowd. The most famous Žižkov pub is probably U vystřeleného oka (At the Shot-out Eye), named in honour of the one-eyed Hussite general Jan Žižka.

Theme bars, such as Irish, English or American bars, have cropped up in recent years, and are popular with young Praguers as well as with expatriates. Guinness is often served in such places, as well as (inexplicably, given the quality of Czech beer) other brews from abroad.

Coffee houses

The coffee house was one of the great institutions of the inter-war First Republic, and Prague café society equal to that of Paris or Vienna. Some have faded into history – for example the Arco, meeting place of "Arconauts" such as Kafka, Werfel and Max Brod. Others are still humming with a vibrant mix that includes students, businesspeople with busy mobile phones, ladies of a certain age, and the inevitable

tourists. Among them are the renovated Malostranská Kavárna and the reopened Café Slavia, filled in its heyday by poets, painters, and actors from the National Theatre opposite. The coffee house is a fine place for people-watching, and the staff won't mind if you spend half the afternoon nursing a single cup while writing in your journal or glancing through the newspapers and magazines provided.

Drinks

The Czech Republic is home to what many consider the world's finest beers (*see opposite*), but it is also wine country, and in addition produces a number of unusual spirits and aperitifs.

Vines once clad the slopes of Prague's Petřín Hill and were responsible for the name of the suburb of Vinohrady ("vineyards"). But they have long since disappeared, and winemaking is concentrated far from the capital in sunny southern Moravia, where the vines spread for almost 113 km (70 miles) between the city of Brno and the Austrian and Slovak borders. Bohemia's vineyards cover a much smaller area, centred on the Elbe and its tributaries north of Prague. The vines growing on the steep slope below the town of Mělník are the descendants of those brought from France and planted here by Emperor Charles IV in the 14th century. They yield white wines rather like those in neighbouring Saxony, dry and rather acidic. Moravian wines are mostly white, though there are plenty of reds too. Among the reds, *Frankovka* (relatively dry) or *Sv.Vavřinec* (plummy and sweetish), can be good, while white *Ryzlink* and *Palava* go well with fish. A so-called "archive" wine (*archivní víno*) may simply be old, not vintage. The most interesting wines are probably found more in specialist shops than in restaurants. The local equivalent of the cult of Beaujolais Nouveau is the arrival in Prague in late September or early October of *burčák*, a cloudy, half-fermented young wine that can pack quite a kick despite its innocent, grape-juice taste. In winter, hot mulled wine, *svařené víno*, will help keep the cold at bay, while special occasions can be celebrated with champagne-type sparkling wines such as *Bohemia Sekt*.

More or less palatable fruit brandies are also distilled. The best is probably *slivovice*, made from plums, traditionally used as a remedy for colds and virtually every other ailment. There is also apricot brandy, *meruňkovice*, and cherry brandy, *třešňovice*. The most popular aperitif is *Becherovka*, a liquor originally served as a restorative to Karlsbad spa guests, and made from a secret herbal recipe. Finally, the Czech Republic is one of the few countries where absinthe is legally made and consumed.

Tap water, while safe, may not be very palatable, and it makes sense in a country with many spas to sample its range of mineral waters. The best known, with a pleasant mildly fizzy character, is Mattoni from Karlsbad. ❏

LEFT: káva in a café.

Czech Beer

The brewing tradition in Bohemia extends over a very long time indeed – in Prague the oldest written record of the brewer's art is found in a document dated 1082. The full-bodied, foamy and flavourful Czech beers of today have been developed from the brew which appeared in the western Bohemian city of Plzeň/Pilsen in 1842, when a group of citizens with brewing rights got together to produce a pale, bottom-fermented beer. The combination of local spring water, famous hops from Žatec in northern Bohemia, and careful cellaring in ideal conditions in the sandstone caves beneath the city yielded a beer that won instant popularity, particularly in Germany, where its name, "Pilsner" or "Pils", is indiscriminately applied to any pale, hoppy brew.

To distinguish the original product from its imitators, its makers gave it the name of "Pilsner Urquell" meaning "original source" (Plzeňský prazdroj in Czech). Highly rated by many native drinkers, and available widely throughout the Czech Republic, Prazdroj is also a major item among the country's exports. Its great rival on the international scene comes from the southern city of České Budějovice, a place of equally venerable brewing traditions. Budějovice is known as Budweis in German and Budvar in Czech. For those who find the distinctive sharp taste of Prazdroj a little too acidic, Budvar is a somewhat sweeter, milder drink.

Pilsen and Budějovice are justly famous as brewing cities, but there are plenty of others, even though numbers are down from the 800 of a century ago when every little town had a brewery or three (the composer Smetana was born in one). Takeovers by international companies and "rationalisations" have taken their toll, but around 70 establishments continue to satisfy the needs of their customers. Pilsen boasts a second big brewery, Gambrinus, while another very popular product comes

from Velké Popovice not far to the south of Prague; called *Velkopopovický kozel*, it features a satisfied-looking goat *(kozel)* on its label. The largest brewery in Prague is Staropramen, founded in 1869 on the banks of the Vltava in the working-class suburb of Smíchov. Many of the capital's host of seasoned drinkers swear by its distinctive product, though other Praguers prefer products from the brewery at Braník in the south of the city or from the *První Pražský městanský pivovar* (first Prague municipal brewery) in Holešovice.

Most Czech beer is of the Pilsner type, and is referred to as *svetlé* (light). It comes

in two strengths, measured in degrees indicating the amount of sugar content. 12o *(dvánactka)* is stronger and heavier with an alcohol content of more than 4%. 10o *(desetka)* is lighter and contains less than 4% alcohol; it has the advantage that more of it can be consumed at one sitting! As well as *svelté*, most breweries also make *tmavé*, a dark and rather sweet beer not unlike British mild. It has declined in popularity, but is sometimes cut with *svelté* in an attempt to combine the advantages of both. A unique dark beer, not to be missed, is brewed in-house in Prague's

RIGHT: Pilsner Urquell being poured.

U fleků pub. ❑

MUSIC

Few other cities can claim musicians of such talent and determination, from the early politically hindered composers to the modern-day jazz buskers

Prague is unquestionably a city of music. The violinist David Oistrakh once described it as the "musical heart of Europe", and the city is still the centre of Bohemia's rich musical heritage, as it has been for centuries.

Bohemian musicians

The great flowering of Czech music, also known as "Bohemian classicism", took place in the 18th century. The popular saying "All Bohemians are musicians" dates from this time, and the fact that it seems to be true – or very nearly true – probably stems from Bohemia's traditional support for musical education. Documents dating from this time show that most cantors (schoolteachers) had a musical education and saw to it that every pupil could play one or more instruments or, at the very least, sing.

In those early days, musical talent and education were an excellent means of obtaining material comforts and advantages. Peasants could be freed from serfdom and exempted from military service if their musical achievements came to the ears of their lords. And once a position as a servant was gained, those who went on to prove themselves as good musicians had the hope of rising to more elevated positions, and perhaps even being released from service altogether.

When the English composer Charles Burnley visited Bohemia in 1772, he was

so surprised by the level of musical skill in the country that he named it the "conservatory of Europe". This musical environment not only produced many folk musicians but also such a surplus of trained performers that they sometimes had difficulty earning their living in their home country.

The unstable political situation of the 18th century, together with religious persecution, forced many people to emigrate. Countless musicians were among them, who, thanks to their skills, easily found work all over Europe. Everywhere these emigrants went, they commanded respect, influenced the new instrumental style of classicism, and left definite

LEFT: Bedřich Smetana.
RIGHT: a bust of Mozart at Bertramka.

traces in the structure of its melodies. At the same time, Bohemian music in turn became exposed to foreign influences, which it incorporated successfully.

Mozart and Figaro

The visits of Wolfgang Amadeus Mozart (1756–91) should be seen in this international context. Mozart left his home town of Salzburg, Austria, to build a career for himself in Vienna, but the Viennese public and the court did not always appreciate him. Prague, however, had gone wild about his opera *The Marriage of Figaro* when it was performed there. An invitation to visit Prague

Although Mozart spent relatively little of his life in Prague, he has become a revered adopted son, as is evident from the Mozart industry in postcards and T-shirts and the interest shown in the Mozart museum, Bertramka, at Mozartova 169 in the district of Smíchov, which holds regular concerts.

The German influence

From the early 19th century on, the aristocracy of Prague gradually lost their position as the most important patrons of the arts. The rising middle classes claimed their share in the process of shaping cultural life. The centre of activity moved from aristocratic salons to

followed, and he came to the city in 1787.

In Prague Mozart witnessed *Figaro*-fever, which had gripped the whole city and led to him receiving a commission for an opera from the impresario of what was then the Nostitz Theatre (now the Estates Theatre, *see page 132*). In contrast to other theatres in Central Europe, the Nostitz was not tied to a court, but was a relatively independent institution. The fact that in Prague opera had been available to the public for a long time explains the interest of the broad mass of people. The Prague premiere of *Don Giovanni* in the autumn of 1787, conducted by Mozart himself, was an unprecedented success.

public concert halls, and a new era dawned. It was shaped by two institutions which both left a definitive mark. One was the Society of Artists, founded in 1803 and modelled on its predecessor in Vienna; the other was the Prague Conservatory, which opened in 1811. This was the first in Central Europe, and set the standards for the rest. The city of Prague, which was still under the strong influence of the Mozart cult, was now being exposed to more new influences.

Carl Maria von Weber, director of the Nostitz Theatre from 1813–16, acquainted Prague with Beethoven's *Fidelio* and the first Romantic operas. In the same theatre, Niccolò

Paganini, the celebrated violinist and composer, enjoyed great successes. Beethoven concerts also took place in the Konvikt, a complex in Bartolomějská (now the Czech Film Archive). Later in the 19th century, a concert hall on the Slavonic Island (Slovanský ostrov), near the present-day National Theatre, became a venue for Berlioz, Wagner and Liszt. The scene was now defined by the flood of German music, and Czech music faded into the background.

Bedřich Smetana

The awakening of national consciousness during the troubled times of the early 19th century saw a generation of Czech artists faced with the task of creating their own culture. They were not alone in this: throughout Europe, nationalists were rediscovering their pasts and forging links between political aspirations and musical and literary expression. In the Czech lands, this cultural resurgence did not take place until the second half of the century.

The name of Bedřich Smetana (1824–84) is inextricably tied with Prague, and in his work Czech music first reached its peak. Born in Litomyšl, Smetana came to the city to study music. He took part in the Czech nationalist revolution in 1848, and shared in the patriotic feelings which engendered it. His wish was to unite artistic expectations with the demands of an independent national culture. It was a long road, but his aim was eventually achieved with his operas. Apart from a five-year stay in Göteborg in Sweden, Smetana remained active in the musical life of Prague, while he tried, at first in vain, to establish himself as a conductor and composer. Not until the success of his opera *The Bartered Bride* (1866) did he achieve the position of conductor to the Czech Opera and widespread recognition.

After the loss of his hearing in 1874, Smetana gave up his career as a practising musician, but he continued to compose and created some notable works, including the symphonic poem *Má vlast (My Homeland)* and the string quartet *Aus meinem Leben (From My Life)*. Smetana received the highest honour when his opera *Libuše* was performed at the official opening of the National Theatre,

a ceremony that symbolised the peak of national aspirations.

Smetana is particularly well represented in Prague's opera houses and concert halls At least one of his romantic operas is generally in production, from the nationalist *Libuše*, to the folk opera *The Bartered Bride (Prodaná nevěsta)*, and *The Brandenburgers in Bohemia (Braniboři v Čechách)*, which celebrated its first success in 1866 and has been in the repertory ever since.

Antonín Dvořák

While everyone in Prague was raving about Smetana, another Czech composer had

already started to show his talent. Antonín Dvořák (1841–1904) was born near Prague, and first attracted attention with his *Hymnus*, a nationalistic cantata based on Halek's poem *The Heroes of the White Mountain*. He attended the organ school in Prague, played in the National Theatre orchestra, and was organist at St Adalbert's from 1874 to 1877.

His talent was recognised by Brahms, who introduced his music to Vienna, sponsoring the publication of the *Klänge aus Mähren (Sounds from Moravia)*, which was followed by a commissioned work, *Slavonic Dances*. His *Stabat Mater*, performed in London in 1883, won him European acclaim. In 1892–5 he was director

LEFT: Smetana playing at a musical salon.
RIGHT: Antonín Dvořák.

York Conservatory. His ninth sym-
... rom the New World had a distinct
Slavonic flavour. Returning to Prague in 1895,
Dvořák remained true to the musical traditions
of Bohemia and influenced the musical life of
the city. His home, Villa Amerika, is now open
to the public *(see page 157)*. The opera
Rusalka and several of Dvořák's other works
are performed regularly at Prague concerts and
in the city's opera houses.

Dvořák could be said to be the founder of a
musical dynasty. His daughter, Otilka, married the Czech violinist, composer and student
of Dvořák, Josef Suk (1874–1935), whose
grandson, also called Josef, is a famous modern violinist. The grandfather was co-founder
of the Bohemia Quartet and is now remem-
bered for his fine orchestral works.

Janáček and Martinů

The two figures that dominated Czech music
during the first half of the 20th century were
Leoš Janáček (1854–1928) and **Bohuslav
Martinů** (1890–1959). Janáček spent almost
all his life in Brno, Moravia, and was little
known in Prague until his *Jenůfa* was performed in the city in 1916 (where it is still a
staple of the National Theatre repertory, as is
his most famous operatic work, *The Cunning
Little Vixen* or *Příhody lišky Bystroušky)*. His
music is known for its use of traditional Czech
song and, in his operas, for his "speech-song",
which he modelled closely on the cadences of
the Czech language. Although most of his
works were premiered in Brno, after 1916
they were all quickly repeated in Prague, and
he became an important figure in the creation
of a national cultural identity around the time
of the emergence of the Czechoslovak state.

Martinů was similarly drawn to using traditional Czech music in his works, but he was
also influenced by developments in contemporary French music. He went to Paris to
study with Albert Roussel, initially to
"escape" from the overbearing influence of
Czech nationalism. In Paris he encountered
Stravinsky, who persuaded him that Czech traditions could be convincingly incorporated
into his compositions, and, after a flirtation
with Neoclassicism, he developed a distinctive and uniquely Czech personal style. This
Czech quality first came to light in the 1930s
with his opera *Julietta* and is especially evident in the works written in exile in the USA
during World War II.

One further composer of the 1930s who
must be mentioned is Vitezslava Kaprálová
(1915–40). After studying composition and
conducting in Brno and Prague she moved to
Paris to continue her studies with Nadia
Boulanger. Her brief but exceptionally
promising career, influenced greatly by Martinů who was one of her teachers, produced
several forward-looking and interesting
works, including the *Six Variations of The
Bells of St. Etienne du Mont in Paris* and the
Military Symphonietta.

ARNOLD SCHÖNBERG

VENUES AND ENSEMBLES

The Czech Philharmonic has its home in the Dvořák
Hall of the Rudolfinum. The Prague Symphony
Orchestra is based in the Smetana Hall at the
Obecní dům. The Czech National Symphony
Orchestra also performs regularly. The National
Theatre, the State Opera and the Estates Theatre
have opera and ballet. As for chamber music, there
are various string quartets, such as the Wihan
Quartet, the Talich Quartet and the Škampa Quartet.
The Suk Chamber Orchestra was founded by vio-
linist Josef Suk, a great-grandson of Dvořák. *(See
also page 221.)*

Modernists

The strength of national culture did not, however, have a detrimental effect on Prague's open-minded attitude to musical developments occurring elsewhere in Europe. The 1908 premiere of *Symphony No. 7* by Gustav Mahler took place in Prague; in 1885 he had been conductor of the New German Theatre's orchestra. The same orchestra was directed from 1911–27 by Alexander von Zemlinsky, who acted as a go-between with the great musical cities, Vienna and Berlin; Alban Berg (1885–1935) and Arnold Schoenberg (1874– 1951) both had the opportunity to get to know Prague. Schoenberg's *Ewartung*

known as Quattro (Sylvie Bodorová, born 1954, Luboš Fišer, 1935–99, Zedeněk Lukáš, born 1928, and Otmar Mácha, born 1922) have produced many interesting works. A good source of further information on contemporary music in Prague is the Czech Music Information Centre (www.musica.cz).

Jazz and popular music

Musical life in Prague has never been restricted to classical music, and its jazz and rock scenes have long had a reputation for lively invention, and have played a significant part in political dissent. Jazz arrived early in Prague, imported American music being noted

(Expectation) was also premiered there.

The avant-garde were heavily circumscribed during the period of Communist rule, yet many of the Czech Republic's most prominent contemporary composers began their careers during this period, often struggling to get their more experimental works performed. Of these one of the most prominent is Petr Eben (born 1929), who is particularly notable for his works for organ, and as a teacher of composition as professor at the Charles University. The Prague-based group of composers

LEFT: Arnold Schoenberg.
ABOVE: *The Bartered Bride* at the National Theatre.

by Karel Čapek at the Café Montmartre in the 1920s. Home-grown talent soon emerged, most importantly in the orchestra lead by Jaroslav Ježek during the 1930s at the Gramoklub. Jazz was banned by the Nazis but emerged again, within limits, under the Communist regime, particularly after Stalin's death. One of the most influential groups of this time was Studio 5. With the clampdown following the Prague Spring, the radical musical mantle passed to rock musicians, in particular the Plastic People of the Universe, formed in 1968. It was the suppression of this group that lead to the setting up of the human rights petition Charter 77. ❑

LITERATURE

From Kafka to Kundera, many Czech writers have won international acclaim. And one – Václav Havel – even became president

Literature has a long history in Bohemia, in both Czech and German. Around 1400, Johannes von Tepl wrote *Der Ackermann aus Böhmen* (The Husbandman from Bohemia), one of the earliest prose masterpieces in German, while Czech was the most productive of all the Slavonic languages in the later Middle Ages, with, among other chivalrous romances, its own version of *Tristram a Izalda* (Tristan and Isolde). The cultural dominance of German was acute during the long *temno* or period of darkness that followed the Battle of the White Mountain in 1620, but Czech underwent a strong revival in the 19th-century period of national awakening. Perhaps the most glorious time for literature came in the early 20th century, when, in a ferment of activity, German – and particularly German Jewish – writers made Prague's Café Arco their headquarters and became known as the "Arconauts". Their Czech counterparts frequented the Café Union, referred to colloquially as the "Unionka". Both factions came together at the famous Café Slavia, with its view of river and castle.

Before this, a growing literature in Czech had produced fine poetry, notably *Máj* (May) by the Byronic and short-lived figure of Karel Hynek Mácha (1810–36). Mácha is still revered today, and lovers traditionally place flowers by his statue on Petřín Hill on 1 May. Prague and its citizenry, particularly the humble denizens of Malá Strana, were celebrated

in an affectionately Dickensian way by Jan Neruda (1834–91) in his collection of short stories called *Tales of the Malá Strana.*

Easily the most famous – and most exploited – of Prague's literary figures is Franz Kafka (1883–1924). As a German-speaker among Czechs, Kafka was in an élite minority; as a Jew among Germans, a smaller minority still. (Look up "Kafka" in several different encyclopedias and you'll find him labelled variously as an Austrian, Jewish, German or Czech writer.) Many believe that the sense of alienation that permeates Kafka's fiction springs from this confusion of identity *(see pages 144–5).*

LEFT: Franz Kafka, a German speaker among Czechs.
RIGHT: Jaroslav Hašek, an emblematic Prague writer.

Kafka wrote in German, and thus belonged to Prague's glittering circle of German-speaking intellectuals, along with such literary contemporaries as Franz Werfel (1890–1945) and Egon Erwin Kisch (1885–1948). Werfel is best known for his book *Song of Bernadette*, but was regarded in his lifetime primarily as a poet. Kisch was called the "Roving Reporter", a journalist whose scathing critiques of society often took him into the back-alley underworld of Prague, and whose personal exploits in getting a story were legendary. But perhaps the key figure in this early-20th-century literary circle was Max Brod (1884–1968). Brod is known today less for his literary works, which are more or less forgotten, than for his tireless championing of other writers and artists. As Kafka's literary executor, it was Brod who brought the writer's great novels to the public after his death. Brod's energy and enthusiasm enabled him to cross the Czech/German language and culture barrier; he was a tireless promoter of the works of composer Leoš Janáček, and helped to achieve the wider acclaim of the quintessential Czech novel, *The Good Soldier Švejk*, by Jaroslav Hašek (1883–1923).

The Good Soldier Švejk

Published in 1921, Hašek's story relates the serial misadventures of the hapless Josef

A LITERARY TOUR

Aside from visiting the obligatory Kafka sites, fans of Czech literature can find many cafés and bars in the city which boasted writers among their clientele, and soak up the atmosphere that inspired these observers of Prague life. Both Hašek and his famous character, the Good Soldier Švejk, are today almost over-immortalised at the pub U kalicha (The Chalice), where, in the novel, Švejk and a friend make a date to meet at "six in the evening after the war". The pub, which features a huge collection of Švejk memorabilia on its walls, now caters mainly to the hordes of tourists wishing to drink in some of the spirit of the good soldier.

Many people today still visit Bohumil Hrabal's favourite pub, U zlatého tygra (The Golden Tiger), where the well-known bon viveur was a regular fixture for many years.

The Café Slavia, which in turn was immortalised by the poet Jaroslav Seifert, was a second home for many prominent Czech artists around the turn of the 20th century. Later, during the Communist era, it was a hotbed for dissident writers whose works were banned by the government. After standing abandoned for many years, the Slavia was finally restored in the 1990s to the glory of its halcyon days, and today retains its unique air of Art Deco sophistication.

Švejk, who frustrates the Austrian army's attempts to make a soldier out of him by his unique form of smiling, servile sabotage. By appearing to follow all orders to the letter, Švejk makes a fruitful career of getting out of whatever work he is supposed to do, meanwhile getting into some very amusing scrapes along the way. It is a dark comic novel that offers very little in the way of optimism.

Because of its questionable hero, *The Good Soldier Švejk* has been criticised by some as being insulting and presenting a negative picture of the Czech national character. But don't tell that to the 23 Czech literary scholars, writers and historians who, in a 1998 survey published in *Týden* magazine, voted *Švejk*, by a wide margin, the greatest Czech prose work of the 20th century. The broad, beaming face of Švejk has been immortalised by the illustrations of the popular Czech artist Josef Lada that appeared in the first edition (and most editions since), images that have become as much of a Prague icon as the brooding face of Kafka (although Švejk is much more likely to take the humorous form of a souvenir puppet).

In his own way, Švejk's creator, Jaroslav Hašek, was as emblematic a Prague figure as Kafka. An anarchic boozer and prankster, Hašek invented imaginary animals to bulk out the pages of *Animal Life*, a magazine of which he was – briefly – editor. His contribution to Austrian political life was to stand for election as a candidate for his own "Party for Moderate Progress within the Bounds of the Law". In World War I he survived the rigours of the eastern front, going over to the Russians and becoming a Red Army commissar before returning home to die of drink. Grotesquely overweight, his bloated body had to be winched out of his bedroom.

Another Czech writer who made his mark was the prolific Karel Čapek (1890–1938). A confidant of President Masaryk, a radical journalist and author of numerous works of fiction, including *An Ordinary Life*, *Meteor* and *Stories from Two Pockets*, he was also a playwright who is perhaps best known for having coined the international word "robot" in his play *RUR* (Rossum's Universal Robots).

LEFT: Masaryk meeting with Karel Čapek.
RIGHT: Kafka with Felice Bauer.

Modern voices

Contemporary Czech literature lost perhaps its brightest light with the death of Bohumil Hrabal (1914–97). The author of many works, including *I Served the King of England* and *Too Loud a Solitude*, Hrabal is probably best known outside of his homeland as the author of *Closely Watched Trains*, set at the end of World War II and made into an Oscar-winning film by Czech director Jiří Menzel in 1966 with whom he forged a fertile creative partnership. Hrabal's life came to an end in characteristic Prague manner – by defenestration. In 1997 he fell to his death from a fifth-floor hospital window, a demise eerily

presaged in several of his later writings, particularly the disturbing collection of essays entitled *Total Fears*.

Also prominent was the Czech writer Jaroslav Seifert (1901–86), the only Czech to date to win the Nobel Prize for Literature, in 1984. A pro-Communist who later turned his back on the movement, Seifert is best known for his poetry, including an ode to the Café Slavia.

Notable among contemporary writers is Ivan Klíma (b. 1931), author of many works that focus on Prague, including *The Spirit of Prague*, *My Merry Mornings* and, perhaps most notably, *Judge on Trial*, which concerns a judge working within the Communist regime. Athough he lives in Prague and writes in Czech, Klíma is generally more popular outside the Czech Republic than he is in his homeland.

Writers in exile

Another Czech writer who is perhaps more revered abroad than at home is the expatriate author Milan Kundera (b. 1929), who may be, after Kafka and Švejk, the name most closely associated with Czech literature for foreigners. His novels, such as *The Book of Laughter and Forgetting* and, most notably, *The Unbearable Lightness of Being*, were

extremely well received in the West. The latter was made into a popular film in 1987 starring Daniel Day-Lewis and Juliette Binoche, and provided many westerners with their first glimpse of what life was like in Czechoslovakia during the dark days of the Iron Curtain. Kundera left Czechoslovakia after the 1968 Warsaw Pact invasion, and chose to remain abroad after the revolution, taking French citizenship and writing his recent works in French. Many Czechs feel that his earlier books, such as *The Joke*, about the Stalinist regime, are more important than those with which he gained an international reputation.

Czechs have similar feelings about another émigré, the witty and disrespectful Josef Škvorecký (b. 1924), who is generally regarded in his homeland more for his 1950 novel *The Cowards* than subsequent works such as *The Engineer of Human Souls*, written in self-imposed exile in Canada.

The new wave

These more established authors are now beginning to have strong competition from a new wave of Czech contemporary writers who have found their voices in the post-Communist era. One of the most popular of these younger writers is Michael Vieweigh, whose novels *The Wonderful Years that Sucked* and *Bringing up Girls in Bohemia* were not only best-selling books, but were also made into extremely popular films.

And then there is Jáchym Topol (b. 1962) – son of the playwright Josef (best known for his play *Nightingale for Dinner*) and brother of the firebrand underground rock musician and actor Filip – who has made an intense impression on the Czech literary scene with his works, including the lacerating novel *City Sister Silver*.

The philosopher president

One of the distinctions of the Czech Republic is, of course, that its first president, Václav Havel was, before the revolution, a well-known playwright and political dissident. His works for the stage, such as *Private View*, *Garden Party* and *Largo Desolato*, functioned not only as drama but as allegorical tools of sabotage against the repression of the Communist regime. Havel also produced several books of thoughtful essays, philosophical reflections that draw on the experiences of his own life, among them *Letters to Olga*, a compilation of his letters from prison to his first wife.

Although Havel's main body of work was produced before his entry into political life, it is likely that the works of this "philosopher president" (as he became known), which spoke so eloquently to his times, will maintain their place among the classic works of Czech literature. ❑

LEFT: Václav Havel, playwright and president.

Czech Film

Prague is well known as a backdrop to Hollywood blockbusters (in *Mission: Impossible,* 1996, or *Amadeus,* 1984, for example); what are less well known to visitors are the home-grown products. The nascent Czech film industry expanded rapidly at the beginning of the 1930s with the building of the Barrandov studios (1931–2) in the south of Prague *(see page 185).* By and large its products were light and entertaining, although *Extáze* (Ecstasy, 1933) by Gustav Machatý caused a scandal for its nude scene, acted by Hedwig Eva Marie Kreisler (later known as Hedy Lamarr). When the invading Germans arrived in 1939 they took over and expanded the Prague studios, not only using them for propaganda films but also continuing the production of feature films (albeit for their own ends).

With the advent of Stalinist rule, filmmaking became turgid, and it was only with the thawing of the regime towards the end of the 1950s that new ideas began to emerge. Presaged by films such as František Vlácil's *Holubice* (The White Dove, 1960), these coalesced into the movement known as the "Czech New Wave". Focusing on everyday life and using real locations, its main exponents included Miloš Forman, Jiří Menzel and Vera Chytilová. In the west, the best known of these is Forman, chiefly for his subsequent work in Hollywood. However, his trio of films made between 1963–7 (*Černy Petr, Lásky Jedné Plavovlásky* and *Horí, Má Panenko*) were made in Czechoslovakia. *Černy Petr* (Black Peter, 1963) is a coming-of-age movie about a boy who becomes a store detective (aka the secret police), while *Lásky Jedné Plavovlásky* (Loves of a Blonde, 1965) was more overtly critical of the regime, attacking centralised planning. The most bitter of the trio, however, is *Horí, Má Panenko* (The Fireman's Ball, 1967) in which almost everyone is corrupt.

Jiří Menzel had a close professional relationship with the writer Bohumil Hrabal, the most fruitful product of this collaboration

being *Ostre Sledované Vlaky* (Closely Watched Trains, 1966), about a young station master on the eastern front during World War II. Vera Chytilová was probably the most adventurous of the trio, especially with her *Sedmikrásky* (Daisies, 1966), about two teenage girls who exploit and sexually tease older men. One Slovakian film (albeit made in Barrandov) that must be mentioned is *Obchod na Korze* (The Shop on Main Street, 1965) by Elmar Klos and Ján Kádar, about a Slovakian carpenter forced to spy on a Jewish woman during World War II.

With the clampdown following the Prague Spring (during which a number of ascerbic

films were made about the authorities) some filmmakers retreated into the world of fairytales, a genre brilliantly subverted by Jaromír Jireš in *Valerie a Tynden Divu* (Valerie and Her Week of Wonders, 1970) which is more like a Gothic horror film, and the animator Jan Švankmajer with his surreal *Neco z Alenky* (Alice in Wonderland, 1988).

Since 1989 there has been a re-examination of the regions's Jewish history, as in Jan Hrebejk's *Musíme Si Poméhat* (Divided We Fall, 2000) about the Holocaust, and a concentration on new social problems, such as teenage prostitution in *Mandragora* (1997) by Wiktor Grodecki. ❑

RIGHT: Miloš Forman, embraced by Hollywood.

ART AND ARCHITECTURE

Prague conjures up images of medieval buildings and alleys, but modern artists and architects have not been shy to experiment in this traditional city

Prague is essentially a Gothic city with a Baroque face. Nearly all of its numerous churches were either built or remodelled during the Baroque period, and many of the original Gothic houses were given a new Baroque facade in the frenetic period of building and reconstruction initiated by the Habsburgs in the 17th century. That said, Prague's historic centre is also remarkable for its harmonious blend of styles, from the Gothic to the avant-garde. It is this lively interplay that gives the city its unique profile.

Little survives of the early Romanesque architecture of the city. Two notable exceptions are the interior Bazilika sv. Jiří, which dates from the 12th century (the façade is a Baroque addition; *see page 86*), and the Rotunda sv. Martina on Vyšehrad (11th century; *see page 161*). The Romanesque, in vogue from the 10th to 13th centuries, was characterised by its heavy walls, round arches and small, slit-lke windows.

The Gothic

The Central European Gothic style has some of its greatest exemplars in Prague. The style, which originated in northern France, has at its heart techniques of building using a "skeleton" of pointed arches, joined by cross-ribs and, often, supported on the outside by a series of flying buttresses. The result of this was a

LEFT: Dientzenhofer's Church of St Nicholas and Myslbek's statue of Jan Hus, Old Town Square.
RIGHT: the tower of the Koruna Building, Wenceslas Square.

light and airy structure that left a great deal of room for windows (there was no longer any need to use the solid stone construction of the earlier Romanesque) and enabled the master builders to construct high, vaulted chambers.

Although most of Prague's original Gothic buildings may not be recognisable as such today, several fine examples of the style that flowered during the reign of Charles IV still stand in the heart of the city. The best-known architectural legacy, to most visitors at least, of the 14th-century ruler is the bridge named after him, Charles Bridge (Karlův most; *see pages 116–17*). Commissioned in the 1350s to replace the earlier Judith Bridge, it was built by Petr Parléř, the architect of much of that other great Gothic landmark, St Vitus's Cathedral. Parler's nave in St Vitus is one of the miracles of the age, showing perfectly the complex yet elegant system of vaulting that enabled the builders to create such a light and airy space *(see page 82)*.

Close by is another superb example of Gothic vaulting, Benedict Reid's late-Gothic Vladislav Hall in the Old Royal Palace. Two other fine Gothic structures are on Old Town Square: the Church of Our Lady before Týn (Kostel Panny Marie před Týnem), and the Old Town Hall, with its clock tower and elaborately carved Gothic doorway.

The Renaissance

Elements of an Italianate style had started to creep in with the late Gothic (for instance the Renaissance doorways in Reid's Vladislav Hall). Indeed, Bohemia was one of the main conduits through which new ideas from Italy and France were spread; even as far as England when Richard II married Anne of Bohemia in 1382. However, it was not until 1537 that Paolo della Stella started work on what is Prague's most characteristically Renaissance building, the Belvedér in the Royal Gardens *(see page 89)*. Also in the Royal Gardens is the Míčovna by Bonifác Wohlmut (1565–9), covered in Italianate

Petr Parléř, the Imperial Architect

In 1344, Charles had already managed to use his good relationship with Clement VI to have Prague promoted from a bishopric to an archbishopric. In the same year the building of St Vitus's Cathedral began, on the site of the former basilica. The cathedral was conceived as a triple-aisled nave church, in the French idiom. Charles obtained the services of the French architect, Matthias of Arras.

Following the latter's death in 1352, the masons' and sculptors' workshop of Petr Parléř (1332–99) took over the building. Under his direction the famous triforium arcade was created, along with the choir, the South Tower, and particularly the vaulting, for which Parléř was famous.

The Wenceslas Chapel and the Golden Door, both evidence of a new synthesis of architecture and sculpture, can be attributed wholly to Parler.

After finishing St Vitus's Cathedral, Parléř completed the Týn Church (begun in 1365). Also designed by Parléř's workshop are the windows of the Martinic chapel, the Bridge Tower of the Old Town and the chapel of Charles Church, modelled on the chapel of Charlemagne in Aachen. In 1357, under Parléř's direction, work began on the Charles Bridge. Petr Parléř was one of the most notable architects of the late-Gothic period, and his style greatly influenced subsequent architecture.

sgraffito (it was Wohlmut who added the Belvedere's idiosyncratic copper roof). Another impressive example of sgraffito work can be seen on the Schwarzenberský palác on Hradčanské náměstí.

The Baroque

Although it was the Habsburgs who brought the Renaissance style to Prague, they more thoroughly stamped their mark on the city after the Thirty Years War when an all-out attempt was made to Catholicise Bohemia, and nowhere is this more apparent than in the predominance of Baroque architecture. The Baroque relied heavily on classical motifs but

early 1700s by Christoph Dientzenhofer, continued by his son Kilián Ignaz, and finished by Kilián's son-in-law Anselmo Lurago. Kilián Dientzenhofer also built Prague's "other" St Nicholas's Church, the much more modest church that anchors the north-west side of Old Town Square.

So many fine examples of Baroque architecture exist within the city, much of it as façades on or remodellings of older buildings, it is hard to single out individual examples. However, it would be a mistake to miss out on the Clam-Gallas Palace (1713) in the Old Town, deigned by the great Viennese architect Johann Bernard Fischer von Erlach.

in a great proliferation of ornament and decoration. A masterly handling of light and shade is also a notable feature of much Baroque architecture and painting.

By building grand Baroque churches the Habsburg rulers meant to inspire awe – and obedience – among the masses. The best of these churches is, without doubt, St Nicholas's Church (Kostel svatého Mikuláše) on Malá Strana's Malostranské náměstí, begun in the

LEFT: the eastern end of Petr Parléř's Cathedral of St Vitus.
ABOVE: the Baroque ceiling of the Church of St Nicholas, Malá Strana.

If many of the major architects working in the Baroque style were foreign, in painting and sculpture there were many fine local artists. Among the sculptors, mention must be made of Johann Georg Bendl (1630–80) and Ferdinand Maximilián Brokoff (1688–1731). However, perhaps the finest sculptor working in Prague during this period was the Austrian-born Matthias Bernard Braun (1684–1738). Of the painters the three greatest of the time were Karel Škréta (1610–74), Petr Brandl (1668–1735) and Jan Kupecký (1667–1740). Many examples of their work can be seen in Prague, especially in the National Gallery's collection of Baroque and Mannerist art.

Revivals

The Habsburgs dominated architectural style in Bohemia until Czechoslovakia's independence in 1918, but towards the end of the 19th century there were rumblings of national feeling appearing on the Prague cityscape. The three most notable examples of the National Revival style of the late 1800s, marked by its monumental Classicism, are the National Theatre (Národní divadlo), the Rudolfinum and the National Museum (Národní muzeum).

Prague's Art Nouveau

Along with Paris, Vienna and Berlin, Prague was one of the centres where the avant-garde

One beautiful example is the Hotel Evropa on Wenceslas Square, designed by Alois Dryák and Bedřich Bendelmayer and built in 1903–4. But the greatest gem of Art Nouveau in Prague is Municipal House (Obecní dům) on Náměstí Republiky, by Antonín Balčánek and Osvald Polívka, completed in 1911, with salons decorated by Alfons Mucha and a huge mosaic, *Homage to Prague* by Karel Spillar. Wilsonova Station (Hlavní nádraží) designed by Josef Fanta and built between 1901 and 1909, is another outstanding example of Art-Nouveau architecture.

A student of the Viennese master Otto Wagner, Jan Kotěra was one of the first to intro-

used revolutionary ideas to shape architectural styles in a way which would reflect their ideals and reject tradition. A progressive atmosphere was created by close cultural and economic ties between the cities. In this environment, architecture flourished, and Czech architecture soon won a place in European artistic journals. The various building styles that emerged in pre-World War II Prague were both internationally influenced and Bohemian-inspired.

The beginning of the modern period came with the advent of Art Nouveau (variously called *Jugendstil* and Secessionist – *secese* in Czech), with its organic and flowing lines.

duce new trends to Prague. At first Kotěra was strongly influenced by Vienna, as can be seen in his Peterka House at Wenceslas Square No. 12, built in 1900. With its slender windows and elegant ornamentation, it is considered one of the purest examples of Art Nouveau architecture in the city. Further development of Kotěra's ideas can be seen in the office block on Růžová and U půjčovny in the New Town, dating from 1924, in which he incorporates Baroque forms.

The Štenc House at Salvátorská 8, near Old Town Square, is by Kotěra's pupil Otakar Novotný. Built for the photographer Jan Štenc in 1909–14, the house's striking appearance is due not to ornamentation but to the play of proportions and light across its fine brick façade.

Another Otto Wagner pupil, Bohumil Hübschmann, marked the courageous transition to a starker architecture with his vertically articulated apartment house at Široká 5–7, built in 1910–11. Hübschmann also designed the covered entrance to the adjacent Jewish Cemetery.

Cubism

The second chapter of modern architecture in Prague was sparked by the exhibition of the first Cubist paintings by Picasso and Braque in Paris in 1909. The shock waves emanating

architects. In a short but frenetic period, Cubist architecture flowered in Bohemia, the only place that the movement caught on.

In the heady atmosphere of the times, people saw Cubism, with its prism-like dissection and abstraction of surfaces, as a way projecting an image of the new age, and architects sought to translate the movement's formal qualities, such as fragmentation, spatial ambiguity and multiplicity, into habitable structures.

In addition to incorporating influences of the Parisian avant-garde, Czech Cubist architecture also had formal roots in the Art-Nouveau style. Art Nouveau's later tendency

from Paris soon reached Prague, and changed not only the development of painting, but also the style of buildings. By 1914, when the Mánes Society art gallery held an important Cubist exhibition, Prague had become the most fertile ground for Cubism outside Paris. It is perhaps not surprising that Cubism found ready adherents among Prague's painters and sculptors, but nowhere else in Europe did Cubism also spark such enthusiasm among

LEFT: the splendid Baroque Philosphers' Library in the Strahov Monastery.
ABOVE: heroic Nationalist sculpture on the National Theatre.

CUBIST LIVING

Rondocubism was not confined to public buildings; there are many residential buildings which were worked on by noted architects. Novotný, for example, designed the facade for an apartment block at Kamenická 35 in the residential Holešovice district in 1923–4. With František Zavadil, Gočár and Janák designed a group of detached houses in the Strašnice district; Rudolf Hrabě used National Style forms and colours in the Prague Municipal Houses complex in the Holešovice district; the style can also be admired here and there in the neighbourhoods of Dejvice, Žižkov, Bubeneč and Vinohrady.

towards a stronger geometric expression marked a transitional phase to the even starker geometry and dynamism of Cubism.

Perhaps Prague's best-known architectural work in the Cubist style – if for no other reason than its prominent location along the Royal Way – dates from 1912: the House of the Black Madonna (Dům u černé Matky Boží), by Josef Gočár, a pupil of Kotěra and one of the most important Czech architects of the 20th century. Located at Ovocný trh 19, the building was Prague's first Cubist building, and originally housed a department store and a café. Today it contains a branch of the National Gallery and features a permanent exhibition of Czech

Baroque statue adjoining the 18th-century Church of the Holy Trinity next door. Though controversial in its day, today we can see it as a sensitive solution to harmonise vastly different periods and styles.

One of the 20th century's most notable and radical architects among those working in the Cubist style was Josef Chochol, who had trained for two years in the Vienna studio of Otto Wagner. His buildings in the neighbourhood below Vyšehrad Hill, all constructed in the heyday of Czech Cubism, rate as some of the primary examples of the style. Don't miss the Hodek Apartment House (1913–14) at Neklanova 30, with its bold cornice.

Cubist painting, sculpture and furniture. The house derives its name from the statue of the Madonna relocated from a former Baroque building at that site. This early Cubist work demonstrates that it was possible to build anew in the modern idiom without destroying the optical harmony of a historic district.

Emil Králíček was responsible for designing another striking Cubist structure, the Palác Diamant at Spálená 4 on the corner of Lazarská – a building whose ground floor now houses a showroom. The Diamant building (1912) straddles the border between the late Art Nouveau and Cubist styles. Notable is the Cubist frame around a

A short walk away is another example of Chochol's work, the 1912–13 villa at Libušina 3, situated between two other noteworthy Cubist houses, one by Králíček to the south and one by Otakar Novotný to the north. The villa and its garden, originally landscaped in the Cubist manner, are surrounded by a gate that echoes the geometric planes of the house. Also worth a look is the architect's so-called Cubist Triple House (1913–14) – three connected private villas on Rašínovo nábřeží 6–10.

Rondocubism

The Cubist movement came at a time when the country was dissolving its centuries-old ties with the Habsburg monarchy and founding the Czechoslovak state. Against this political background, leading architects tried to create an independent national style, using Cubist methods combined with forms of vernacular architecture such as arches, cylinders and shapes in high relief. In their new designs, they were inspired by folk art: brightly painted Moravian portals, elaborately decorated cottages and the like. Roundness and colour were used as a counterpoint to the sharp edges and greyness that to them symbolised the Germanic monarchy.

The style arising from this unlikely marriage of national feeling and radical modernity is known to art historians as Rondocubism –

Both of these buildings are situated opposite the Urbánek House (also called the Mozarteum) by Kotěra. Built in 1912 as a house and concert hall for the music publisher Mojmír Urbánek, this building now contains a gallery exhibiting contemporary Czech and international art, and is well worth a visit to admire its interior.

Otakar Novotný designed a number of buildings in the Rondocubist style, including three apartment houses of 1919–21 located at Elišky Krásnohorské 10–14 in the Old Town. Sometimes called simply the Cubist House, it has an effective colour scheme and geometric designs.

Gočár also produced one of Rondocubism's finest exemplars – the Czech Legion Bank on

known locally as the National Style – and has had a strong influence on many buildings in Prague. A brief but fruitful period produced a number of notable houses, especially the colourful Adria Palace at Jungmannova 31 by Pavel Janák (1922–5), built for the Italian Riunione Adriatica insurance company. Its neighbour at Jungmannova 29, built in 1923–6 by the same architect, features a similar, though more monumental, façade.

LEFT: stained glass by Alfons Mucha in the Cathedral of St Vitus.
ABOVE: the elegant, early-Functionalist Mánes building.

Na poříčí 24, built between 1921–3, with its dramatic red-and-white facade and semicircular window arches. Visitors can step inside to admire the bank hall, which combines lively elements of folk ornamentation with straightforward modernity and features a vaulted glass roof. The frieze *Return of the Legionnaires* is by Otto Gutfreund, arguably the greatest 20th-century Czech sculptor and one of the nation's pre-eminent Cubist artists.

Modernism and Functionalism

During the course of the 1920s, the so-called National Style reached a blind alley, and architects sought to reconnect with European modernism. Adolf Loos, the Viennese architect active in Prague and an early opponent of Art Nouveau, believed that architecture devoid of ornament represented pure and lucid thought, going so far as to state that "ornament is a crime". The influence of Loos, as well as Gropius and Le Corbusier, began to take hold.

Throughout the 1920 and 1930s, these ideas found expression in the movement known as Functionalism, a doctrine stressing purpose, practicality and utility. One of Prague's most prominent examples of Functionalism is the Mánes Artists' Association House, built between 1927–30. Named in honour of Josef Mánes, the 19th-century

ments built in 1938–9, with its lively interplay of vertical and horizontal planes.

Several other notable examples of Modernism's streamlined aesthetic can be seen on Wenceslas Square, for example the former Hotel Juliš by Janák dating from 1928–33 and the Lindt Department Store by Ludvík Kysela from 1925–7. The glass facade of the Lindt house was restored in 1998. Another notable building by Kysela on Wenceslas Square is the Bat'a Department Store (1927–9), with a glass curtain wall over a reinforced concrete skeleton.

A remarkable building of a different style dating from this period is the Church of the

artist and nationalist, this white, puristic building designed by Otakar Novotný protrudes into the Vltava river and forms a bridge between the embankment and Slovanský Island. It is still in use today as an art gallery and terraced restaurant.

Many of Prague's best examples of the Functionalist style – typified by simple white facades, flat roofs, ribbon windows, elegant entrances and fine attention to detail – are located in the city's outlying districts (see pages 164–5), but right off Wenceslas Square, tucked behind the church Our Lady of the Snows at Jungmannovo náměstí 17, is the small three-storey House of Musical Instru-

Holy Heart, designed between 1929–32 by Josip Plečnik, a Slovene architect who also initiated additions and adjustments to Prague Castle in his role as chief architect there. This bold creation is a major landmark in the area. Its lower two thirds are lined with vitrified bricks, while the top third continues the effect with a white-plastered band that features a rhythmical sequence of windows.

Post-war architecture

The architecture of the post-war years after the Communist takeover in 1948 yielded few buildings that are still admired today, although some of the works of this period are now starting to be reassessed *(see pages 186–7)*. In fact, very little was done to the city centre during this time. Mention should be made, though, of the design of the Prague Metro (underground) stations, completed in 1974. Although no rival to the opulence of Moscow's system, several of the stations deserve mention. On line B (Yellow), for example, walls are covered with glazed ceramic tiles and decorated with mosaics: especially worth a look is the stop Anděl (formerly Moskevská, or Moscow), which was designed in cooperation with a Soviet architect. Coloured marble and bronze figure reliefs were used to evoke scenes from Moscow such as Red Square and the Kremlin.

Hollywood duo, the swooping glass-and-steel "Ginger" tower – a magnificent flight of fancy – plays off against the concrete tapering cylinder of the "Fred" tower. Even before it opened in 1996, the building attracted its share of critics, who charged that it clashes with the landscape and that it smacked of grandstanding. Visitors can decide for themselves: the top floor contains one of the city's more expensive restaurants, La Perle de Prague, and the view over the river, with its sweeping vista of the city's many architectural styles, is wonderful.

One of the most recent additions to the Prague skyline is the prize-winning Danube

Post-Communism and Postmodernism

The fall of Communism in 1989 freed up architects to experiment, not always with an eye on quality and aesthetic worth, however. One exciting and controversial addition to the Prague cityscape in recent years is the curvaceous "Fred and Ginger" building (in Czech, Tančící dům, or dancing building), co-designed by American architect Frank O. Gehry and his Zagreb-born colleague Vlado Milunič. Created to resemble the immortal

House, part of a large riverside development along Rohanské nábřeži in Karlín, the industrial district to the north of Žižkov. The sharply pointed glass structure, designed by Kohn Pederson Fox, is certainly exciting, and bodes well for the future of architecture in the city.

Painting and sculpture seemed to have fared less well since the fall of Communism. Largely derivative of developments elsewhere in Europe, many of the pieces are lacking in ideas and meaning. It has been suggested that, denied the need to fight back against a repressive regime (which in the recent past gave artists much of their creative impetus), Prague artists feel somewhat lost at present. ❑

LEFT: the Art Deco interior of the Café Slavia.
ABOVE: the "Fred and Ginger" building.

PLACES

A detailed guide to the city with the principal sites
clearly cross-referenced by number to the maps

Prague used to be known as the "Five Towns", and although it has now been divided into 10 separate districts, most visitors concentrate on the five historic towns: Hradčany; Staré Město (Old Town); Malá Strana (Lesser Quarter); Nové Město (New Town); and the former ghetto of the Jewish Quarter, or Josefov. City administration was not unified until the rule of Joseph II (1780–90), and the separate town halls are reminders of previous autonomy. Gradually the city began to expand and by the beginning of the 19th century, some 80,000 people lived in the city. Gradually more districts were added to the original five towns, and the population grew steadily. The incorporation of Vyšehrad, Holešovice and Bubeneč brought the population to around 200,000 by 1900. After World War I, the city's area tripled to a size of 550 sq. km (190 sq. miles). New suburbs such as Severní Město (North Town) and Jižní Město (South Town) were built, and the southwestern suburb of Jihozápadní Město is a site of ongoing expansion. The present population is around 1.2 million.

Each individual district of the city still has its own special appeal. Hradčany Castle and its surroundings, especially the Loreta Church and the Strahov Monastery, have a distinct atmosphere. Malá Strana and the island of Kampa, with its ostentatious palaces built in the shadow of the rulers in Hradčany, is another, quite separate place, dotted with elegant bars and restaurants. The gardens of the hillsides of Petřín and Hradčany, the view of the Vltava River and the Charles Bridge all have a romantic fascination.

In earlier times, the inhabitants of the congested Old Town and Jewish Quarter must have felt envious when they looked across to the other bank of the Vltava, though today Old Town Square has been beautifully restored and Pařížská is a splendid avenue lined with expensive shops. However, in the narrow alleys and courtyards you can still easily imagine old Prague, the city of Franz Kafka. The far-sighted designs of Charles IV (1346–78) and his architects, which you see when you walk through the New Town and the broad open spaces of Charles and Wenceslas Squares, are evidence of planning well ahead of its time. ❏

PRECEDING PAGES: looking down the Vltava from Letná Park; trams at Sídliště Barrandov. **LEFT:** the wonderful Art Nouveau Obecní dům.

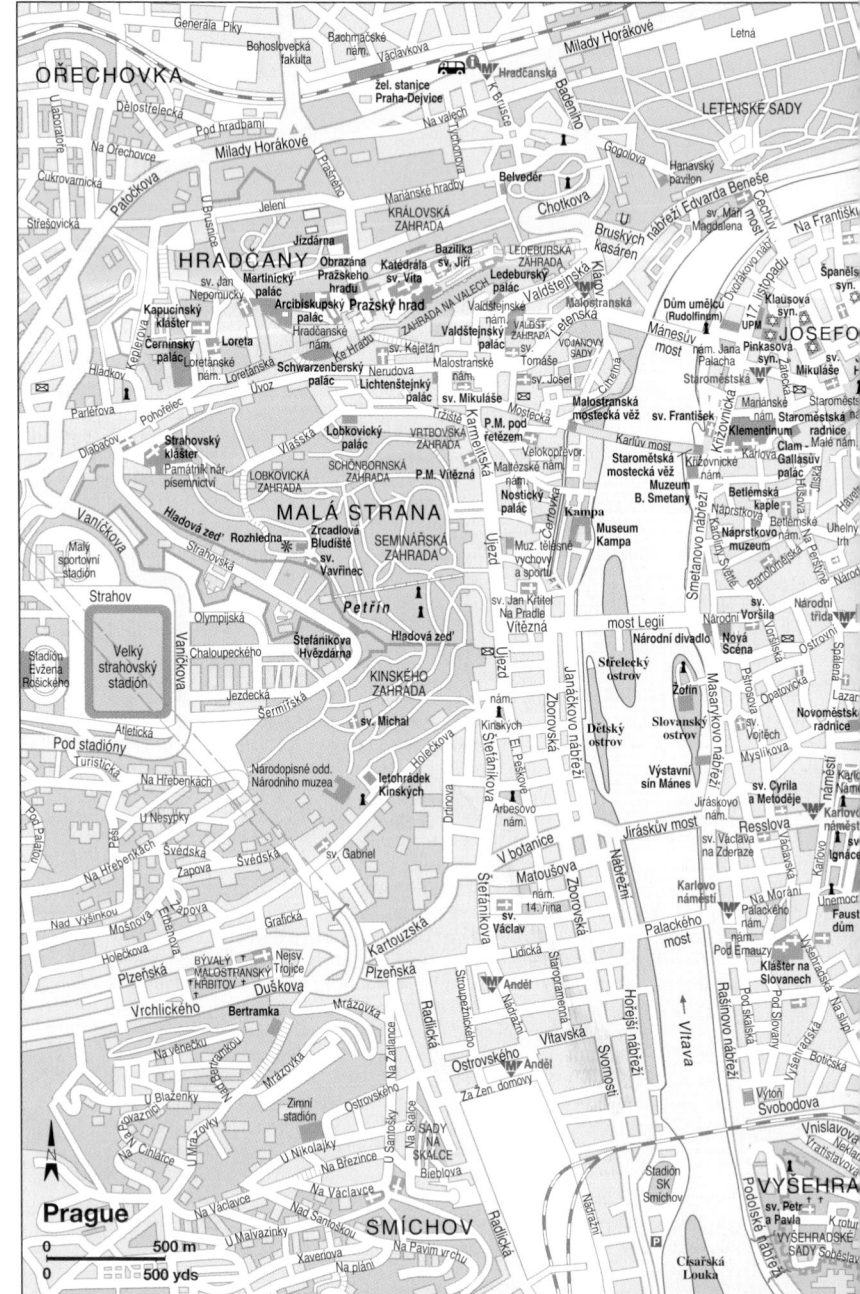

Prague

0 ————— 500 m
0 ═══ 500 yds

HRADČANY

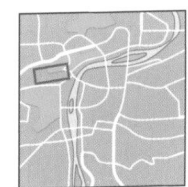

The history of Prague began with the construction of its castle in the 9th century, and even today the area is at the heart of Czech politics as the seat of the nation's president

The silhouette of Hradčany (the castle district) is perhaps the best-known view of the city. With the advantage of its exposed position, the castle dominates the skyline of the left bank of the Vltava. It is particularly impressive when floodlit at night, with the cathedral in the background.

The historical importance of this royal residence matches its imposing appearance. Its history is not only tied up with that of the city, but also with the history of the first independent Czech state and its destiny. A thousand years ago the fate of the country was decided here and, after several centuries of being ruled from Vienna, it regained its status as the ruling heart of the city. The castle is the seat of the president of the republic and still a centre of political power.

The building of the castle dates from the same period as the first historically documented prince of the Přemyslid dynasty, Prince Boleslav. He built what was at first a wooden fort on the site of a pagan place of worship. It then became the seat of the dynasty and secured the crossroads of important European trade routes which met at the ford of the Vltava. At the same time, Boleslav built the first church on the hill to replace the pre-Christian burial ground, as a sign of progressive Christianisation. In AD 973, when the bishopric of Prague was founded, the castle also became the bishop's seat.

After the turn of the millennium a Romanesque castle gradually evolved on the site, with a princely (later a royal) palace, a bishop's palace, several churches, two monasteries and a series of fortifications. Every period has added its contribution to the castle's development, but its appearance today is due mainly to Empress Maria Theresa (*see page 82*).

Map on page 78

LEFT: the nave of St Vitus.
BELOW: the distinctive skyline of Hradčany.

Hradcany Square

Before entering the grounds of the castle, take a look at the vast **Hradčanské náměstí ❶** (Hradčany Square). A few interesting palaces have been built since the fire of 1541, which destroyed all of Hradčany and much of Malá Strana lying below. Most notable for their façades are the Rococo **Arcibiskupský palác ❷** (Archbishop's Palace; open to visitors once a year on Maundy Thursday, the Thursday before Easter) next door to the castle, and on the opposite side of the square the Renaissance **Schwarzenberský palác ❸** (Schwarzenberg Palace). This has fine sgraffito decoration on its façade, in keeping with the Italian style. No longer housing the Vojenské historické muzeum (Military Museum), it is due to become the new location of the National Gallery's collection of Old Masters in 2007, after an extensive period of renovation.

This ornate lamp post stands in the centre of Hradčanské náměstí.

The bold proportions of its façade draw attention to the early Baroque **Toskánský palác ❹** (Toscana Palace), which ends the square to the west. Where Kanovnická joins the square you will see the Renaissance **Martinický palác ❺** (Martinic Palace). When the building was restored, sgraffito decorations portraying Biblical and classical scenes were discovered.

To the left of the Archbishop's Palace as you face it, a little alley leads off to the hidden **Sternberský palác ❻** (Sternberg Palace). This is the main building of the **Národní galerie** (National Gallery), which houses a fine collection of European art, including Old Masters, from Antiquity to the 18th century *(see pages 90–1)*.

To the south, Hradčany náměstí opens up to the ramp (**Ke Hradu**) which leads up to the castle from Nerudova; from here you get a superb view across the city.

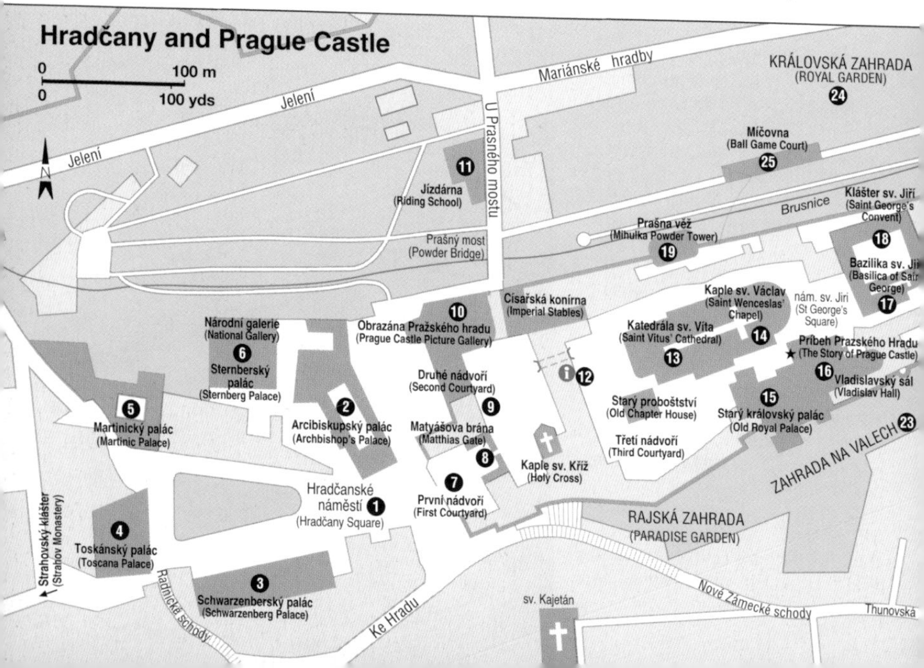

Hradčany and Prague Castle

```
0        100 m
0        100 yds
N
```

Mariánské hradby

KRÁLOVSKÁ ZAHRADA (ROYAL GARDEN) ㉔

Jelení

Jelení

U Prašného mostu

Míčovna (Ball Game Court) ㉕

Brusnice

Jízdárna (Riding School) ⑪

Klášter sv. Jiří (Saint George's Convent) ⑱

Prašný most (Powder Bridge)

Prašná věž (Mihulka Powder Tower) ⑲

Bazilika sv. Jiří (Basilica of Saint George) ⑰

Císařská konírna (Imperial Stables)

Kaple sv. Václav (Saint Wenceslas Chapel)

nám. sv. Jiří (St George's Square)

Obrazárna Pražského hradu (Prague Castle Picture Gallery)

Druhé nádvoří (Second Courtyard) ⑨

⑩

Kaledrála sv. Víta (Saint Vitus' Cathedral) ⑬

⑭

Příběh Pražského Hradu ★ (The Story of Prague Castle) ⑯

Národní galerie (National Gallery) ⑥

Sternberský palác (Sternberg Palace)

Vladislavský sál (Vladislav Hall)

Arcibiskupský palác (Archbishop's Palace) ②

Matyášova brána (Matthias Gate) ⑧

Starý proboštství (Old Chapter House)

Starý královský palác (Old Royal Palace) ⑮

⑤

Martinický palác (Martinic Palace)

Třetí nádvoří (Third Courtyard)

㉓

ZAHRADA NA VALECH

Strahovský klášter (Strahov Monastery)

Hradčanské náměstí ① (Hradčany Square)

První nádvoří (First Courtyard) ⑦

Kaple sv. Kříž (Holy Cross)

RAJSKÁ ZAHRADA (PARADISE GARDEN)

④ **Toskánský palác** (Toscana Palace)

③ **Schwarzenberský palác** (Schwarzenberg Palace)

Radnická schody

Ke Hradu

sv. Kajetán

Nové Zámecké schody

Thunovská

Entering the castle grounds

The main entrance to the castle is the **První nádvoří** ❼ (First Courtyard), which opens onto Hradčany Square. You enter this so-called Ceremonial Courtyard through a gate under a wrought-iron decoration. Two guards of honour *(see box on page 80)* are posted in front of the statues, copies of the *Battling Titans* by Ignaz Platzer.

This is the most recent of the courtyards and was built on the site of the western castle moat during the alterations of Maria Theresa's reign (1740–80). The **Matyášova brána** ❽ (Matthias Gate) is considerably older; indeed, it is the oldest Baroque building in Hradčany Castle. It originally stood apart, like a triumphal arch, between the bridges that led over the moats. During the rebuilding it was elegantly integrated into the new section as a relief. Since then, the Matthias Gate has been the

entrance to the Second Courtyard. To the right of the gate a staircase leads to the reception rooms of the presidential apartments, which are closed to the public.

The **Druhé nádvoří** ❾ (Second Courtyard) has a somewhat plain appearance. In the centre is a Baroque fountain by Hieronymus Kohl (1686). In the south eastern corner is the **Kaple sv. Kříž** (Chapel of the Holy Cross) built 1756–63 by Anselmo Lurago. It now serves as a shop and a box office selling tickets for concerts.

The symmetrical, closed impression given by the Second Courtyard is thanks to Maria Theresa's innovations. Behind it, however, lies a conglomeration of buildings which has grown up gradually over the centuries. Each has its own complicated history. In the right-hand passage to the Third Courtyard you can see some excavated remains of the Romanesque castle fortifications.

Map on page 78

The castle grounds, which are free, are open Apr–Oct 5am–midnight, Nov–Mar 6am–11pm.

BELOW: a Titan guarding the gateway.

Prague Castle Picture Gallery

The remains of an even older building, St Mary's Church, dating from the 9th century, were discovered in the **Obrazárna Pražského hradu** (Prague Castle Picture Gallery; open daily, Apr–Oct 9am–5pm, Nov–Mar 9am–4pm; admission charge). Access to the gallery is from the passage where the north and west wings meet.

Here you can see a collection largely put together by art lover Emperor Rudolf II (1583–1611). This Emperor has gone down in history as something of an eccentric *(see page 24)*, yet he was a great patron of the arts and sciences and collected a huge amount of art treasures, as well as countless curiosities. His collection was one of the most notable in Europe in his day. When the Imperial residence moved to Vienna, a great part of the collection went with it. Still more fell to the Swedes as loot during the Thirty Years War. Yet another valuable collection was created, during the 16th century, from what

remained, but much of it was also taken to Vienna, or sold to Dresden. What was left was auctioned off, and was thought to be totally lost. After a long and tortuous history, the remnants of the Rudolfine collection, that decorating the castle apartments, were finally brought together and put on display in 1965. The gallery was closed 1993–8 to reconstruct the space that you can now see.

The small but valuable collection contains almost 4,000 paintings (some of the most important are on permanent loan to the National Gallery), of which around 70 are on display at any one time. Among these are pieces by, among others: Hans von Aachen (*Head of a Girl*, 1611); Titian (*Young Woman at Her Toilet*, 1512–15); Tintoretto; Veronese; Rubens (*Assembly of the Gods at Olympos*, 1602); Matthias Bernard Braun; Adriaen de Vries; and the Bohemian Baroque artists Jan Kupecký and Petr Brandl. Temporary art exhibitions are housed in the next-door **Císařská konírna** (Imperial Stables), decorated with Renaissance-style vaulting, and **Jízdárna**

When an inventory of Rudolf's collection was made after the Swedish siege of 1648, two of the most famous pieces had not been taken: Dürer's Feast of the Rosary *(now in the National Gallery, see page 90); and fragments of Lucas Cranach's altarpiece that had been in St Vitus until its dismemberment by Calvinist iconoclasts in 1619.*

BELOW: the Castle Guards in their summer outfits.

The Camp Guards

The changing of the guards at Prague Castle always draws a crowd, especially at midday when it is accompanied by music. Far from being steeped in military tradition, this faintly ludicrous Ruritanian ceremony was invented after 1989. The uniforms, dripping with braid and tassels, were designed by Theodor Pištěk (the English pronunciation of his surname is suspiciously appropriate), who was responsible for the costumes in *Amadeus*. The Hollywood feel is enhanced by the trumpets, trombones and tuba playing from surrounding windows; the score, composed by Michal Prokop, sounds like a bad soundtrack to a war flick.

⓫ (Royal Riding School) across the Powder Bridge *(see page 89).*

The Information Centre

Tickets for entry to St Vitus's and the castle buildings are sold in the Third Courtyard (entered via the passageway on the eastern side of the Second Courtyard) in the **Informační středisko pražského hradu** ⓬ (Information Centre of Prague Castle; tel: 224 373 368; www.hrad.cz).

Four different tickets (valid for 1 day) are available, covering: a) St Vitus's, the Old Royal Palace (Starý královský palác); the Basilica of St George (Bazilika sv. Jiří), the Powder Tower (Prašná věž), Golden Lane (Zlatá ulička) and the Story of Prague Castle (you can also pay separately for this); b) St Vitus's, the Old Royal Palace and Golden Lane; c) Golden Lane; and d) the Basilica of St George. The buildings are open daily, Apr–Oct 9am–5pm, and Nov– Mar 9am–4pm.

St Vitus's Cathedral

As soon as you have entered the Third Courtyard, you can hardly avoid stopping and letting your eyes follow the daring vertical lines of **Katedrála sv. Víta** ⓭ (St Vitus's Cathedral); the towering western façade is only a few steps away. The cathedral, the largest church in Prague, is the metropolitan church of the Archdiocese of Prague, the royal and Imperial burial church and also the place where the royal regalia are proudly kept.

The 600-year history of the building of the cathedral began when the archbishopric was founded in 1344. Ambitious as ever, Charles IV used this opportunity to begin the construction of a cathedral which was intended to be among the most important works of the 14th-century Gothic style that was spreading from France. To this end, Charles employed the French architect

Matthias of Arras, who had trained in the French Gothic school and was working in Avignon (at that time a papal city). Arras died after eight years and the work was taken over by Petr Parléř, who influenced all later Gothic architecture in Prague.

After Parléř's death, his sons continued the work, giving the building their own individual stamp, until construction was interrupted in the first half of the 15th century by the Hussite Wars. It was in this period that the choir, its chapels and part of the south tower were completed. Only a few alterations were made during the years that followed. For instance, the top of the tower was given a Renaissance look sometime after 1560. This was replaced by a Baroque roof some 200 years later.

The task of completing the cathedral was not attempted until the 1860s, when a Czech patriotic association took it up. Following old plans and consulting Czech artists, they completed the building in 1929. The additions carried out across the centuries explain why the cathedral lacks a unity of style.

Map on page 78

This impressive gilded Renaissance grill is high up on the cathedral tower.

BELOW: the Neo-Gothic western façade.

Before entering the cathedral through the western portal, take a look at its exterior, which dates from the last few years of the completion process. The **Rose Window**, more than 10 metres (30 ft) in diameter, portrays the creation of the world. On either side of the window are carved portraits of the cathedral architects. The towers are decorated with the statues of 14 saints. In the centre of the bronze gates the history of the building has been portrayed, and on the sides are images relating to the legends of St Adalbert and St Wenceslas.

The silver tomb of St John of Nepomuk by Johann Emanuel Fischer von Erlach.

Inside the cathedral

In the splendid interior of the cathedral the most notable features are the stained-glass windows and the **Triforium**, a walkway above the pillars with a gallery of portrait busts. Leading Czech artists took part in creating the windows, among them Max Švabinský, who was responsible for the window in the first chapel on the right, the mosaic on the west wall and the great window above the south portal. The window in the

third chapel on the left was designed by Alfons Mucha, who is perhaps best known outside the Czech Republic for his Art Nouveau posters featuring the actress Sarah Bernhardt (*see page 151*). However, all 21 of the chapels contain several notable works of art.

St Wenceslas's Chapel

The main attraction inside the cathedral and generally overcrowded is the **Kaple sv. Václava** ❶ (St Wenceslas's Chapel), which protrudes into the south transept (entry to the chapel is not possible; it must be viewed from its doorways). It was built by Petr Parléř on the site of a 10th-century Romanesque rotunda, in which the national saint Wenceslas was interred. In keeping with the importance of the Wenceslas cult, the saint's sacred place is exceptionally ornate.

The wall frescos, which are decorated with semi-precious stones and gold bezants, portray (in the upper half) Christ's passion and (in the lower) the story of St Wenceslas, prince of Bohemia. A little door leads to the **Treasure Chamber** directly above the chapel. Here the Bohemian royal regalia are kept, behind seven locks, the seven keys of which are held by seven separate institutions. The precious jewels are put on display only on special occasions.

The nave

The three central chapels of the choir, behind the main altar, contain the Gothic tombs of the princes and kings of the Přemyslid dynasty, and are the work of Petr Parléř's masons. In the choir itself, on the left side is a kneeling bronze statue of Cardinal von Schwarzenberg, by the Czech sculptor Josef Myslbek (1848–1922), who also created the Wenceslas Monument in Wenceslas Square (*see page 147*). On the right hand side of the choir is the ostentatious

Architects of the Castle

The 14th-century architect Petr Parléř was one of the most influential in creating the medieval image of Prague, much of which can still be seen today. As well as his founding work on St Vitus's Cathedral and the Royal Palace, Parléř designed the original Charles Bridge, including the Gothic tower that still stands at the entrance to the Old Town. As well as work in the city, Parléř completed the St Barbara's Church in Kutná Hora. In the second half of the 18th century, Empress Maria Theresa commissioned the Viennese court architect Nicolo Pacassi to give the various buildings a unified, Neoclassical facade and extensions. As a result, the original eclectic character of the castle has been transformed into something resembling a massive palace. Then, in the 1920s, Josip Plečnik was appointed chief architect of the castle, and made various additions to the complex, including the granite obelisk in the Third Courtyard, as well as designing the presidential apartments. Although unpopular at the time, Plečnik is now hailed as a postmodern genius. It is a credit to these three architects, and many others over the centuries, that the varying styles have blended harmoniously within the complex.

silver tomb of the 17th-century cleric St John Nepomuk, designed by the Baroque architect Johann Emanuel Fischer von Erlach. Also remarkable are the wooden reliefs in the choir showing the city of Prague, masterpieces of Baroque woodcarving. Beyond the tomb of St Nepomuk is the extraordinary late-Gothic **Royal Oratory**. The balcony is supported by a fantastic complex of intertwined foliage.

Opposite the tomb of Count Schlick, designed by Matthias Bernard Braun, a staircase leads down into the **Royal Crypt**. Here you can see the remains of the walls of two Romanesque churches that previously stood on the site of the cathedral, as well as the sarcophagi of Charles IV, his children and his four wives, George of Poděbrady and other rulers. Emperor Rudolf II lies in a Renaissance pewter coffin. Sitting above the Royal Crypt – just in front of the Neo-Gothic high altar – is the impressive white marble Imperial tomb of the Habsburgs, built for Ferdinand I, his wife Anna and their son Maximilian.

Glance upwards to admire the lozenges adorning the roof of the choir. Petr Parléř displayed a masterly ability to combine revolutionary technical solutions with elegant caprice. This is particularly evident on the south side of the choir, where the interplay of columns and struts and the remarkable complexity of the tracery are especially impressive. The organ loft originally marked the end of the choir on the west side. Once the Neo-Gothic part of the cathedral was completed, however, it was moved to its present position.

On the southern side of the neo-Gothic nave is the entry to the **Great South Tower** (open Apr–Sept, last entry 4.15pm). The views from the top are stupendous and give a fascinating view of the cathedral's roofs and buttresses; beware, however, of the narrow, spiral staircase with its 287 steps. In the room at the top is a clock made for Rudolf II in 1597.

The Third Courtyard

In order to see more sights, you have to walk around the former Old Chapter House which is pressed up

Map on page 78

You can enter the cathedral without a ticket, but may only go as far as the transept, beyond which lies the Gothic section for which you must have paid an entrance fee at the Information Centre.

BELOW: the Gothic statue of St George opposite the southern façade.

The 14th-century mosaic of the Last Judgement.

against the side of the cathedral. Of special interest to art historians is a copy of the **Equestrian Statue of St George** which stands prominently in the courtyard. The original Gothic sculpture – now in the Lapidarium *(see page 175)* – is evidence of the highly developed art of 14th-century metal casting. The flat-roofed shelters next to the cathedral are to protect archaeological discoveries which have been made in the lower levels of the castle courtyard, visible through the grille.

From here you can get an impressive view of the complex system of buttresses and the south facade of the cathedral, which is dominated by the almost 100-metre (300-ft) tower. Its stylistically unusual top includes a gilded window grille, the letter "R" and the two clocks (the upper shows the hours, the lower the quarter-hours) date from the time of Rudolf II. The tower contains four Renaissance bells, among them Bohemia's largest, weighing 18 tons.

Unusual in both position and execution is the **Zlatá brána** (Golden Gate), the distinctive portal that leads into the south transept. It is the ceremonial entrance to the cathedral, and it was through here that monarchs passed on their way to their coronation *(see page 7)*. Its remarkable triple-arched anteroom has an exterior mosaic, thoroughly cleaned in the early 1990s, depicting the Last Judgement. It was created by Italian artists around the year 1370.

The anteroom itself is fitted with a grille illustrating the months of the year. The covered staircase in the left-hand corner leads to the Castle Gardens. These, in turn, lead to the **Starý královský palác ⓯** (Old Royal Palace), which should not be missed.

Old Royal Palace

In keeping with the rest of the castle complex, this was also built by many generations of rulers. New storeys of the palace were layered one above the other on top of the original walls, which now lie deep under the level of the courtyard. A tour of the present building will enable you to gain deeper insights into the castle's past.

Go past the fountain decorated with an eagle, and from the courtyard you will be able to ascend the staircase leading to the anteroom. From here, you can start your tour of the palace, which until the 16th century was the residence of the Czech rulers. The first three rooms to the left of the entrance constitute the **Green Chamber**, a former law court and the audience hall, with a ceiling fresco, *The Judgement of Solomon.* Further along is the **Vladislav Bedchamber** and the **Land Records Depository**. The Land Records were books in which not only the details of property ownership but also the decisions of the Bohemian Estates and the law courts were recorded.

Leave the anteroom and go on to the **Vladislavský sál** ⑯ (Vladislav Hall), named after King Vladislav II. This most imposing late-Gothic throne room was built by the architect Benedikt Ried between 1493 and 1502. Numerous coronations and tournaments took place under the 13-metre (43-ft) high pillars. Immediately to the right of the entrance of this hall another wing of the building is joined.

Continue on the same level and you reach the **Bohemian Chancellery**. In the first room is a model showing how the castle looked in the 18th century and comparing it to today's complex. Go through a Renaissance portal and you enter the office of the former Imperial Governor. Ascending a spiral staircase, you come to the **Imperial Court Chancellery**. This is situated above the Bohemian Chancellery; in Rudolf II's reign, the whole of the Holy Roman Empire was ruled from here.

Saints and fortifications

Under the three Renaissance windows on the narrow wall of the Vladislav Hall a staircase leads off to **All Saints Chapel**, which con-

tains three remarkable works of art: *Triptych of the Angels* by Hans von Aachen, *All Saints*, the painting on the high altar, is by Václav Vavřinec Reiner and, in the choir, a cycle of paintings by Dittmann. The last portrays 12 scenes from the life of St Procopius, who is buried in the chapel. The next room leading off from the Vladislav Hall is the **Council Chamber**, in which the Bohemian Estates and the highest law court assembled. The royal throne and the furnishings date from the 19th century. To the left of the throne is the tribunal of the chief court recorder, built in the Renaissance style. The wall is decorated by the portraits of the Habsburg rulers.

The last room open to the public in this wing is the **New Land Records Office**, with the heraldic emblems of the Land Rolls officials decorating the ceiling and walls.

The **Riders' Staircase**, built to allow rulers and guests to enter and take part in riotous festivities on horseback such as jousting, leads out of the most recent part of the palace. The early-Gothic levels on the lower

Map on page 78

In the Vladislavský sál, take a look at the doors and windows; in contrast to the highly ornate Gothic ceiling, these draw on the Classical forms of the Renaissance.

BELOW:
the Dalibor Tower.

storeys are accessible as part of the **The Story of Prague Castle** *(see below)*, as is the lowest level, the Romanesque palace which contains the remains of fortifications dating from the end of the 9th century.

The Story of Prague Castle

There is a version of the Castle Game available on CD-ROM. This teaches children the history of the castle by introducing them to its famous inhabitants.

BELOW: *The Assumption* by Johann Christoph Lischka (*c.* 1695).

This newly opened exhibition – beautifully displayed – can be reached by the ramp to the left of the entrance to the Old Royal Palace. This highly recommended introduction to the castle site (*see* www.story-castle.cz) has two parts: the first leads you from room to room describing the development of the castle in chronological order; the second tells the "Story of …" various subjects, such as residences, learning, burials, the Church and patronage. The exhibits are well-labelled in English and Czech, and there is a "Castle Game" for children to play that takes them around the displays gathering information, role-playing, and writing and drawing.

The story of the castle site is told from prehistory to the 20th century. Among the exhibits that illustrate

the history of the castle are: a helmet and chainmail coat said to have belonged to St Václav; the tympanum of the Bazilika sv. Jiří *(see below)*; the grave dresses of Rudolf II and Eleonora of Toledo; and some amazing examples of 16th- and 17th-century costume.

St George's Basilica

Leaving the Royal Palace by the Riders' Staircase brings you into **Náměstí sv. Jiří** (St George's Square). The red Baroque facade opposite the choir of St Vitus's Cathedral belongs to the **Bazilika sv. Jiří** ⑰ (St George's Basilica). This is the oldest church still extant on the site of the castle and, together with the adjoining monastery, it formed the hub of the complex in the early Middle Ages. It was founded in about AD 920 and rebuilt after a fire in the 12th century. Despite rebuilding programmes during the Renaissance and Baroque periods, the church has largely retained its Romanesque appearance and, following renovations at the beginning of the 20th century, it has been restored to its former glory.

The interior, in which concerts are held to take advantage of the excellent acoustics, is closed off by a raised choir. Remnants of the original Romanesque ceiling paintings can still be seen. To the right of the choir you can look through a grille into the **Ludmilla Chapel**, housing the tomb of the saint, the grandmother of Prince Wenceslas.

The tombs of two Bohemian nobles are in front of the choir. The Baroque statue in front of the crypt – a corpse with snakes in its intestines – is an allegory of the transitory nature of life. The Baroque **Chapel of St John Nepomuk** is incorporated into the outer facade of the basilica. Its portal is decorated with a 17th-century statue of the saint by Ferdinand Maximilian Brokoff.

Baroque and Mannerist art

Adjoining the basilica on the left is the former Benedictine **Klášter sv. Jiří** (St George's Convent). Founded in AD 973 but rebuilt several times, today it houses the National Gallery's substantial **Collection of Baroque and Mannerist Art in Bohemia** (open Tues–Sun 10am–6pm; admission charge; www.ngprague.cz). The fine collection is displyed on the upper floor. Although most items on display are paintings, one of the most extraordinary exhibits is an intricately carved wooden Tree of Life (*c.* 1650) from southern Germany.

Of the Mannerist pieces here, some of the most attractive are by: **Bartholomeus Spranger** (*Resurrection*, 1576), **Hans von Aachen** (*Portrait of Painter Joseph Heintz*, 1585–7) and **Roelant Savery** (*Woodland Stream*, 1608). The first signs of Baroque painting in Bohemia are seen in the works of **Karel Škréta** (1610–74): notable in the collection is his *Family Portrait of the Gem-Carver Dionysio Miseroni* (*c.* 1663). There are some fine works by the contemporaries **Petr Brandl** (1668–1735) and **Jan Kupecký** (1667–1740). Notable-works are, by the former, *Bust of an Apostle* (*c.* 1725) and, by Kupecký, *Self-Portrait* (1711), which shows the artist working on a portrait of his wife. The Rococo is represented by a large collection of the works of **Norbert Grund** (1717– 67); see his *Galant Scene with a Lady on a Swing* (*c.* 1760).

The Powder Tower and Golden Lane

Along the north side of St Vitus' Cathedral runs Vikářská, which contains the **Prašná věž** (Mihulka Powder Tower). In the late 15th century, while parts of the northern fortifications were being built, it served as a gunpowder workshop.

Another part of the fortifications which can be seen behind St George's Convent, is the atmospheric **Zlatá ulička** (Golden Lane), also known as Goldmakers' Alley. This is one of the most popular – and crowded – attractions of the castle. In the part of the fortifications between

The Powder Tower now serves as a museum, part of which is a reconstruction of an alchemist's workshop; there are also a number of fine royal portraits.

BELOW: Golden Lane.

The Daliborka is the setting for Smetana's nationalist opera Dalibor, *inspired by the imprisonment of Duke Dalibor in the tower during the 15th century. According to legend, the music he made while locked up was so exquisite it attracted people to the foot of the tower.*

the central **Bílá věž** (White Tower) and the outermost **Daliborka** ㉑ (Dalibor Tower), tiny houses crouch under the walkway on the castle wall, making a romantic backdrop. Legend has it that this is where the alchemists employed by Rudolf II tried to discover both the secret of eternal life and how to make gold. What is fact, however, is that Franz Kafka (*see page 145*) lived and worked for a while in No. 22, which now houses a tiny exhibition and Kafka-orientated bookshop. The castle ends at the **Cerná věž** (Black Tower), where Jiřská reaches the eastern gate.

The Lobkowicz Palace

Just before the gate, on the right-hand side, you come to the **Národní Muzeum Lobkovický palác** ㉒ (Lobkowicz Palace; open Tues–Sun 9am–5pm; admission charge; www.nm.cz). This large building, parts of which have now been renovated, contains the Historical Museum. The rooms run chronologically from the early part of the first millennium AD to the revolutions of 1848, and while the labelling is in Czech you can ask

BELOW: the Belvedér.

to borrow a booklet that gives all the captions in English. Although the information is rather dense, it is worth picking through to discover the interesting archaeological finds and early documents relating to the history of the city. These displays are on the upper floors; the floors below are given over to temporary exhibitions, and in the courtyard by the entrance is a pleasant café.

Across the street is the rather dull **Muzeum hraček** (Toy Museum; open daily 9.30am–5.30pm; admission charge), although parts of the surrounding buildings have been attractively converted into a gallery space. On the other side of the eastern gate, the Old Castle Steps and the street Na Opyši lead down to Malá Strana (*see page 101*) and Malostranská Metro.

The Rampart Gardens

A more pleasant way to descend to Malá Strana is go through the gardens that line the hill above Valdštejnské náměstí. On your right after you exit below the Cerná věž are the **Zahrada na valech** ㉓ (Gar-

dens on the Ramparts; open daily Apr–Oct 10am–6pm). About halfway along the path below the castle is the entrance to the **Palácové zahrady pod pražským hradem** (Palace Gardens below Prague Castle; open daily Apr–Oct 10am–6pm; admission charge; www.palacovezahrady.cz). Consisting of five separate but linked formal Baroque gardens (the Ledeburská zahrada, Malá Pálffyovská zahrada, Velká Pálffyovská zahrada, Kolowratská zahrada and Malá Fürstenberská zahrada) these were laid out following the Swedish occupation of the city in 1648. They replaced the Renaissance Italianate gardens that had initially replaced the vineyards that lined the hill. The gardens have been beautifully restored and are full of small follies and statues.

The Palace Gardens

On the other side of the castle are the **Královská zahrada** ㉔ (Royal Gardens; open daily Apr–Oct 10am–6pm). Leave the Second Courtyard by the Picture Gallery *(see page 80)*, and cross the **Prašný most** (Powder

Bridge); the entrance to the gardens is on your right. Famous for their azaleas, they are a lovely place to sit and wander; there is also a modern glasshouse stretching along the side opposite the castle. In the gardens is the **Míčovna** ㉕ (Ball-Game Court). Built in 1565–9 and designed by Bonifác Wohlmut, it has an Italianate sgrafitto façade and has recently been restored. At the end of the gardens is the **Belvedér** ㉖ (Summer Palace), which art historians consider to be the only example of a purely Italian Renaissance building north of the Alps. Emperor Ferdinand I had the palace built in 1537 for his wife Anna.

In winter the Belvedér can be reached from Mariánské hradby.

In the park beyond the palace is a large, rather strange, monument in the form of a grotto to Julius Zeyer (1841–1901). Steps below the Belvedér take you down to the tree-lined Jelení příkop (Stag Moat). It is possible to return to the Prašný most by walking up the vale and through a beautifully designed modern tunnel; you can then make your way up to the right.   ❑

Map on page 78

In front of the Belvedér is a Renaissance fountain made by Francesca Terzio in 1563. Known as the "Singing Fountain" (after the sound made by the water dropping into the bowl), if you hold your head under the bowl you can detect a faint hum.

BELOW: the Palace Gardens below Prague Castle.

RESTAURANTS AND CAFÉS

Lví dvůr
U Prašného mostu 6
Tel: 224 372 361
Open: daily 11am–midnight. €€
Previously the castle menagerie and now a decent restaurant, and small outdoor café, with views over the cathedral and the palace gardens from its terrace. The food on offer is mosty hearty and Czech (duck, dumplings and roast suckling pig), with the odd Italian-inspired starter, served up by pleasant staff.

● ● ● ● ● ● ● ● ● ● ● ● ● ● ● ● ●

Prices are for a three-course meal for one, including a glass of wine or beer.
€€ 300–600 Kč

THE NÁRODNÍ GALERIE

The Czech National Gallery has some world-class paintings, from Dürer and Holbein to Rubens and Rembrandt

While the Old Masters section of Prague's National Gallery (open Tues–Sun 10am–6pm; admission charge; www.ngprague.cz) may not have the breadth of other national collections, it nonetheless contains some exceptionally fine works. At present the works are on display in Sternberský palác *(see page 78)*, though there are plans to move them to the renovated Schwarzenberský palác in 2007. The gallery is set out on three levels: the ground floor houses German and Austrian art from the 15th to the 18th centuries; the first floor comprises the art of antiquity, icons and the art of the Netherlands and Italy of the 14th–16th centuries; the second floor has Italian, Spanish, French, Dutch and Flemish art of the 16th–18th centuries.

ABOVE: Rubens's painting *The Marchese Ambrogio Spinola* (*c.* 1627) is one of the finest portraits in the collection. Close by is another highlight, Rembrandt's *The Scholar in His Study* (1634), perhaps showing the 16th-century physician Paracelsus.

LEFT: Albrecht Dürer's large-scale *Feast of the Rosary* (1506) is perhaps the most outstanding work in the gallery. One of the greatest paintings of the northern Renaissance, it combines the innovations of light and colour of Italian art, while retaining the northern Gothic tradition of the truthful portrayal of landscape and nature. Dürer himself can be seen on the right-hand side, holding a sheet of paper. Other wonderful pictures of the German and Austrian collection include the left and right wings of the *Hohenburg Altarpiece* (1509) by Hans Holbein the elder, and a number of paintings by Lucas Cranach the elder, including *St Christina* (*c.* 1520–2) and *Adam and Eve* (*c.* 1538).

RIGHT: *The Garden of Eden* (1618) by Roelant Savery is just one of the large holdings of Flemish and Dutch paintings. Important works include Geertgen tot Sint Jans's *Triptych with the Adoration of the Magi (c. 1490–5)* and a panel by Jan Gossaert's (Mabuse) *St Luke Drawing the Virgin (c. 1513)*, which clearly shows the technique of perspective he learnt from Italian painters.

OTHER NATIONAL COLLECTIONS

The Old Masters collection is not the only section of the National Gallery in Prague; to display all the holdings in one place would take a vast space. The collections are spread across the city, the closest section to the Sternberský being the Collection of Baroque and Mannerist Art, on display in the Klášter sv. Jiří, also in Hradčany *(see page 87)*. The collections of Medieval Art in Bohemia and Central Europe are held in the Anežský klášter in Staré Město *(see page 127)*. The Veletržní palác in Holešovice, an important piece of Functionalist architecture, is home to the Collection of 19th, 20th and 21st Century Art *(see page 171)*. Another outstanding Modernist building, Dům u černé Matky Boží, holds the Museum of Czech Cubism *(see page 125)*, while at Zbraslav there is the stunning collection of Asian art *(see page 210)*.

ABOVE: Bronzino's wonderful portrait of *Eleonora of Toledo (c. 1540–3)* is one the finest Italian paintings in the collection. Other works of interest include the *Portrait of an Elderly Man* (1580–90) by Bassano and *St Jerome (c. 1550)* by Tintoretto.

LEFT: This *Still Life with a Goblet of Wine* by the German-Dutch painter Abraham Mignon (1640–79) is one of a number of exquisite still lifes in the gallery, including *Flowers in an Earthen Vase* by Jan Brueghel the elder (1568–1625). Of the gallery's holdings of French and Spanish paintings, three in particular stand out: Simon Vouet's *Suicide of Lucretia (c. 1624–5)*; a painting by El Greco (Domenikos Theotokopoulos), *Christ in Prayer (c. 1595–7)*; and, finest of all, Goya's *Portrait of Don Miguel de Lardizabal* (1815).

THE LORETA AND STRAHOV

Prague's main centre of Christian pilgrimage is
enclosed within a Baroque setting worthy
of its religious importance. Nearby is the
quaint 17th-century street Nový svět

I f you climb from Hradčany
Square towards the Strahov
Monastery *(see page 96)*, as you
walk between the palaces you can
hear, every hour on the hour, a delicate tune played by bells. Many
years ago, during an outbreak of
plague, there lived in Prague a
mother and her children. One child
after another fell sick, and with the
last few coins that she had left she
paid for the church bells to be rung
whenever a child died. After they
were all dead, she herself fell ill
and died, but of course there was
no one to have the bells rung for
her. Then, all of a sudden, all the
bells of Loreta rang out, playing
the tune of a hymn to Mary. The
same tune has been played up to
the present day.

This story gives some indication
of the importance that this shrine
has for many people. It is not merely
of historic and artistic importance,
but is still considered to be a place
of Christian pilgrimage.

The Santa Casa

In the mid-13th century the armies
of Islam reconquered the Holy
Land. At that time two brothers
were priors of the Franciscan
monasteries in Haifa and Nazareth.
According to legend, when they fled
the brothers removed the Santa Casa

(Holy House) stone by stone, and
rebuilt it near Renecati, now Loreta,
in Italy. The house was visited by
many pilgrims on their way to
Rome, and was later decorated with
rich marble reliefs, as the many
copies show.

When the Catholic Habsburgs tried
during the Counter-Reformation to
convert their Hussite subjects back to
the "true faith", they used the pious
legend to serve their cause. They had
replicas of the Santa Casa built
throughout the land. The best-known

Map
on page
102

LEFT:
the Strahov Monastery.
BELOW:
the entrance to the
Sternberg Palace.

and most attractive of these is Prague's **Loreta ❶** (open Tues– Sun 9am–12.15pm, 1–4.30pm; admission charge). It stands on the Loretánske náměstí and was founded by Kateřina of Lobkovic, who laid the foundation stone on 3 June 1626. The Casa Santa itself was designed by Giovanni Battista Orsi and built 1626–31.

Unlike the simple original, the shrine became, across the centuries, an entire complex consisting of various buildings with several chapels, ornate cloisters and the Church of the Nativity. Dominating the group is the early Baroque tower, built in 1694, which has a carillon that rings out every hour.

Just as in Italy's Loreta, the shrine's outer walls are decorated with Renaissance reliefs. The interior also strictly follows the Italian model. As a result, you can see inside the Prague Loreta a small, bare building which is probably the copy of a house in Palestine, and in which the **Loreta Madonna** is honoured by the numerous pilgrims. Dressed in a long cloak, she carries the infant Jesus in her arms.

The Diamond Monstrance in the Loreta's Treasure Chamber.

BELOW: frescos in the Loreta cloister.

The two-storey **Cloisters** surrounding two courtyards were enlarged by the Bavarian Baroque architect Kilián Ignaz Dientzenhofer in 1740. The paintings in these cloisters have been a little over-restored. However, the poetic – and at times amusing – images of the supplications to Mary are impressive: look for "Tower of David", "Gate of Heaven", and "*Oroduj za nas*", (Pray for us).

Between the portal and the Santa Casa you can see the **Kostel Narození Páně ❷** (Church of the Nativity), with frescos by Baroque artist Václav Vavřinec Reiner, and some macabre skeletons. The elaborately decorated church was consecrated on 7 June 1737, exactly 111 years after the laying of the foundation stone.

Treasure Chamber

The Loreta's main attraction is the **Treasure Chamber**. As in other places of pilgrimage, pilgrims over the years have given votive gifts to the treasury as a sign of thanksgiving. The gifts of the Bohemian nobility were commissioned from notable goldsmiths of the time and include some of the most valuable works of liturgical art in Central Europe. The most remarkable is the **Diamond Monstrance**, which was a legacy of Ludmilla Eva Franziska of Kolowrat.

The monstrance, made in 1699 by Baptist Kanischbauer and Matthias Stegner of Vienna to a design by Johann Bernard Fischer von Erlach, is studded with 6,222 diamonds and sends out its rays like the sun. It is almost 1 metre (3 ft) in height and weighs more than 12 kg (26 lbs).

Černín Palace

If you leave the Loreta and walk right up to the square, you will be struck by the massive facade of the **Černínský palác ❸** (Černín Palace), an incredible counterweight to the light buildings surrounding the Santa Casa, which, seen from this point, almost seem to cower. Twenty-nine half-pillars run along the whole length of the palace facade, which is more than 150 metres (500 ft) long.

Map on page 102

In 1666, Humprecht Johann, Count of Černín, bought the land, and work started on the palace, under the direction of Francesco Caratti. In 1673, Emperor Leopold I came to Prague to see the building about which there was so much talk in Vienna. It seemed as if the count, who had not received the Imperial favour he expected, was building a palace out of pique. The Emperor was displeased when the count claimed that it was nothing but a barn and he was going to replace the wooden doors with bronze ones. "For a barn, those wooden doors are quite good enough," the Emperor retorted.

The Černín were an old Bohemian family and their members had excelled time after time in the service of the Bohemian crown. The house in Prague was to become a "Monumentum Cernín", and construction work continued for several generations until financial collapse put a stop to the project. During the Napoleonic Wars it was used as a military hospital, and in 1851 the state bought parts of it and turned it

The Loreta's Casa Santa.

BELOW:
a snow-bound Loreta.

The narrow streets around Nový svět are very atmospheric.

BELOW: ecclesiatical symbols on the Strahov.

into a barracks. In 1929, the authorities of the young Czechoslovak Republic had the palace renovated and made it the home of the Foreign Ministry, which it still is today. It was here that Jan Masaryk fell – or was pushed – to his death in 1948 *(see page 31)*.

Nový svět

Below the gardens of the palace is part of the old settlement in front of the castle. In the middle of this former poor quarter is the exceptionally attractive alley of **Nový svět** ❹ (New World; take either Kapucínská or Černínská from beyond the palace and church), which has drawn many an artist and intellectual in the past. Many of the houses have names displayed on house signs and often include the adjective "golden", a Prague tradition. You will see The Golden Leg, The Golden Star and The Golden Pear (U zlaté hrušky), which is now a hotel and restaurant serving good Czech food. Famous previous inhabitants of the small but colourful houses include the Danish astronomer Tycho Brahe and the later astronomer Johannes Kepler, who both lived at number 1.

The Strahov

Outside the castle fortifications, away from the castle complex on the age-old trade route from Nürnberg to Krakow, lies the **Strahovský klášter** ❺ (Strahov Monastery; open daily 9am–midday, 1–5pm; admission charge; www. strahovsky klaster.cz). The oldest monastery in Bohemia, the complex sits on the slopes of Petřín Hill, the crown of the gently sloping valley, in a square now called Strahovské náměstí.

The two towers of the Strahov, along with the green of the Petřín Hill and its miniature Eiffel Tower replica, and the long line of the roof of the Černín Palace, together make up part of the distinctive skyline of the left bank of the River Vltava.

The first monastery of the district monks of the Premonstratensian Order was founded in 1140 by King Vladislav II, but was completely destroyed by fire in 1258. The wars of the ensuing centuries also left their mark, with the result that very little remained of the original Romanesque building. Today, the monastery is predominantly Baroque in style, although it contains early Gothic and Renaissance elements. Only St Mary's Church, also known as the Church of Our Lady, retains visible traces of the Romanesque original.

The monastery continued to function until 1952. After the dissolution of all religious orders in Czechoslovakia under the Communist regime, it was declared a museum of literature and opened to the public on 8 May 1953. The monastery complex was returned to the Order with the downfall of the Communist government in 1989, and the Premonstratensian monks are back in charge.

Strahov library

The rapid transformation of the Strahov library into a museum of national literature was possible because of the vast resources of the monastery library, which had been slowly gathered over the centuries. Today, although no longer a national literature museum, the monastery possesses the one of oldest, most extensive and most valuable libraries in the country. The collection was established at the time of the foundation over 800 years ago. Gradually added over the years were examples of almost the complete literature of western Christianity up to the end of the 18th century.

Entering the harmonious enclosure of the monastery, the first thing you will see is **chrám sv. Rocha** (St Rochus's Church), built from 1603 to 1612 during the rule of Emperor Rudolf II, and now used as a gallery. On the facade of the New Library (built from 1782 to 1784) is a medallion with the portrait of Emperor Josef II, the ruler whose support of the Enlightenment led to the dissolution of the majority of monasteries in his domains (1783). Josef's memory is honoured here because he allowed Strahov to escape the dissolution, and the monks of Strahov were permitted to buy the equipment for a new research library from another famous monastery in Moravia, the Bruck monastery near Znojmo. These brown-and-gold gleaming shelves equipped the new hall, which was then designated the Philosophers' Hall, while the older hall was renamed the Theologians' Hall.

Theologians' and Philosophers' halls

The monastery's greatest attractions are these two library halls, the entrance to which is on the southern side of the square, by the Church of St Mary *(see below)*. The of first the libraries is the **Filozofický sál** (Philosophers' Hall), built by Ignaz Palliardi in 1782–4. The ceiling fresco (1794) is beautiful but less easy to understand than that in the next-door Theologians' Hall. The work of Franz Anton Maulbertsch, it is in concept and technique a monumental finale to Rococo ceiling

Map on page 102

The walk from the Strahov across Petřín Hill and down to the Kinsky Gardens in Smíchov (see page 183) is one of the finest in the city.

BELOW:
the Theological Hall.

painting in Europe, and is remarkable in that it was completed in only six months. The fresco shows the development of humanity through wisdom – a theme that borders on the ideas of the Enlightenment. At the two narrow ends you can see Moses with the tablets of law and, opposite, St Paul preaching at the pagan altar. The lines of figures on the longer sides of the hall introduce great personalities of history who have made progress possible through their achievements.

The **Teologický sál** (Theologians' Hall) next door was built by Giovanni Domenico Orsi in 1671–9 in a rich Baroque style at a cost of 2,254 guilders. It was painted with splendid ceiling frescos by Siardus Nosecký, a member of the Order, between 1723 and 1727. The theme is true wisdom, rooted deeply in the knowledge of God. The brightly coloured scenes in their sturdy stucco frames radiate warmth and cheerfulness. In the middle of the room stand a number of valuable astronomical globes from the Netherlands, dating from the 17th century.

A chimera is a mythical beast made up of parts of various animals. The one in the Strahov is not so much fierce as rather sweet, looking a bit like a duck-billed platypus.

BELOW:
the roofs and gardens of Malá Strana below the Strahov.

The closest end of the corridor linking the two library rooms is lined with display cabinets of "curiosities". They are mostly specimens of marine creatures from a collection owned by Karel Jan Erben, and were acquired by the monastery in 1798. One of the more bizarre pieces is a faked chimera.

The Strahov collection

In 1950, the library contained 130,000 books. This number has now increased to around 900,000, as the Strahov has taken in the contents of a number of other monasterial libraries, particularly from central and northern Bohemia. One of the most famous of all the manuscripts is the **Strahov Gospels**, the oldest manuscript in the library, dating from the 9th to 10th centuries, which was acquired during the reign of Charles IV. A facsimile of the gospels is on display in the corridor.

Also among the most valuable treasures are rarities such as the New Testament printed in Plzeň in 1476, one of the first printed works in the Czech language. Another is the

beautifully illustrated story of the journey of Frederick von Dohna to Rome, dating from the 17th century.

The **Strahov Collection of Art**, comprising the monastery's newly renovated picture and sculpture galleries, is upstairs above the cloister. Although a small collection, it is well worth a look. The works of art are mostly religious, but there are a number of secular works by Baroque and Rococo painters; these include Norbert Grund (1717–67) and Franz Anton Maulbertsch (1724–96).

One of the most important works owned by the monastery is the wooden **Strahov Madonna** by a Bohemian sculptor, dating from the second third of the 14th century. There is also a wonderful painting of *Judith* from the workshop of Lucas Cranach the elder (1472–1553).

St Mary's Church and gardens

Nanebevzetí Panny Marie (St Mary's Church), next door to the monastery, is usually closed to the public, although the interior can be seen through a grille in the porch.

This impressive Romanesque building was vastly altered and richly redecorated in the Baroque style during the 17th and 18th centuries. Much of the decorative work by Czech artist Jiří Neunhertz depicts scenes from the life of St Norbert, Archbishop of Magdeburg and founder of the Premonstratensian Order in northern France in 1120. It is believed that his remains were brought to this church during the 17th century. The organ, often heard in the monastery grounds, was once played on by Mozart.

Also forming part of the monastery grounds are the large gardens, offering a wonderful vista of the city. These gardens fill the valley between Petřín Hill (once part of the monastery) and Castle Hill, right up to the edge of the Malá Strana. Beyond the gardens, over the summit of Petřín, is the enormous **Velký Strahovský Stadión** ❻ (Strahov Stadium). Built in the 1920s and designed by Alois Dryák, it was used by the nationalist Sokol (Falcon) organisation for mass gymnastic displays. ❑

Map on page 102

The Sokol movement, and its mass gatherings, was banned by the Communist regime, in part because of the uneasy similarities between the Czech movement and organisations in Nazi Germany, and in part because of its nationalist aspirations. The Sokol movement has now been reformed.

RESTAURANTS AND PUBS

Restaurants

Malý Buddha
Úvoz 46
Tel: 220 513 894
Open: Tues–Sun
1–10.30pm. €–€€
A popular, non-smoking cellar tea house which also serves a variety of noodle and rice dishes, many of them vegetarian. The food is a bit bland, but healthy and dished up in pleasant surroundings which try to emulate a Buddhist temple (including a shrine at the back). Aside from the food there is a large range of healthy juices and teas.

U zlaté hrušky
Nový Svět 3
Tel: 220 514 778
Open: daily 11.30am–3pm, 6.30pm–midnight. €€€
The 'Golden Pear' is an attractive cellar restaurant on one of Hradčany's loveliest streets. The building has been renovated and is now very comfortable, while the menu, courtesy of chef Vladimír Šalanský, is a good mix of international and Czech dishes, including, fittingly, pear soup with cinnamon gnocchi, venison and roast duck; there are even some vegetarian options.

Pubs

U černého vola
Loretánské náměstí 1
Tel: 220 513 481
Open: daily 10am–10pm.
This traditional pub, tucked away near the Loreto Church, is one of the best-loved in the city. It consists of a couple of smoke-filled rooms lined with long, wooden benches and tables, and usually packed with locals. The Velkopopovický Kozel beer (both dark and light) is extremely tasty; the food doesn't extend much beyond sausages, bread and mustard, but it goes well with the beer and unpretentious air of the place.

● ● ● ● ● ● ● ● ●
Price includes a three-course dinner and a glass of wine or beer. €€€ over 600 Kč, €€ 300–600 Kč, € under 300 Kč.

MALÁ STRANA

One of the best-preserved areas of Prague, Malá Strana abounds with ornate Baroque architecture and landscaped gardens, as well as contemporary art and excellent restaurants

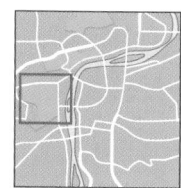

Malá Strana (the Lesser Quarter) lies at the foot of Prague Castle *(see page 77)*. It is a totally individual quarter, almost like a picturesque island, separated from the rest of the city by broad parks and the wide, steady flow of the Vltava. Looking down from the hills, the impression gained is of a landslide of roofs which started to roll between the Hradčany and Petřín hills and came to a stop on the river bank. In 1257, Malá Strana was made a city, and is thus the second-oldest of the five historic cities that make up Prague. Malá Strana experienced its first boom during the rule of Charles IV. During this time it was extended considerably and received new fortifications.

However, not until catastrophic damage was inflicted by the great fire of 1541 was there any sign of a major rebuilding programme. This rebuilding shaped the individual characteristics of the quarter which we can still see today.

Malá Strana truly blossomed after the victory of the Catholic League over the Bohemians in the Battle of White Mountain in 1620, when many wealthy families loyal to the House of Habsburg settled here. True, most of the palaces were deserted once the political administration of Bohemia had moved to

Vienna, but they have been spared major alteration to this day. Even the town houses, which often have much older foundations, have kept their mainly Baroque facades with their characteristic house signs. For this reason, Malá Strana can be described as an architectural jewel, indeed as a complete work of art representing the Baroque style of Central Europe. The different creative styles of the town houses, the small, quiet squares, and the mansions with their attractive

Map on page 102

LEFT: tram 22 enters Malostranské náměstí.
BELOW: the dome and tower of St Nicholas dominate the skyline.

gardens designed to blend in with the slopes of the hill all came together harmoniously to form an original style, "Prague Baroque".

The district is home to a number of embassies (including those of Italy, the UK and USA), and not a few of the city's best restaurants. However, by no means everything revolves around the tourist here, and Malá Strana still has its own everyday life to live, even if the character of this is changing as new businesses move in; once off the main streets, you can enjoy the special atmosphere of the place.

St Nicholas's Church

The centre of Malá Strana always was and still is Malostranské náměstí, a square which is actually divided into two parts by the **Chrám sv. Mikuláše** ❼ (St Nicholas's Church; open daily 9am–5pm; admission charge) and the neighbouring former Jesuit college. The church, Prague's greatest Baroque building, has recently undergone a restoration, and the spectacular interior is bright and gleaming. During the summer it is possible to ascend the church tower, with its great view over the surrounding rooftops.

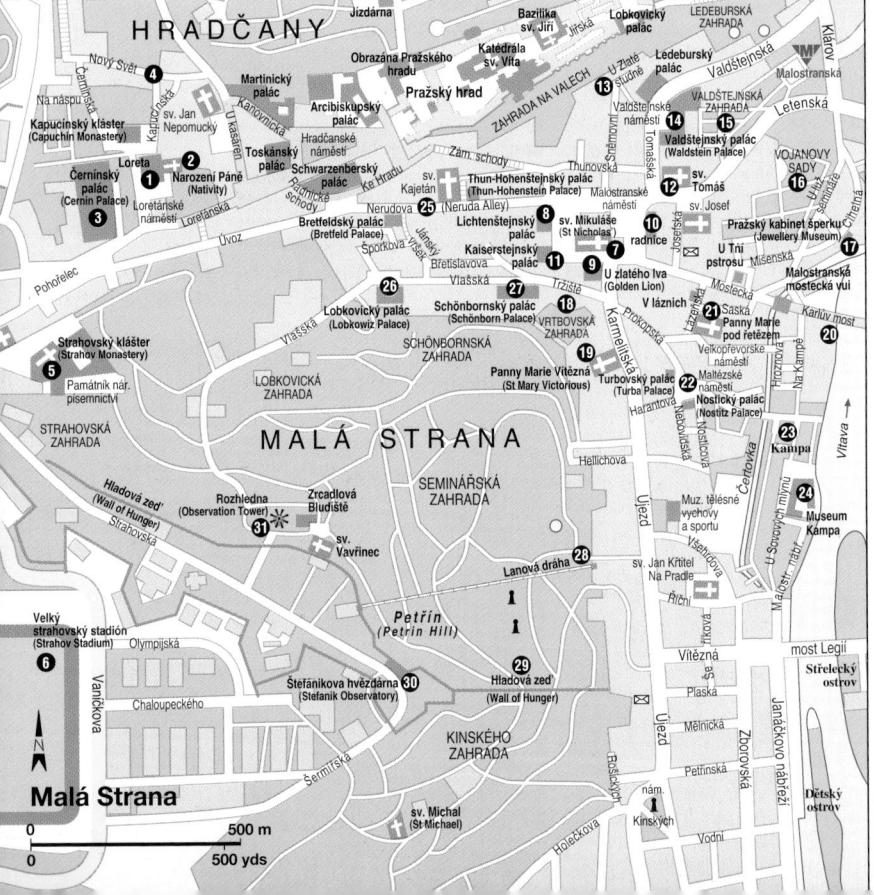

Malá Strana

0   500 m
0   500 yds

The conspicuous dome of St Nicholas's Church and its slender tower can be seen from many different viewpoints in an ever-changing perspective. This unequal couple has become the symbol of the whole of Malá Strana. The church itself is a masterpiece of Baroque architecture and one of the most beautiful examples of its kind.

In the early 18th century the famous Bavarian architect Christoph Dientzenhofer built the nave and side chapels on the site of a Gothic church. The choir and the dome were added later by his son Kilián Ignaz. The building was completed in the mid-18th century by the addition of the tower, which was the work of Carlo Lurago.

Particularly outstanding among the special features of the interior is the monumental ceiling fresco by Johann Lukas Kracker in the nave. It is one of the largest in Europe and portrays scenes from the life of St Nicholas. Another valuable fresco, *Celebration of the Holy Trinity* by Franz Xaver Karl Palko, decorates the dome. The dome itself is 75 metres (247 ft) high – tall enough to accommodate the tower on Petřín Hill inside it *(see page 113)*. A particularly fine view of the ceiling frescos can be had from the gallery above the nave, where there is also a collection of paintings by Karel Škréta (the entrance to the steps lies to the left of the main altar).

The impressive sculptures of the Eastern Church Fathers that stand in front of the four supporting pillars of the dome (clockwise from the right St Cyril Alexandrijsky, Jan Zlatoústý, Řehoř Naziánský and Basil Veliký, 1755–69) are the work of František Ignác Platzer. He was also responsible for the gilded statue of St Nicholas (1765) which is by the high altar. The wooden altar itself is to the design of Andrey Pozza and dates to the first quarter of the 18th century. Also worthy of note is the stunningly ornate pulpit, made of artificial marble and covered with gilt (from the workshop of R.J. Prachner, 1762–6).

In front of the church, in the middle of the square, is a plague column by Giovanni Alliprandi (1715).

Map on page 102

The 18th century Plague Column in front of the church.

BELOW: the wonderfully ornate interior of St Nicholas

The sleek café-restaurant Square on Malostranské náměstí was previously the Malostraská kavárna, a favourite hang-out of Jan Neruda, author of Tales of the Lesser Quarter.

BELOW: façades on Malostranské náměstí.

Malostranské náměstí

Opposite St Nicholas's is the **Lichtenštejnský palác ❽** (Lichtenstein Palace) with its broad Neoclassical façade. From 1620 to 1627 it belonged to Karl von Lichtenstein, the so-called "Bloody Governor" who was mainly responsible for the execution of the leaders of the 1618 rebellion *(see page 25)*.

From St Nicholas's Church you will also notice the **U zlatého lva ❾** (Golden Lion House) at No. 10. It is one of the few purely Renaissance houses in the Malá Strana and also contains the somewhat touristy wine bar and restaurant U mecenáše. Small wine bars like this, whose charm lies mainly in their ancient walls, are typical of Malá Strana; some have been serving drinks since 1600.

On the lower side of this busy square (at No. 21) is the quarter's old **radnice ❿** (town hall), The building dates back to the late 15th century but, like much else here, was given its present façade in the early 17th century. The **Smiřický-Montág palác** (at No. 18) was once a hotbed of 17th-century Protestant plotting, while on the right is the **Kaiserštejnský palác ⓫** (Kaiserstein Palace). A memorial plaque outside the house proclaims that the world-famous opera singer Ema Destinová once lived here.

St Thomas

Following the tramlines out of the square to the north (along Letenská) brings you to the church and former monastery of **Sv. Tomáše ⓬** (St Thomas; open Mon–Sat 11am–1pm, Sun 9am–midday, 4.30–5.30); the entrance is on the small road to the left. The former monastic brewery (founded in 1358) is no longer in existence; though there is still a touristy beer cellar further down Letenská. The church is the most impressive part of the former Augustinian monastery, and was first built in the 13th century. Its present Baroque form (late 1720s) is the work of Kilián Ignaz Dientzenhofer.

However well-conceived on the outside, it is the interior that is the finest part of the church. A beautifully ornate example of Central European Baroque, the church orig-

Map on page 102

inally had two altarpieces by Rubens (the *Martyrdom of St Thomas* and *St Augustine*), now replaced by copies (the originals are in the National Gallery; *see page 90*). The ceiling frescoes are by the Bohemian artist Václav Reiner.

Just before the church of Sv. Tomáše is, to the left, the street of Tomášská, which leads down to Valdštejnské náměstí (Waldstein Square). Here are The Golden Pretzel (No. 12) and the Baroque house **The Golden Stag**, which bears one of the most beautiful and house signs in Prague. The sculpture shows St Hubert with a stag, and is the work of Ferdinand Maxmilian Brokoff. Before house numbers were introduced, during the reign of Empress Maria Theresa in the 18th century, these house signs were used for identification. They were based on the profession or craft of the house owner, his status or the immediate environment of the house. Animal and other symbolic signs, of both a secular and a religious nature, were popular. If the house owner changed, the house retained its original sign.

Sometimes the new owner even took over the name of the house.

Leading off Tomášská is the small street of Thunovská, which heads up the hill. From there, make a short excursion into Sněmovní. This street and the adjoining cul-de-sac, **U zlaté studně ⓭** (The Golden Well) form a picturesque corner. Hidden away at the end of the little alley is an excellent restaurant with the same name as the street. Also noteworthy is the Renaissance house **The Golden Swan** at No. 10, which hides a beautiful inner courtyard. Go back in the direction of Thunovská, which leads to the Zámecké schody (New Castle Steps). These so-called "new" steps are not to be confused with the Old, which lead to the other end of the castle. The British Embassy is located here in the 17th century **Thunovský palác** (at No. 14).

The Waldstein Palace and Gardens

Valdštejnská and Valdštejnské náměstí (Waldstein Square) lie at the end of Tomášská. These border the large **Valdštejnský palác ⓮** (the

A Waldstein Palace door relief.

LEFT:
the fake grotto in the Waldstein Gardens.

Albrecht von Waldstein

General Albrecht von Waldstein (also known as Wallenstein, the eponymous hero of a play by the German playwright Schiller) was a man who made his way to the top by skilful strategy and leadership on the one hand, and by intrigue and treachery on the other.

During the Thirty Years War he enlisted under the Habsburg Ferdinand II. He won many important victories for Ferdinand and these brought him not only power and a ducal title, but also considerable wealth, which as a court favourite he was particularly well placed to increase. By 1625, he owned one quarter of all Bohemia. This process was helped not least by his participation in a grandiose coin swindle, so that in the end he was able to raise his own private army. Eventually, his services became so expensive that parts of the Empire had to be mortgaged to afford him. But Waldstein's rapid rise came to an equally rapid end when, in secret deals with the enemy, he initiated tactical manoeuvres which would have eventually led him to the Bohemian crown. However, Emperor Ferdinand saw through him and organised a group of mercenaries to get rid of him. They murdered him in his bed in the town of Cheb in 1634.

Walking in the delightful Waldstein Gardens.

BELOW: looking over a wintry Vltava from Malá Strana.

Waldstein Palace, or Wallenstein, as it is also called) on two sides. This was the first Baroque palace in Prague, built between 1624–30 for General Albrecht von Wallenstein.

The grandiose residence matches Wallenstein's grand political ambitions – it was intended to rival Prague Castle that looms above. He acquired the site for the building by buying up and dispossessing the inhabitants of more than 20 houses. Even the city gate had to go, in order to give the architects (all Italians) enough space to provide their patron with a palace featuring all possible luxuries available at the time. The palace today is used as one of the buildings of the Czech Parliament, however; there is some access allowed (open Sat–Sun 10am–4pm; admission charge).

The rooms open to the public include the Mannerist and early-Baroque main hall, with superb ceiling paintings by Baccio di Bianca. Off the main hall is the Knights' Hall, with its unusual 19th-century leather wall covering, which leads on to the beautifully ornate circular audience chamber and mythological passage decorated with scenes from Ovid and Virgil.

The rather restrained outer façade and walls facing the square do not give anywhere near the same impression as a visit to the **Palace Gardens** ⓯ (open daily Apr–Oct 10am –6pm; entrances on from Valdštejnské náměstí, Letenská and by Malostranská Metro). The greatest pride of the gardens was the triple-arched loggia *(sala terrena)*, richly decorated with frescos. Also in the gardens are a large aviary (home to some beautiful owls), a delightful pond and an extraordinary artificial grotto which spreads along most of the garden walls.

The bronze statues of mythological gods and goddesses scattered about the garden are the work of Adriaen de Vries, court sculptor to Emperor Rudolf II. They are, however, copies; the originals were taken to Sweden as spoils of war in 1648 and are now located in the park of the Drottingholm palace near Stockholm.

Another work by de Vries is the figure of Hercules fighting the Hydra in the middle of the pond.

The fountain with the sculpture of Venus and Cupid is also remarkable. Opposite the loggia is the former Riding School, where temporary exhibitions are held.

The Malostranská Metro station contains a copy of Matthias Bernard Braun's *Hope*. Some sculptures from his workshop can be seen in the courtyard garden. Along Valdštejnská are palaces whose gardens lie on the slope beneath the castle. Three of these terraced gardens, built for the nobility after Italian models, can be visited. The entrance is next to the Koloratský palác (Kolowrat Palace, No. 10; *see page 89*). On U lužického semináře, which runs parallel to Letenská, is the entrance to **Vojanovy sady** ⑯ (Vojan Park), the former garden of a nearby palace. In this park, with its two Baroque chapels, modern sculptures are often exhibited.

Towards the river is the street of Cihelna. In the same complex as the **Hergetova Cihelna** restaurant ⑰ *(see page 114)* are the recently opened **Pražský kabinet šperku** (Prague Jewellery Collection) and **Franz Kafka Museum** (both open daily 10am–6pm; admission charge; www.cihelna.info, www.kafkamuseum.cz). Among the glittering jewellery exhibits (which date from the 17th century to the present) are original Fabergé eggs and Czechoslovak items displayed at the Brussels Expo of 1958 *(see also page 175)*.

Karmelitská

Running in the opposite direction (south) from Malostranské náměstí is the street of Karmelitská. On the corner of Tržiště, by the U Malého Glena jazz club, is the lovely Baroque terraced **Vrtbovská zahrada** ⑱ (Vrtba gardens; open daily, Apr–Oct 10am–6pm; admission charge) of the Vrtbovský palác (Vrtba Palace). This World Heritage Site has a *sala terrena* (pavilion) with frescoes by Václav Reiner and a number of sculptures by

Matthias Bernhard Braun. The views of the castle hill from the stepped gardens – especially the final terrace – are magnificent.

A little further along Karmelitská is the **Kostel Panny Marie Vítězná** ⑲ (Church of St Mary Victorious; open Mon–Sat 8.30am–6pm, Sun 9am–7pm), the first, although by no means the best, Baroque church to be built in Prague. It was constructed as a monument to the Counter-Reformation brought to the city by the Habsburgs. The furnishings, which are all of a unified style, date from the 17th century; the saints' pictures by the altar are the work of Petr Brandl.

It is in this church that the famous **Bambino di Praga** is kept, a 16th- to 17th-century wax figure of Spanish origin of the infant Jesus, dressed in one or another of its 72 costly robes. This rather unprepossessing little figure is revered by Catholics, and believed to work miracles, thus ensuring a constant stream of pilgrims, all of whom are subjected to the hard-sell of the nuns running the tacky gift shop attached.

Map on page 102

Almost everyone travels by tram.

BELOW: Mostecká leads down to the Charles Bridge.

The Brunsvík stands beside the Charles Bridge (see page 117).

BELOW:
the main square
on Kampa Island.

Mostecká

Mostecká is the street running from Malostranské náměstí down to the river. This previously elegant street (part of the Royal Route that once led from the Prašná brána, *see page 125*, to the castle) is now lined with a selection of rather tacky souvenir shops, a McDonald's and places to change money. At No. 15 is the 18th-century **Kaunicův palác** (Kaunitz Palace), now the embassy of Serbia and Montenegro.

At the bottom of Mostecká is the **Karlův most** ⑳ (Charles Bridge, *see pages 116–17*) with its two towers, one from the 12th-century Judith Bridge that used to span the Vltava at this point, the other dating from the 15th century.

Without leaving the bridge you can see **U tří pštrosů** (The Three Ostriches), with the remains of the sgraffito decoration which gives it its name. In the late 16th century the house belonged to a merchant who supplied feathers to the royal house. There was a coffee house established here in 1714 and it is now a hotel and restaurant.

The Maltese Square

Leave Mostecká on its southern side and you will find that the streets have become quieter. Here you enter one of the still quiet, dreamy corners of the Malá Strana. Take Saská, or turn off straight into Lázeňská, where house No. 6, **V láznich** (The Spa), was a luxurious hotel up until the 19th century. Among the celebrities to have stayed here were Tsar Peter the Great and, as a memorial plaque proclaims, the French poet François-René de Chateaubriand. The house called **U zlatého jednorozce** (The Golden Unicorn), is the place where the composer Ludwig van Beethoven once stayed.

On the junction between Lázeňská and Maltézské náměstí (*see below*) a beautiful Baroque interior can be found in the **Kostel Panny Marie pod řetězem** ㉑ (Church of St Mary Beneath the Chain), the oldest church in Malá Strana. The 12th-century remains of its Romanesque predecessor can still be seen in the right-hand wall of the forecourt. The church behind was built in the 17th century by Carlo Lurago;

the altar painting, of Mary and John the Baptist, is by Karel Škréta.

On your right is the long sprawl of the **Maltézské náměstí ㉒** (Maltese Square), with its sculpture representing St John the Baptist, the work of Ferdinand Maxmilian Brokoff. Two palaces in this square are worthy of your attention: the **Turbovský palác** (Turba Palace), now the Japanese Embassy, with its Rococo façade, and the early-Baroque **Nostický palác** (Nostitz Palace), now occupied by the Dutch Embassy, to the south.

Adjacent to the Church of St Mary Beneath the Chain is another square, the Velkopřevorské náměstí. On one side is the **Buquoyský palác** (Buquoy Palace), home of the French Embassy, and opposite is the former **Palace of the Grand Prior of the Knights of Malta**, one of the most beautiful in the area. The wall of the Palace of the Grand Prior, facing the French Embassy, is known as the **John Lennon Wall**.

During the 1980s this graffiti-strewn wall was the focus of Prague's Beatles-worship. The "mural", with its depiction of John Lennon, was twice under threat; firstly from the secret police, who painted it over, and then from the Knights of Malta, after it had been repainted and they had been given the property back under the post-1989 restitution. The wall was finally saved from respectability by the intervention of the French ambassador, who appealed to the authorities to let it be.

Kampa island

A little bridge connects the square with the island of **Kampa ㉓**, separated from the Malá Strana by a canal branching off the Vltava, the **Čertovka** or Devil's Stream. This district of the city is also known as Little Venice on account of its situation, watermills and gardens.

The park has been formed by linking up the gardens of former palaces and offers a beautiful view of the Old Town. The small group of houses lying directly by the water between Charles Bridge and the mouth of the Čertovka are also known as the Venice of Prague, and

Map on page 102

The name of the church Sv. Jana na prádle (St John at the Laundry) at the southern end of Kampa Island refers to the previous use of the Čertovka for washing clothes.

BELOW: the Čertovka and its water mill.

Map on page 204

The museum is as impressive inside as out.

BELOW: Museum Kampa.

are much sought after. Kampa was one the areas most affected by the 2002 floods, although little is left to suggest the scale of devastation.

Much of the southern section of the island is given over to **Kampa Park**, a lovely green space on the banks of the river that is a good place to laze around in summer. Within the park is the **Museum Kampa** ㉔ (open daily 10am–6pm; admission charge; www.museumkampa.cz), set in an old water mill. The building has been beautifully converted – the uncharitable might say this is the finest exhibit – by Helena Bukovjanská. Two of the most impressive parts are the additions by Czech artists. The first is the glass cube, designed by Marian Kasměla, that tops the building (an open staircase takes you up to the cube from where there is a lovely view), and the second a glass footbridge, by Václav Cigler, that appears to lead you out over the river. The proximity of the river ensured that the museum was inundated by the 2002 floods, and the large sculpture of a chair that stands on the embankment outside the building

was found washed 40 km (25 miles) downstream.

Based around the collections of wealthy Czech ex-pats Jan and Meda Mladek, the museum has large holdings of the works of the abstract painter František Kupka (1871–1963) and the Expressionist and Cubist sculptor Otto Gutfreund (1889–1927). A good proportion of the exhibition space is given over to displays of contemporary Central European art. The museum has a very pleasant café and restaurant with seating overlooking the Vltava.

The northern part of the island is largely taken up by the square of Na kampě (one of the locations that starred in the film *Mission: Impossible*), lined with restaurants and shops that have now mostly reopened after the repair of the flood damage. At the northern end of the square are a double flight of steps onto Karlův most (Charles Bridge). By the steps is a replica (1884) of the late-Gothic column with a statue (now in the Lapidarium) of the hero **Brunsvík**, better known in English as Roland.

Nerudova

Parallel to the Castle Steps *(see page 105)* lies the street of **Nerudova** ㉕, named after the famous Czech poet, author and journalist Jan Neruda (1834–91), who lived in the upper part of the street, in house No. 47, U dvou slunců (The Two Suns). His work, particularly the book *Tales of the Lesser Quarter*, was inspired by the everyday life of Malá Strana. Much of the street is now home to iffy restaurants and shops selling tourist tat.

Many of the middle-class houses were originally built in a Renaissance style and later given Baroque additions. They often bear house signs which don't match the names of the houses. For instance, house No. 6, The Red Eagle, has a sign showing two angels. In the case of house No. 12, The Three Violins, however, it is known that several generations of violin-makers lived here. More signs can be seen on The Golden Chalice (No. 16), St John Nepomuk (No. 18), and The Donkey and the Cradle (No. 25). A pharmacy was formerly housed in The Golden Lion at No. 32.

As is often the case in Prague, two embassies have settled into the Baroque palaces in this street. On the left is the **Morzinský palác** (Morzin Palace), the Romanian Embassy. Its unusual facade ornament – the heraldic Moors which support the balcony, the allegorical figures of Day and Night and the sculptures representing the four corners of the world – are the work of Ferdinand Maximilian Brokoff.

Somewhat higher up is the **Thun-Hohenštejnský palác** (Thun-Hohenstein Palace), the Italian Embassy, which is decorated with two eagles with outspread wings, and is the work of Matthias Bernard Braun. The statues of Roman deities represent Jupiter and Juno. The palace is connected by two passages to the neighbouring church and monastery of St Cajetan, creating an architectural unity typical of the closing years of the 17th century.

From the top of Nerudova you can enjoy a splendid view of the Schwarzenberg Palace *(see page 78)*. The street gives way to a romantic but steep stairway leading up to the cas-

Map on page 102

Jan Neruda's name was adopted by Ricardo Eliecer Neftalí Reyes y Basoalto, the Nobel Prize-winning poet Pablo Neruda.

BELOW: grafitti on Kampa Island.

The small funicular railway that runs up Petřín Hill.

tle; to the left, Loretánská street leads out of Malá Strana up in the direction of Strahov Monastery and the Loreta Shrine *(see pages 93–9)*.

Below Nerudova

A maze of courtyards lies hidden at the back of the last houses of Nerudova. They fall in a series of terraces into the valley between the two hills. At the bottom are a few alleys that have almost a village character. If you go back a little, you will reach, at No. 33, the Rococo **Bretfeldský palác** (Bretfeld Palace), with a relief of St Nicholas on the portal. In earlier years famous balls took place in this building, some of which both Mozart and Giacomo Casanova are said to have attended. The palace is not open to the public.

From here the steps Jánský vršek lead down and then turn right into Šporkova, which leads us along the slope mentioned above. It then curves and leads into Vlašská, directly opposite the **Lobkovický palác ㉖** (Lobkowicz Palace). This magnificent Baroque palace now

contains another embassy: this time representing Germany. This was a scene of chaos during 1989 when many East Germans came to Prague and camped out in neighbouring buildings, and even the grounds of the embassy, until they were given leave to enter the Federal Republic.

This area was settled by Italian artists and craft workers invited by Rudolf II, and they still have a presence here; just beyond the Lobkowicz Palace, on the other side of the square, is the **Italian Cultural Institute**. Set in an old church it holds temporary exhibitions sponsored by the Italian Embassy.

Descending Vlašská brings you to Tržiště. On Tržiště is the **Schönbornský palác ㉗** (Schönborn Palace), which now houses the heavily guarded US Embassy (all passing cars are stopped and searched). It has a splendid garden, which can be seen from the Castle Ramp.

Petřín Hill

Above Nerudova is one of Prague's favourite parks, Petřín Hill. One fun way of ascending is to take the **Petřín Funicular Railway ㉘** *(lanová dráha)* from Újezd (a continuation of Karmelitská which lies at the bottom of Tržiště). Although also known as a cable car, the cars don't actually hang on cables, they run on rails. The fact that the contraption looks so curious is due to the original method of locomotion. The old cars had a water tank, which was always filled at the top and emptied at the bottom. In this way, the cars going up were powered solely by the weight of the cars going down.

The cable car was inaugurated in 1891. In the 1960s the water tanks were done away with; the hill slope was repaired (it had partially collapsed) and the railway reopened in 1985, powered by more modern means; normal tram and Metro tickets are valid on the funicular.

The park on **Petřín Hill** was formed by linking up the gardens which had gradually replaced what had once been vineyards. On the level of the upper cable car station, a path offering a marvellous view of the castle and the Old Town below it leads all the way through the park to the Strahov Monastery. But apart from the delightful views of the city, the park also has many sights of its own which are worth taking the time to explore.

In the most southerly corner is the Villa Kinský (actually in the district of Smíchov to the south; *see pages 182–5*). Also on the Smíchov side of the hill is the little wooden **church of Sv. Michal** (St Michael), a wonderful example of folk art of the 18th century. It comes from the Carpathian Ukraine and was rebuilt on this spot in 1929, a gift from the inhabitants of the small Ukrainian village of Mukacevo, which had become part of Czechoslovakia after World War I and was annexed by the Soviet Union after World War II. A belfry from Wallachia stands next to the church.

The **Hladová zed'** ㉙ (Hunger Wall) which leads down the slope is part of the fortifications built by Charles IV. According to legend, this project was undertaken to provide work for the starving and impoverished. Near the wall lies the **Štefánikova hvězdárna** ㉚ (Stefanik Observatory; admission charge; www.observatory.cz). During the day you can go and observe the sun, while at night (depending on the weather, of course) the telescopes are focused on the moon and planets.

On top of the hill are two attractions built for the Prague Jubilee Exhibition in 1891: one is the **Rozhledna** ㉛ (Observation Tower), a scaled-down replica of the Eiffel Tower 60 metres (197 ft) high, and the other the **Zrcadlová bludiště**, a labyrinth of distorting mirrors inside a miniature castle (both open, daily Apr–Oct, 10am–7pm, Nov–Mar Sat–Sun 10am–4.30pm; admission charge). The view from the top of the tower is quite stunning. Not far away is **Chrám sv. Vavřinec** (St Lawrence's Church), a Romanesque building with a Baroque façade. ❏

Map on page 102

The observatory is open Nov–Feb, Tues–Fri 6–8pm, Sat–Sun 10am–midday, 2–8pm; Mar and Oct, Tues–Fri 7–9pm, Sat–Sun 10am–midday, 2–6pm, 7–9pm; Apr–Oct, Tues–Fri 2–7pm, 9–11pm, Sat–Sun 10am–midday, 2–7pm, 9–11pm; and Sept, Tues–Fri 2–6pm, 8–10pm, Sat–Sun 10am–midday, 2–6pm, 8–10pm.

BELOW: a quiet Malá Strana backstreet.

RESTAURANTS, CAFÉS AND BARS

Restaurants

Alchymist
Hellichova 4
Tel: 257 312 518
Open: daily 8–11am,
noon–3pm, 7pm–midnight.
€€€
Decorated with esoteric
symbols as befits its
name, this restaurant
manages to stay just the
right side of kitsch. The
food is very good, with
large starters (tasty salads), as well as excellent
pasta and a delicious
risotto Milanese. Very
good service and a large
wine list round off its
attractions.

Bakeshop Diner
Lázeňská 19
Tel: 254 534 244
Open: daily 7am–7pm. €
Just off Mostecká, this

modern little place
with retro formica tables
has a selection of
reasonably priced burgers, omelettes, sandwiches and salads, as
well as decent coffee and
fresh juices. It is a good
place for breakfast, but
avoid the rather leaden
croissants.

Café kafíčko
Míšeňská 10
Tel: 724 151 795
Open: daily 10am–10pm. €
A very pleasant, nonsmoking café not far
from the Charles Bridge.
There is a good range of
teas, coffees, and some
lovely cakes.

C'est la vie
Říční 1
Tel: 257 321 511
Open: daily 11.30am–1am.
€€€

At the end of a small
street on the edge of
Malá Strana, you can
either dine in the attractive minimal interior or on
the atmospheric terrace
overlooking the river and
most Legíí. The food here
consists of very well-prepared, if expensive, international dishes given an
East Asian twist.

Cukrkávalimonáda
Lázeňská 7
Tel: 257 530 628
Open: Mon–Fri 9am–7pm,
Sat–Sun 10am–7pm. €
A clean, modern space
with a nicely painted ceiling, set on a small square
just off Mostecká.
Friendly and laid-back it
serves decent coffee,
good breakfasts (excellent ham and eggs) and a
selection of good-value
simple meals (pasta,
omelettes and pancakes).

David
Tržiště 21
Tel: 257 533 109
Open: daily 11.30am–11pm.
€€€
Tucked away down a
quiet, atmospheric backstreet, this is a lovely
place, decorated with
paintings by the Czech
artist Michael Halva. The
service is discreet but
friendly, and stylishly-executed, and the Czech
and modern European
dishes are beautfully
presented. It is all
backed up by an excellent selection of Moravian and French wines.

Hergetova Cihelna
Cihelná 2b
Tel: 257 535 534
Open: daily 10am–2am.
€€–€€€
Part of the Kampa Park
empire, with a similarly
good view of the Charles
Bridge. The food is predominantly Italian (pizza
and pasta) with a few
modern Czech dishes
(potato soup). The
desserts include delicious vodka-marinated
raspberries. There is a
well-stocked bar and the
surroundings are modern and clean.

Kampa Park
Na Kampě 8b
Tel: 257 532 685
Open: daily 11.30am–1am.
€€€
One of the best places to
eat in Malá Strana, and
the viewis certainly spectacular. The restaurant
has restrained and tasteful decor, and a predominance of fish on the
menu. Expensive and
much frequented by the
visiting "great and
good", but do try the
excellent-value set lunch
for a taste of the well-regarded food.

Pálffy Palác
Valdštejnská 14
Tel: 257 530 522
Open: daily 11am–11pm.
€€–€€€
Go through the door in
the right-hand side of the
imposing gateway and all
the way up the stairs.
The dining hall exudes a

faded opulence – a gilded chandelier and palms setting off the yellowing walls – and it comes across as a mixture of a gentlemen's club and grand railway buffet. The food is competent but nothing special, a combination of French and Czech; it's the surroundings that really count.

Restaurant Gitanes
Tržiště 7
Tel: 257 530 163
Open: daily 11am–11pm. €€
A quirky and comfortable Bosnian/Serbian/Montenegran restaurant with a prettily painted floral ceiling and furnishings, plus a cosy hideaway for two behind a curtain. The excellent and homely Balkan dishes (stuffed peppers, homemade lamb sausage, grilled mushrooms) and an eclectic and interesting wine list make this well worth a visit.

Square
Malostranské náměstí 5
Tel: 257 532 109
Open: daily 8am–1am. €€
A famous café given a modern look with a well-thought-out and stylish interior. This is a good place for reading the papers over breakfast before heading up the hill to the castle, or for a light lunch or dinner from the bistro-style menu.

U Maltézských rytířů
Prokopská 10
Tel: 257 530 075

Open: daily 11am–11pm. €€€
An atmospheric, intimate cellar that houses a delightful restaurant. The Czech food, including pike-perch, duck and vension, is well prepared and tasty, with especially good strudel to finish off with. There are some great local wines, and the staff and owner are very friendly and helpful.

U Modré kachničky
Nebovidská 6
Tel: 257 320 308
Open: daily noon–4pm, 6.30–11pm. €€€
Oozing Bohemian charm, this Malá Strana restaurant serves some of the best Czech dishes in the city. The emphasis is very much on duck and game, such as venison with bilberries and spinach or duck with walnut stuffing, and they also do lovely fruit dumplings for dessert.

U Patrona
Dražického náměstí 4
Tel: 257 530 725
Open: daily 11am–midnight. €€€
These elegant little dining rooms close to the Charles Bridge are a good place to try some well-prepared Bohemian specialities. They include a tasty game consommé with juniper berries and an excellent roast goose with red cabbage. All helped along by the comfortable interior and very smooth service.

U Zeleného čaje
Nerudova 19
Tel: 257 530 027
Open: daily 11am–10pm. €
While pretty much everywhere on Nerudova is best avoided as a tourist trap, this is an honourable exception. A quiet tea house with a large range of teas, simple meals and excellent strudel. The building was used during the filming of Amadeus.

Bars

St Nicholas Café
Tržiště 10
Tel: 257 530 204
Open: daily midday–3pm. €
A pleasant, laid-back cellar bar, complete with arched roof. There is decent Pilsner Urquell on tap and a very extensive list of cocktails. Freshly cooked pizzas are available if you need something to keep you going in the small hours. All in all, one of the nicest places in Malá Strana for a relaxing evening's drinking.

Tato
Kampa Park
Open: daily 10am–midnight. €
This convivially run-down bar is set in the mlýn Huť (Works Mill) beside the Čertovka, home to a mixture of students and artists. As well as friendly place for a drink, it also gives you a opportunity to lhave a look around one of Kampa Island's old watermills.

PRICE CATEGORIES

Prices for three-course dinner per person with a glass of wine or beer:
€ = under 300 Kč
€€ = 300–600 Kč
€€€ = above 600 Kč

LEFT: great wine and lovely service at David.
RIGHT: alfresco at Square.

KARLŮV MOST

One of the loveliest sights in Prague, the Charles Bridge combines in unique fashion its original Gothic architecture with Baroque sculpture

The first stone bridge was constructed here during the second half of the 12th century, in the place of a 10th-century wooden bridge which was situated somewhat further to the north. Known as the Judith Bridge after the consort of King Vladislav I, it still exists today in the pillar foundations in the Vltava and the smaller of the bridge towers on the Malá Strana side. In 1342 the Judith Bridge collapsed. In 1357, Charles IV laid the foundation stone for the new Gothic construction. Building began under the supervision of the cathedral architect, Petr Parléř, who was only 27 at the time. However, the bridge was not completed until 1399, after Parléř's death in the same year.

ABOVE: the view of the bridge from the Old Town Bridge Tower (Staroměstská mostecká věž). This was Parléř's last work, its vast construction, standing on the first bridge support, decorated with fine sculptures on its east side. High up, in a gallery of tracery, stand St Adalbert (left), the second bishop of Prague, and St Wenceslas (right). Below, in a rounded arch, is Charles IV (left); on a foreshortened representation of the Charles Bridge is St Vitus (centre) and finally Wenceslas IV (right). Further down again is a row with the coats of arms of the Holy Roman Empire (inside left), Bohemia (inside right) and the Luxembourg domains. Here – and elsewhere on the tower – is Wenceslas IV's personal emblem: a kingfisher in a 'love knot', a knotted handkerchief. Equally elaborate sculptures on the bridge side of the tower were destroyed in 1648 during the Swedish occupation. A memorial plaque recalls the Thirty Years War.

LEFT: looking back from the bridge towards Malá Strana, with the dome of St Nicholas appearing between the two towers at the western end of the bridge. The Lesser Quarter Bridge Tower, on the left (south) side is a relic from the Judith Bridge (1158–72); the right-hand (north) tower was erected later, in 1464. The bridge itself is 510 metres (558 yds) long and 10 metres (33 ft) wide. Slightly curved, it spans the Vltava by means of 17 pillars, strengthened on both sides and forming 16 arches. All is not well with the bridge, however, as the foundations are slowly crumbling, and a reconstruction programme has been started to save this medieval treasure.

RIGHT: Prague is known both for defenestrations and depontefications. In 1393, Wenceslas IV believed that the Vicar General, John of Nepomuk, was organising monks against his treatment of the Church. The king had him thrown over the Charles Bridge, and according to legend a ring of seven stars appeared in the water where he sank. The martyr was later made a saint, and it is said that touching the relief of the death scene on his statue (No. 15; modelled by Johann Brokoff, 1683) will assure your return to Prague.

SCULPTURES

During the Middle Ages the bridge had no sculptural decoration, the only adornment being a crucifix (5 on map), subsequently renewed on several occasions. The 30 statues adorning the bridge were added over a period of 250 years. Nonetheless, visually they form a harmonious whole in spite of their widely varying artistic merits. Many are replicas; the most valuable are now in the Lapidarium of the National Museum. The first statue to be added was that of St John of Nepomuk (15). Between 1706–14, a further 21 statues were erected on the bridge. The most important Baroque works that can be seen here are by Johann Brokoff (15), his son Ferdinand Maximilian Brokoff (4, 10, 14, 20, 23, 27, 28), and the accomplished Tyrolean artist Matthias Bernhard Braun (2, 16, 24).

THE BRIDGE STATUES: 1 The Virgin Mary with St Bernhard; 2 St Ivo; 3 The Virgin with SS Dominic and Thomas Aquinas; 4 Ss Barbara, Margaret and Elizabeth; 5 Crucifixion group with a crucifix; 6 Pietà; 7 St Anne with the Virgin Mary and Infant Jesus; 8 St Joseph; 9 SS Cyril and Methodius; 10 St Francis Xavier; 11 St John the Baptist; 12 St Christopher; 13 SS Wenceslas, Norbert and Sigismund; 14 St Francis Borgia; 15 St John of Nepomuk; 16 St Ludmilla; 17 St Anthony of Padua; 18 St Francis the Seraphic; 19 St Judas Thaddeus; 20 SS Vincent of Ferrer and Procop; to the left is a late-Gothic column with a statue of Brunsvík, the patron of the bridge; 21 St Augustine; 22 St Nicholas of Tolentino; 23 St Cajetan; 24 St Luitgard (considered the statue with most artistic merit); 25 St Philip Benitius; 26 St Adalbert; 27 St Vitus; 28 SS John of Matha, Felix of Valois and Ivan (the figure of the Turk is particularly well-loved); 29 SS Cosmas and Damian; 30 St Wenceslas.

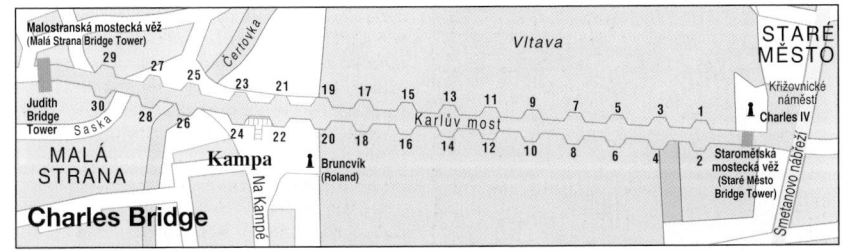

Malostranská mostecká věž (Malá Strana Bridge Tower)
Čertovka
Vltava
STARÉ MĚSTO
29 27 25 23 21 19 17 15 13 11 9 7 5 3 1
Judith Bridge Tower
Saská
30 28 26 24 22 20 18 16 14 12 10 8 6 4 2
Karlův most
Křižovnické náměstí
Charles IV
MALÁ STRANA
Kampa
Na Kampě
Bruncvík (Roland)
Staroměstská mostecká věž (Staré Město Bridge Tower)
Smetanovo nábřeží

Charles Bridge

STARÉ MĚSTO

Prague's Old Town has always been the centre of activity in the city, as well as the site of many historic events. Today it is the tourist hub, where medieval buildings rub shoulders with souvenir shops

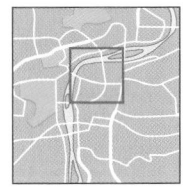

The Old Town (Staré Město) of Prague is spread along the right bank of the Vltava and around the Old Town Square. The area's main streets – Národní třída, Na příkopě and Revoluční – mostly follow the course of the city fortifications, which no longer exist. The name Na příkopě, which means "on the moat", indicates that it was built on the site of the moat which separated the Old Town from the New. Together, these two districts form the actual city centre of Prague.

The Old Town has kept much of its original character; the pattern of streets and squares has remained largely unaltered since the Middle Ages. Originally the Old Town lay some 2–3 metres (6–9 ft) below the modern street level. But the area was subject to repeated flooding, which is why the street level has been raised little by little since the late 13th century. Many houses have Romanesque rooms hidden in their basements.

The historic core of the Old Town is built on these foundations, and every age has left its signs for us to read. The influence of the Baroque cannot be overlooked, but it only finds its expression in individual buildings and has not altered the basic structure of the district. The only large intrusion in the area is the massive building of the Jesuit College, the Klementinum. Here and there you can also see traces of the 19th and 20th centuries, for the development of the river bank gave the modern city a chance to break in. However, apart from the demolition of most of the Jewish Quarter at the end of 19th century, the district has retained much of its medieval and Baroque architecture.

The present-day appearance of the streets is marked by the succession of houses with a great variety

Map on page 120

LEFT:
the Astronomical Clock and Old Town Hall.
BELOW:
the golden lion, a symbol of Prague.

of façades, and generally it is a vibrant district with a well-balanced mixture of homes, offices, shops, small businesses, several schools and leisure facilities.

Prague's first settlement

The first settlements on the site of the Old Town for which there is any historical evidence date from the 10th century. They concentrated around the crossing of three important trade routes, which met at the ford across the Vltava, a little downstream from where the Charles Bridge stands today.

According to a contemporary report, a large market place with numerous stone houses covered the site of the present Old Town Square. As the years went by this market place grew, and was fortified with a city wall in the early 13th century. Around 1230, the settlement received its city charter. By this time it was possible to speak of a large town, in European terms. In 1338, John of Luxembourg granted the citizens of the Old Town the right to their own town hall, and in the years that followed under Charles IV the city experienced an immense eco-

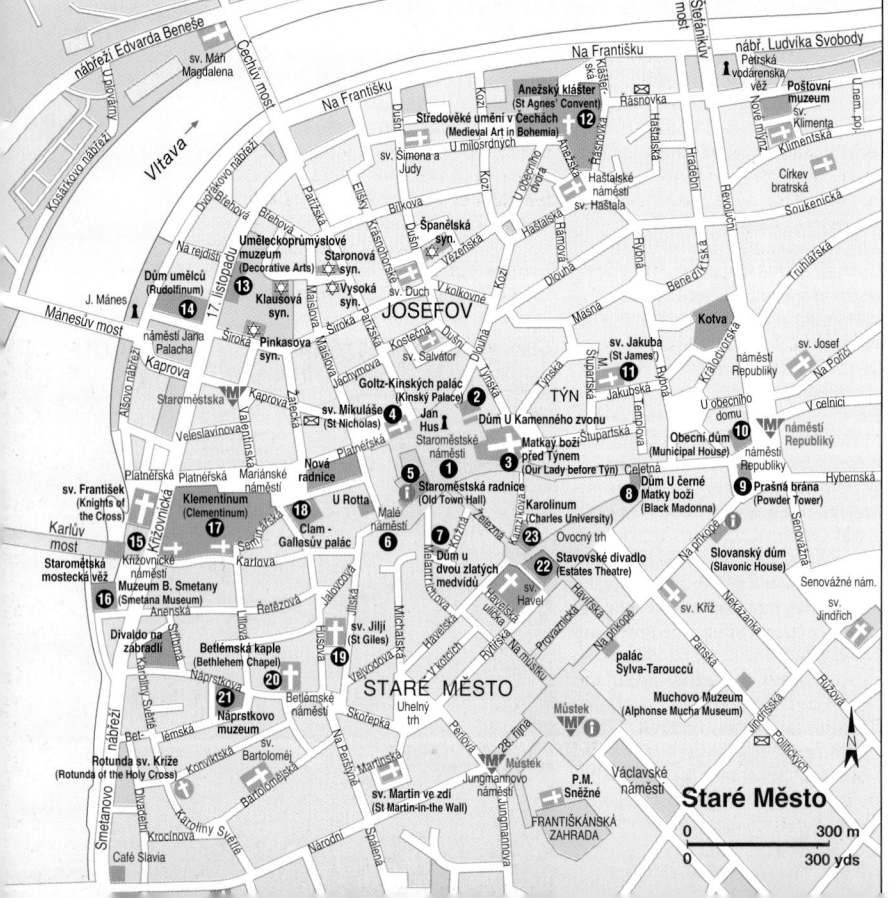

Staré Město

nomic and cultural boom. The Karolinum (Charles University), the oldest university in Central Europe, was founded in 1348 *(see page 132)*. Even if the importance of the imperial residence diminished later on, the Old Town kept its leading position in Prague. When the five independent towns became one unit in 1748, it was the town hall in the Old Town that became the seat of the administration.

Old Town Square

The busy streets near the border of the New Town lead to the **Staroměstské náměstí ❶** (Old Town Square). They approach the square from all sides like the rays of the sun and make it the natural centre of the district. The mix of architectural styles tend to complement, rather than confuse, the overall effect, and even if much of the square is given over to tourist traps it still remains a beautiful and impressive sight.

The imposing memorial in the middle of the square honours the great reformer Jan Hus *(see page 20)* and was erected on the 500th anniversary of his death, 6 July 1915. The work of Czech sculptor Ladislav Šaloun, Hussites and Protestants surround the figure of Hus, while a mother and child symbolise rebirth. Since its unveiling it has formed a symbol of resistance to foreign occupation, from the fall of the Habsburg Empire to the invasion of the Warsaw Pact troops in 1968. In a sign of the changing times, the steps at its foot now form a central meeting and resting place for young backpackers.

The houses on the east side of the square form a singular backdrop. This juxtaposition of contrasting building styles is typical of the Old Town and, together with the towers of the Týn Church, give the Old Town Square its special character.

To the left you can see the **palác Goltz-Kinských ❷** (Kinský Palace) with its late-Baroque façade, which incorporates some Rococo elements. It was designed by Kilián Ignaz Dientzenhofer and built by Anselmo Lurago. It was from here that Prime Minister Gottwald made his speech to the nation that brought in the Communist regime. The building was used for the National Gallery's collection of prints and drawings but is closed at present (for up-to-date information see www. ngprague.cz). On the ground floor of the palace is a bookshop, once the premises of Franz Kafka's father.

To the right of the palace, at No. 13, is the Gothic house **Dům u kamenného zvonu** (House at the Stone Bell), which has been restored and has had its original facade replaced. It is used to hold temporary exhibitions put on by the Prague City Gallery (open Tues–Sun 10am–6pm; for details check www.citygallery prague.cz). The two neighbouring houses are connected by an arcaded passage with ribbed vaulting. To the left, the former Týn School, originally

A beautiful example of sgrafitti on Old Town Square.

BELOW:
the façade of the Clam-Gallas Palace.

a Gothic building, was rebuilt in the style of a Venetian Renaissance loggia. On the right is the early Neoclassical house, U bílého jednorožce (The White Unicorn).

Týn and St Nicholas's churches

Taking the Týn School passageway in the line of houses at the eastern side of the square gives you access to the **Chram Matky Boží před Týnem ❸** (Our Lady Before Týn Church; open for mass and Mon–Fri 9am–midday, 1–2pm; if the church is shut, as it often is, you can usually see the interior from the glass partition in the porch). The church is a source of national pride to the Czechs, and the façade, particularly when floodlit at night, is one of the finest sights in the Old Town.

Built in 1365, it was the third church to occupy this site, the successor to Romanesque and early-Gothic buildings. Until 1621 this was the main church of the Hussites. The paintings on the high altar and on the side altars are by Karel Škréta, the founder of Bohemian

The wonderful façade and towers of the Týn Church dominate Old Town Square.

BELOW:
Old Town Square.

Baroque painting; the tall nave was given Baroque vaulting after a fire. Other remarkable works of art are the Gothic Madonna (north aisle), the Gothic pulpit and the oldest remaining font in Prague (1414). To the right of the high altar is the tombstone of the famous Danish astronomer Tycho Brahe (1546–1601), who worked at the court of Rudolf II. The window immediately to the right of the south portal is a curiosity; through it you can see into the church from the neighbouring house. One resident who had this privilege was Franz Kafka.

George of Poděbrady (1458–71) had a gold chalice set into the gable niche between the church's two towers as a symbol of the Hussite faith. When the Catholic Habsburgs took over after 1620 it was replaced by a statue of the Virgin; the chalice was melted down to make her crown, halo and sceptre.

The beautiful, white Baroque façade of **Kostel sv. Mikuláše ❹** (St Nicholas's Church; open Tues, Thur–Fri 10am–midday, Wed 2–4pm), on the other side of the

square, is the work of Kilián Ignaz Dientzenhofer, built between 1732 and 1735 on the site of an earlier 13th- to14th-century building. The dark statues on the outside are by Anton Braun, a nephew of Matthias Bernhard Braun. The unusual proportions of the church have come about because houses originally stood in front of the building, completely separating it from the square. It is interesting to see how the architect has succeeded in creating so perfect a building in such a relatively small space. However, the sparse interior is somewhat disappointing in comparison, having suffered at the hands of Emperor Joseph II, who ordered the site to be used as a storage warehouse.

The house to the left of the church is built on the spot of a childhood home of Franz Kafka (only the portal survives), and is marked by a bronze plaque with a bust of the author. It has been converted into the small but interesting **Kafka Museum** (open Tues–Fri 10am–6pm, Sat 10am–5pm; admission charge).

Old Town Hall

In times gone by, the area of the small park opposite the church was occupied by a Neo-Gothic wing of the **Staroměstská radnice** ❺ (Old Town Hall; open for guided tours Apr–Oct Mon 11am–6pm, Tues–Sun 9am–6pm, Nov–Mar Mon 11am–5pm, Tues–Sun 9am–5pm; admission charge), which was destroyed by the Nazis in the last days of World War II. If you walk around the Town Hall Tower, which protrudes into the square, you have an unobstructed view of the historic part of the hall. Originally the house next to the tower on the left was purchased by citizens of the Old Town and declared a town hall. Later, three further houses were acquired.

The tower was built in 1364 and later had the oriel chapel added. The interior of the building has been carefully restored, and tours take visitors around the 15th-century council chamber and Petr Parléř's Gothic chapel. Also interesting are the dungeons in the basement. These were used by the Czech resistance during World War II.

Map on page 120

A ceiling mosaic from the Old Town Hall.

LEFT:
the two faces of the Astronomical Clock.

A Centre of Prague's History

The Old Town Square has always been a central focus in Prague, and memorial tablets on the Town Hall Tower are reminders of the various important events that have taken place here over the centuries. Following the second defenestration *(see page 25)* in 1618 and the defeat of the Czech Protestants in the Battle of White Mountain, "27 Bohemian gentlemen" were executed in the square on the orders of Emperor Ferdinand. Their heads were displayed on Charles Bridge, their punishment intended to serve as an example to others. The event led to the Counter-Reformation.

On 8 May 1945, the Nazis set fire to the Old Town Hall in a last-ditch attempt to hold the city. The following day, the Russian Red Army liberated Prague from German occupation by marching on the Old Town Square. The fire damage was repaired almost immediately. Three years later, Gottwald's speech from the Kinský Palace ushered in the Communist government. The Jan Hus monument in the centre of the square is in honour of the 15th-century religious reformer who stood up against the corrupt practices of the Catholic Church.

The Renaissance doorway of the House of the Two Golden Bears.

BELOW:
the Cubist House of the Black Madonna.

However, the most popular feature is the **Orloj** (astronomical clock), which dates in its earliest form from 1410. It consists of three parts. In the middle is the actual clock, which also shows the movement of the sun and moon through the zodiac, in accordance with the geocentric view of the universe that underpinned the Czech understanding of life in the 15th century. Underneath is the calendar, with signs of the zodiac and scenes from country life, symbolising the 12 months of the year. The art work on the calendar is by the 19th-century Czech painter Josef Mánes.

The performance of the upper part of the clock is what draws the hordes of tourists. On the hour the figures play the same scene: Death rings the death knell and turns an hour glass upside down. The 12 Apostles proceed along the little windows which open before the chimes, and a cockerel flaps its wings and crows. The hour strikes. To the right of Death, a Turk wags his head. The two figures on the left are allegories of Greed and Vanity.

Malé náměstí (Little Square) just beyond the Old Town Hall is very evocative of medieval Prague. Surrounding the fountain, with its pretty Renaissance grille, are a number of fine houses, each with its own history. In No. 11, Agostino of Florence established the first documented apothecary in the city (1353), and during the reign of Emperor Charles IV it became the home of a herbalist from Florence.

Most spectacular is the multi-coloured **U Rotta** at No. 3, whose cellar was once the lower floor of a Romanesque town house. The first Czech Bible was printed here in 1488; at the turn of the 20th century an ironmonger had the building renovated; the façade with the original sign of three white roses was designed by the artist Mikuláš Aleš.

Alleys and Backstreets

The area to the south of Staroměstské náměstí is riddled with small winding streets. The best way to explore these is just to wander around; however, an interesting circuit can be made by first heading east on Celetná. Take the small passage at No. 10 to Kamzíkova, a narrow lane leading to Železná. Turn right, walk a few metres and turn left into Kožná. Follow this narrow cobblestoned lane to Melantrichova; the last house on the right, **Dům u dvou zlatých medvídů** (The Two Golden Bears), is a beautiful example of Renaissance architecture.

Across the street, a Gothic archway leads into a courtyard. Continue in the same direction and you will exit from the courtyard at the foot of Michalská. To your left is a wooden gate at No 19, which leads to an adjacent courtyard; this alley is the oldest surviving street in the Old Town. Head off through the final wooden gate and take a right turn leading on to Jilská. Just a few steps along, you'll come across a Gothic

stone passageway leading off to your right marked U kučerů, after the former residents of the house above. The curves, bends and steps of this passage will bring you to Hlavsova, and then back once again to Michalská. From there, turn left through the wooden gateway just ahead and pass through the corridor into a Renaissance courtyard. The passageway continues, bringing you back to Staroměstské náměstí.

Celetná

The street Celetná is named after the medieval bakers of small loaves (calty). It is one of the oldest streets in Prague, and its course follows the line of the old trade route to the east where it left the Old Town markets. It is lined with pastel Baroque façades, one of particular interest being the late-Baroque **Hrzán Palace** (No. 12). Near by is **U zlatého jelena** (The Golden Stag), one of the oldest stone houses in the city.

Another architectural gem is the Cubist **Dům u černé Matky Boží** ❽ (The Black Madonna) at No. 34, designed by Joseph Gočár (1911–12), originally as a department store (see page 64). The first to fourth floors contain the National Gallery's **Museum of Czech Cubism** (open Tues–Sun 10am–6pm; admission charge; www.ngprague.cz).

The entrance is via a beautiful spiralling staircase with a Cubist motif on the bannister supports. While the first floor holds temporary exhibitions, the permanent galleries start on the second floor with a series of reliefs by Otto Gutfreund (look for *Při toaletě*, 1911). Also here is a wonderful display of ceramics by Pavel Janák (1882–1956), a number of Braque-like collage paintings by Emil Filla (1882–1953) and some excellent furniture by Gočár. The third floor contains a number of interesting architectural designs by Janák as well as fine examples of his

furniture. Further examples of Cubist design can be seen in the posters of Jaroslav Benda (1882–1970). The fourth floor is home to a striking series of prints by Bohumil Kubišta (1884–1918) and a collection of African statues from which he was said to have drawn his inspiration. However, the star exhibit is probably the building itself, as beautifully designed inside as out.

At the end of Celetná is the late-Gothic **Prašná brána** ❾ (Powder Tower; open daily Apr–Oct 10am–6pm; admission charge). It was built in the second half of the 15th century as an impressive city gate, replacing an older gate which had previously stood on this site. Its special status among the 13 gates of the Old Town fortifications came about because the Royal Court – the royal residence during the 15th century – was next door. It acquired its name when it was used as a gunpowder storehouse, and the Neo-Gothic roof was added during rebuilding in the second half of the 19th century. Inside is a display of photographs of Prague by Ladislav Sitenský.

Map on page 120

The Black Madonna on the outside of the Cubist building.

BELOW:
the Powder Tower.

Although it is hard to see from walking around the outside of building, the layout of the Obecní dům is very clever. Laid out on a triangular site, the almost symmetrical building is in the shape of an arrow head, with the concert hall neatly placed at its centre.

BELOW: the façade of the Art Nouveau Municipal House.

The Municipal House

In the modern **náměstí Republiky** (Republic Square), which leads to the northern New Town, on the site of the old Royal Court, is the **Obecní dům** ⓾ (Municipal House; open daily 10am–6pm; tours are conducted in Czech and English; tel: 222 002 101; www.obecni-dum.cz), built during the years 1906–11.

The splendid Art Nouveau building was created in response to the politically and economically strengthened national consciousness of the Czech bourgeoisie around the turn of the 20th century. A whole generation of artists worked on this building, including Alfons Mucha, who has left here some wonderful examples of his art. Every corner of the building, both inside and out, is elegantly decorated, and has been carefully maintained over the years. It was also here that the independent Czechoslovak republic was declared in October 1918 *(see page 29)*.

Today, the building is home to the Prague Symphony Orchestra (www. fok.cz), which plays in the ornate **Smetanova síň** (Smetana Hall).

Some idea of the splendour of the its can be gained from the café and restuarants *(see pages 134–5)*.

Another example of Prague's late Art Nouveau (similar to the Viennese Secessionist style) can be seen at the **Hotel Paříž**, which is in Obecního domu, behind the Municipal House. Also on náměstí Republiky is the polygonal **Kotva Department Store** (1966–74), by Věra Machoninová and Vladimír Machonin. This is one of the few striking examples of architecture from the Communist era in the city centre.

St James and the Týn

If you enter the little alleys at the back of these buildings, you soon come to the **Kostel sv. Jakuba** ⓫ (St James's Church; open Mon–Sat 9.30am–12.30pm, 2.30–4pm, Sun 2–3.45pm) in Malá štupartská. You can also get to it from Celetná, through one of two passages in houses No. 17 and No. 25. Like so many churches in Prague, this was originally founded by the Minorites during the reign of Charles IV, and was rebuilt several times until it

attained its present Baroque form. Notable works of art are the reliefs on the main portal, the ceiling frescos and the painting by Václav Vavřinec Reiner on the high altar. Particularly valuable from an artistic point of view is the tomb of Count Vratislav Mitrovic, the work of Johann Bernhard Fischer von Erlach and Ferdinand Brokoff.

A more gruesome feature is the 400-year-old decomposed arm hanging on the west wall, supposedly amputated from a thief who tried to steal the jewels from the altar, but who was stopped, legend has it, by the Madonna grabbing his offending arm. The almost theatrical quality of the interior provides a fine stage for the frequent organ concerts given on the ornamental and powerful instrument dating from 1705.

The cloisters of the former Minorite monastery adjoin the north side of the church. Between St James and the Týn Church lies the pleasant Týn Court, also known simply as the **Týn**. The origins of the whole complex go back to the 11th century, when it offered protection to foreign merchants. To get to Staroměstské náměstí take the street named Týnská, which leads around the Týn Court to the north portal of the church. The covered end of this street, with the Týn Court gateway and the church portal with its tympanum from Petr Parléř's workshop (now a copy), is very attractive.

St Agnes's Convent

To the north of the Týn, just off Haštalské náměstí at the bottom of Rybná, is the **Anežský klášter** ⑫ (St Agnes's Convent). The convent is the first early-Gothic building in Prague (founded 1234). However, the whole complex, which included two convents and several churches, fell into decay over the years and parts of it were completely destroyed. After many years, restorers succeeded in bringing some rooms back to their original state. These were linked to form the present-day historic complex by means of carefully reconstructed additions.

The convent buildings now hold the National Gallery's collection of **Medieval Art in Bohemia and Central Europe** (open Tues–Sun 10am–6pm; admission charge; www.ngprague.cz). The superb collection has been sensitively displayed and fits well into the restored space.

The exhibits are shown in broadly chronological order, starting with a very important early wooden statue, the **Madonna of Strakonice** (*c.* 1300–20), and the painting of the Madonna of Zbraslav (1350–60). Among the star exhibits are the museum's two Bohemian altarpieces: the first from **Vyšší Brod** (1350) with a Nativity showing the founder of the monastery, Peter I of Rosenberg, and Christ on the Mount of Olives; and the second from **Třeboň** (1380–5) whose artist was one of the most important figures of the International Style. Also look out for the series

Map on page 120

The resurrected Christ from the Třeboň altarpiece.

BELOW: the Kotva department store.

When the Nazis occupied Prague they wanted to get rid of the statue of the German Jewish composer Mendelssohn from the Rudolfinum. Unfortunately for them; they removed the statue of the revered German composer Richard Wagner by mistake.

BELOW: the splendid Rudolfinum.

from the Chapel of the Holy Cross at Karlštejn (1360–4) by **Master Theodoricus**. There then follows some very fine Bohemian woodcarving, especially that of the Pregnant Virgin Mary (1430–40) and St John the Evangelist (*c.* 1400–50) by the **Master of the Týn Crucifixion**.

Later works are displayed in the long final gallery. Prominent here are some rather gruesome depictions of the Crucifixion; also look for the **St James Cycle** with souls being dragged from people's mouths and some fierce demons. Influence from the Netherlands can be seen in **Hans Pleydenwurff**'s *Beheading of St Barbara* (*c.* 1470), and, at the end of the 15th century, from the Italian Renaissance in the work of the **Master of Grossgmain**. As well as some fabulous Swabian and Bohemian woodcarving, there are two excellent paintings by **Lucas Cranach the elder** (the *Madonna of Poleň*, 1520, and *Young Lady with a Hat*, 1538). The galleries end with a display of woodcuts, notably **Dürer**'s *Apocalypse* (1511) and the series *The Passion Cycle* (1509) by Cranach.

Museum of Decorative Arts

Following the banks of the river will bring you round to the impressive *fin de siècle* street of Pařižská, with its expensive boutiques and designer shops. Running south from Pařižská is 17. listopadu, on which is the **Uměleckoprůmyslové muzeum** ⓭ (Museum of Decorative Arts; open Tues–Sun 10am–6pm; admission charge; www.upm.cz). The building, itself a fine example of the decorative arts, was built 1897–1900.

This is one of the best, and most interesting, museums in Prague. The beautifully arranged exhibits are displayed by process and material: "The Story of Fibre" (textiles and fashion); "Born in Fire" (ceramics and glass); "Treasury" (metals); and "Print & Image" (graphic design and photography). Each section has some wonderful items, but among the best are the collections of late-19th- and 20th-century women's costume. Among many fine pieces are an adventurous day dress in a hand-woven fabric (1926) by Marie Teinitzerová, a 1930s sunbathing outfit of a bodice, shorts and sleeveless jacket, and two

great 1960s op-art-influenced swimsuits. The collections include not only clothing but an excellent selection of shoes and accessories.

The glass and ceramics collection includes some fine examples of 16th- to 17th-century Venetian glass, but, of course, it is the Bohemian work that is best represented. Of particular interest are the four cases that show the development of faience, glass and ceramic from Art Nouveau, via Cubism, Art Deco and the 1950s, to the present day. Of the imaginatively displayed metalwork, it is probably those pieces of 1900–30 that are most interesting; look out for Josef Gočár's Cubist clock (1913). There are also some interesting examples of 20th century jewellery, particularly those pieces from the 1970s and 1980s by Jozef Soukup.

The Czechs have long had a reputation for good graphic design, and this is borne out by the displays of early-20th-century posters; chief among these are those displaying the influence of Cubism. As well as a display of experimental photography from the *fin de siècle* to the 1940s, there is a case of drawers showing the changes in typographical design from the 15th–20th centuries.

The Rudolfinum

Opposite the museum is the **Dům umělců** ⓮ (Rudolfinum; www.rudolfinum.cz), an impressive Neo-Renaissance building, which faces náměstí Jana Palacha (Jan Palach Square). During 1918–38 it was the seat of the Czechoslovak parliament, but after World War II it was returned to its original use, as the home of the Czech Philharmonic Orchestra, who regularly perform in its magnificent Dvořák Hall. The **Galerie Rudolfinum** (www.galerie rudolfinum.cz) is an important venue for the work of well-known, often foreign, artists and has, perhaps more importantly, a lovely café.

Crusader Knights' Square

At the end of Křižovnická, by the Charles Bridge *(see pages 116–17)*, is **Křižovnické náměstí** ⓯ (the Knights of the Cross Square) with its statue of Charles IV. The **Kostel sv. Františka Serafinského** (Church of St Francis) on the northern side of the square is dedicated to St Franciscus Seraphicus. It once belonged to the monastery of the Order of Knights of the Cross, a Bohemian order of the time of the Crusades. The cupola of the church is decorated with a fresco of the Last Judgement by Václav Reiner.

The buildings on the southern waterfront were originally the municipal waterworks. The last one, actually on Novotného Lávka and reached via Smetanovo nábřeží, now contains the **Muzeum Bedřicha Smetany** ⓰ (Smetana Museum; open Wed–Mon 10am–5pm; tel: 222 220 082; admission charge). The building is decorated with sgraffiti and is possibly of more interest than the small museum dedicated to the nationalist composer's life and work *(see page 49)*.

Map on page 120

The Judith Bridge, which predated the Charles Bridge, crossed the river from the Knights of the Cross Square to Malá Strana; it was the order of the Knights of the Cross that guarded the river crossing.

BELOW: the Klementinum seen from the Knights of the Cross Square.

Opposite the bridge you can see the Baroque facade of **Kostel sv. Salvátora** (St Saviour's Church), which is part of the Jesuit college, the **Klementinum**  (Clementinum). This broad complex was founded by the Jesuits, who were called to Prague in 1556 to help coax the country back into the Catholic fold. But not long after the building was completed, the Jesuits were exiled from the country, in 1773. Nowadays four libraries, including the National Library, are based here. The spectacular Zrcadlová kaple (Mirrored Chapel) is usually closed, but it might be worth attending a concert here to get a glimpse of the inside.

The only interior parts of the complex that are open to the public are the spectacular **Barokní sál** (Baroque library hall) and **Astronomical Tower** (by guided tour, only on the hour, Mon–Fri 2–8pm, Sat–Sun 10am–8pm; admission charge). Dating from 1722, the Klementinum's Baroque library was commissioned by the Jesuits and handed over to the university in 1773. The impressive space holds a collection of valuable books on philosophy and theology. Above the library is the astronomical tower, also built in the 1720s. Its main attraction is the wonderful view of the city from its balcony.

Halfway up the Klementinum Astronomical Tower is a line marking the Prague meridian; when sunlight crossed the line at noon, a flag was hung from the tower.

BELOW:
the Smetana Museum.

Karlova

The narrow and twisting **Karlova** (Charles Alley) has always been the link between the Charles Bridge and the Old Town Square. The astronomer Johannes Kepler lived at No. 4 for a while. A little further on, in **U zlatého hada** (The Golden Serpent), the Armenian Gorgos Hatalah Damashki opened the first Prague café in 1714. Much of the street is now given over to trashy shops selling tat to hordes of tourists.

Following the outer wall of the Klementinum brings you to the **Clam-Gallasův palác**  (Clam-Gallas Palace), at the corner of Husova. This magnificent Baroque building (1713–30) was constructed by the Viennese court architect Johann Bernhard Fischer von Erlach. The portal ornamentation of statues of Hercules is by Matthias Bernhard Braun. Once containing a theatre, where Beethoven reputedly performed, the building now houses the city archives.

Along Husova look for a façade in a Venetian Renaissance style. The buildings (Nos. 19–21) contain part of the **České muzeum výtarných umění v Praze** (Czech Museum of Fine Arts), which holds exhibitions of contemporary Bohemian art (open Tues–Sun 10am–6pm; admission charge; WWW.CMVU.CZ). A little further to the left is the **Kostel sv. Jiljí**  (St Giles's Church). Walking around it gives you the best impression of the clear, Gothic lines of the church exterior (built in the mid-14th century), which contrasts with the ornate Baroque interior, decorated with paintings by Václav Vavřinec Reiner.

A turn to the right down Řetězová brings you to the **Dům panů z Kunštátu a Poděbrad** (House of the Lords of Kunštát and Poděbrady; open daily 9am–10pm; admission charge). Behind the much later façade are a number of well-preserved 12th-century rooms. Those now at ground level, greatly changed, were originally on the first floor, while down below in the cellar the vaulted chambers have been left in their original state. This was the 15th-century residence of George of Poděbrady, and there is a small exhibition relating to his life.

Bethlehem Square

The **Betlémská kaple** ⑳ (Bethlehem Chapel; open daily Apr–Oct 10am–6.30pm, Nov–Mar 10am–4.30pm; admission charge), in the square of the same name (Betlémské náměstí) is an important Hussite memorial. It was here that mass was first said in Czech instead of Latin. The plain interior, which could hold up to 3,000 people, had the pulpit as its focal point and not the altar. The building dates from 1391; it was

Map on page 120

here that Jan Hus *(see page 20)* preached from 1402 until shortly before he moved to Constance (1415). So, too, did Thomas Münzer, the leader of the German peasants' revolt, a century later, in 1521. Taken over by the Jesuits in the 17th century, after Protestantism was banned, the chapel was rebuilt, but then demolished in 1786. It was meticulously reconstructed in its original form in 1950–4, partly making use of original building materials. In the adjoining rooms there is a small display on the life of Jan Hus.

A picturesque courtyard on the western side of the square contains the **Náprstkovo muzeum** ㉑ (Náprstek Museum; open Tues–Sun 9am–5.30pm; admission charge; www.aconet.cz/npm). This ethnographic museum of Asian, African and American cultures is based around the superb collections of Vojta Náprstek (1826–94). In 2002 the museum received two significant donations of African sculpture from Vladimír Piskáček and Roland Hutter, the first with items from Mozambique, Congo and Nigeria, the

The Church of St Martin-in-the-Wall (see overleaf).

BELOW: the dreaming spires of the Klementinum and Old Town.

Map on page 120

The Náprstek Museum's extensive holdings of Asian art are in the chateau of Libĕchov, around 40 km from Prague (closed at present for renovation after the 2002 floods).

BELOW: the Karolinum.

second with some very fine pieces from West Africa.

The ground floor holds temporary exhibitions, while the first floor has the permanent collection of American Indian cultures. A wide range of peoples are represented, from Inuit peoples to the groups of the Plains and the Pueblo peoples of Mexico. Among the many fascinating pieces there are a number of feathered Apache headdresses, some beautiful papooses from California and some wonderful Inuit clothing. The galleries continue with the Central and South American holdings. Notable here are the brightly coloured textiles and the stylised Huaxtec figures.

The collections from Australia, Polynesia and Melanesia on the second floor are beautifully displayed. As well as some wonderful Aboriginal paintings, there are boomerangs and harpoons, and a lovely model of a fish. The Melanesian holdings are particularly rich, with the pieces from Papua New Guinea taking pride of place, particularly the fine body ornaments. Look out also for the decorated skulls from the Solomon Islands

and the intricate pandanus weaving from the Marshall Islands. However, undoubtedly the most striking exhibit is the large totem pole from Papua New Guinea in the final room.

Just a little out of the way, on the corner of Karoliny Světlé and Konviktská, lies the **Rotunda sv. Kříže** (the Rotunda of the Holy Cross), a Romanesque round church dating from the beginning of the 12th century. There is another curious church building in Martinská. Originally Romanesque, later rebuilt in a Gothic style, **Sv. Martin ve zdi** (Church of St Martin-in-the-Wall) was, as the name suggests, incorporated into the city walls. Here, in 1414, Holy Communion was first administered "in both forms" (i.e. both bread and wine given to the laity).

The Estates Theatre

Martinská leads into the **Uhelný trh** (Coal Market) – now home to the city's red-light district – and some narrow old streets, like the attractive V kotcích. Between **Ovocný trh** (Fruit Market) and Železná lies the Neoclassical **Stavovské divadlo** ㉒ (Estates Theatre; www.narodni-divadlo. cz), which was opened in 1783 as the Nostitz Theatre. The oldest theatre building in Prague, it has played a large part in the cultural life of the city; Mozart himself conducted the premiere of *Don Giovanni* here in 1787. It was also the site, in 1834, of the first performance of the Czech national anthem, *Kde domov můj?* (Where is My Home?), as part of a musical, *Fidlovačka*.

To the left of the theatre lies the **Karolinum** ㉓, the central part of the Charles University. The magnificent oriel window is the only true remnant of the original 14th-century Gothic building, although the courtyards were reconstructed in this style after World War II. The building is used for graduation ceremonies and is closed to the public. ❑

RESTAURANTS, CAFÉS AND PUBS

Restaurants

Allegro
Four Seasons Hotel,
Veleslavínova 2
Tel: 221 427 000
Open: daily 6.30–11am,
11.30am–midnight. €€€
Generally considered the
best restaurant in the
city, eating is either in
the refined dining room,
or (during the summer
11.30am–9.30pm) on
the outdoor terrace with
its stunning view across
the river to the castle.
The menu, from break-
fast to dinner, has a delicious array of varied and
well-thought-out dishes,
many given an Italian
twist courtesy of chef
Vito Mollica. Sunday
brunch is served
11.30am–3pm.

Ariana
Rámová 6
Tel: 222 323 438
Open: daily 11am–11pm.
€€
A bit of a rarity, an Afghan
restaurant set in an old
Prague building. However,
this incongruity doesn't
affect the food. The Per-
sian-inspired dishes com-
prise kebabs, curried
vegetables and speciali-
ties such as steamed
bread stuffed with veg-
etables. Big mounds of
rice accompany most
dishes, and you can wash
it down with a yoghurt
drink or sweet chai.

Arzenal Siam-i-Sam
Valentinská 11
Tel: 224 814 099
Open: daily 10am–midnight.
€€
The brainchild of Czech
designer Bořek Šípek,
the front of the shop
sells furniture, glass and
ceramics while the back
is given over to an excellent Thai restaurant with
good service and a lovely
interior. The spicy,
authentic dishes are
beautifully presented –
the idea is that you can
also buy the dishes and
glasses out front – and
the substantial menu
includes a good number
of vegetarian items.

Au Gourmand
Dlouhá 10
Tel: 222 329 060
Open: daily 9am–7pm. €
A beautiful little café and
patisserie with a fully-
tiled interior. Wonderfully
prepared, authentic
French quiches and
cakes (one counter is for
savoury, the other for
sweet items), and
decent coffee, which you
eat in or take away.

Bellevue
Smetanovo nábřeží 18
Tel: 222 221 443
Open: Mon–Sat noon–3pm,
5.30–11pm, Sun
11am–3.30pm, 7–11pm.
€€€
A classic restaurant that
has a balcony terrace with
a splendid view over the
river. Smooth and effi-
cient service brings beautifully presented
international dishes with
a modern touch (for exam-
ple, cod with puréed
sweet potato). The
desserts are excellent,
especially the wild berries
with walnut ice cream.

Byblos
Burzovní palác, Rybná 14
Tel: 221 842 121
Open: Mon–Fri 8am–mid-
night, Sat–Sun 11am–mid-
night. €€–€€€
This Lebanese restau-
rant, beside the Kotva
shopping centre, is cen-
tred on an indoor garden.
The food runs from a
wide selection of meze,
to grilled meat dishes
and some seafood. For
dessert there is sweet
and sticky baklava.

Café Montmartre
Řetězová 7
Tel: 222 221 244
Open: Mon–Fri 9am–11pm,
Sat–Sun midday–11pm. €
A legendary café, once
frequented by the likes
of Jaroslav Hašek and
Egon Erwin Kisch. In the
past the café played an
important part in the
city's cultural life and
although that is long-
over, it remains a pleas-
ant place to sit, read
and drink.

PRICE CATEGORIES

Prices for three-course
dinner per person with a
glass of wine or beer:
€ = under 300 Kč
€€ = 300–600 Kč
€€€ = above 600 Kč

Chez Marcel
Haštalská 12
Tel: 222 315 676
Open: Mon–Fri 8am–1am,
Sat–Sun 9am–1am. €
Very French and good
value (no credit cards),
this bistro just opposite
St Agnes's Convent has
all the expected dishes
(omelettes, steaks with
various sauces, salads
and cheese-and-ham
sandwiches), plus
French wines by the
glass. Tasty, simple food
of the sort it is easy to
find in France can be had
from early in the morning
until late at night.

Country Life
Melantrichova 15
Tel: 224 213 366
Open: Mon–Fri
10am–6.30pm. €
A haven for desperate
vegetarians and health
food addicts close to Old
Town Square. Line up and
take what you want from
the large and varied salad
bar and hot dishes. When
you get to the checkout,
your plate is weighed and
the cost is calculated.
Tasty and healthy, there
is also a variety of juices,
a free water filter and
good desserts.

Dahab
Dlouhá 33
Tel: 224 827 375
Open: daily noon–1am. €
An Arab coffee house,
lovingly recreated in central Prague complete
with narghiles, mint tea
and couscous. There is a
large selection of teas,
excellent Turkish coffee
and a wide-ranging and
varied menu of Middle

Eastern food, including
some good vegetarian
dishes.

Don Giovanni
Karolíny světlé 34
Tel: 222 222 060
Open: daily 11am–midnight.
€€€
A long-standing Italian
restaurant with very
tasty and surprisingly
authentic food. The
dishes range from
straightforward pasta to
expensive seafood.
There is also a good
range of Italian wines,
including one from the
owner's vineyard, and
some excellent
grappa. The surroundings
are comfortable and the
service pleasantly
relaxed.

Ebel Coffee House
Týn 2
Tel: 224 895 788
Open: daily 9am–10pm. €
In a courtyard behind the
Týn Church is some of
the best coffee in
Prague, with a huge vari-
ety of roasts. All of these
can be bought, along
with a wide variety of
teas, at their nearby
shop Vzpomínky na
Afriku (on Rybná/
Jakubská). The café also
serves a selection of
tasty light meals.

Flambée
Betlem Palais, Husova 5
Tel: 224 248 513
Open: daily 11.30am–1am.
€€€
An expensive but excel-
lent French restaurant in
the heart of the Old
Town, running Allegro a
close second for the best
place to eat in Prague.

Beautifully cooked, but
rich, food of the foie gras
and truffle and Madeira
sauce variety dished up
in a stylish cellar.

Káva Káva Káva
Národní třída 37
Tel: 224 228 862
Open: Mon–Fri 7am–10pm,
Sat–Sun 9am–10pm. €
A pleasant, quiet café in
a courtyard opposite
Tesco. The friendly staff
will bring you excellent
coffee (some of it in vast
mugs) as well as a selec-
tion of limited, but tasty,
snacks such as quiches
and cheesecake. There
is also internet access
downstairs.

Kavárna Slavia
Národní třída/Smetanovo
nábřeži
Tel: 224 220 957
Open: daily 8am–11pm. €
This famous café, with
its views over the river
and National Theatre,
was previously the haunt
of many famous Czech
artists, including Václav
Havel. The spacious and
elegant Art Deco interior
encourages you to linger
here, and there is a
range of salads, pan-
cakes and Czech dishes
to go with the coffee.

Klub Architektů
Betlémské náměstí 5a
Tel: 224 401 214
Open: daily 11.30am–mid-
night. €–€€
Just opposite the Bethle-
hem Church and under
an architecture book-
shop. As well as a few
meaty things, there are
lots of vegetarian offer-
ings, salads, soups and
more exotic dishes,

served up in a minimal-
ist, bare-walled cellar.
Friendly staff and low
prices add to its attrac-
tions, as does the no-
smoking area.

Le Terroir
Vejvodova 1
Tel: 602 889 118
Open: daily 11am–11pm.
€€€
This beautifully restored
cellar is now home to a
superb modern French
restaurant. The classic
dishes are prepared with
a light touch and, aside
from being delicious, are
nicely presented. How-
ever, pride of place must
go to the wine list, which
is both extensive and
lists some impressive
vintages.

Mlýnec
Novotného lávka 9
Tel: 221 082 208
Open: daily noon–3pm,
5.30–11pm. €€€
If you possibly can, dine
outside on the terrace
over the river, giving
unparalleled views of the
Charles Bridge and Old
Town Bridge Tower. The
food is very tasty, mostly
international dishes
given an East Asian
twist, as well as surprisingly good sushi and
some lovely desserts.

Obecní dům
Náměstí republiky 5
Tel: 222 002 770
Open: (**Francouzscá
restaurace**) Mon–Sat
noon–4pm, 6–11pm, Sun
11.30am–3pm, 6–11pm;
(**Plzeňská restaurace**) daily
11.30am–11pm; (**Kavárna
Obecní dům**) daily
7.30am–11pm. €–€€€

Prague's most opulent Art Nouveau building is home to three eateries. The finest – Francouzscá restaurace – is an expensive French restaurant that serves excellent food amidst a stunning gilded and chandeliered interior. In the basement is the cheaper, and charmingly decorated, Plzeňská restaurace serving tasty Czech dishes, while opposite the French restaurant is the café Kavárna Obecní dům with basic meals and cakes and equally impressive surroundings.

Orange Moon
Rámová 5
Tel: 222 325 119
Open: daily 11.30am–11.30pm. €€
One of a cluster of decent restaurants in this part of town, Orange Moon concentrates on South-East and South Asian food. The dishes range from chicken satay and spring rolls to phad thai and fish masala; all of them hot, spicy and tasty.

Pizzeria Rugantino
Dušní 4
Tel: 222 318 172
Open: Mon–Sat 11am–11pm, Sun noon–11pm. €
Conveniently close to Old Town Square, this decent restaurant serves large, tasty pizzas at very reasonable prices. There is a no-smoking section at the front, overlooking the

RIGHT: French dining at the Obecní dům.

street, and the staff are friendly and efficient.

V zátiší
Betlémské náměstí/Liliová 1
Tel: 222 220 155
Open: daily noon–3pm, 5.30–11pm. €€€
This lovely restaurant has a pleasant, warm atmosphere. The food consists of Czech and modern European dishes, beautifully cooked meat and fish, although you can ask for the daily vegetarian specials. The desserts are particularly good and range from rhubarb and apple pie to hot chocolate fondant.

Pubs

Radegast
Templová 2
Tel: 222 238 069
Open: daily 11am–12.30am. €
This smoky, ursatz beer hall is still holding its

own. Full of locals, who appreciate the well-kept beer and the cheap-but-tasty Bohemian food, it is one of the best places in Staré Město for a traditional night out.

U medvídků
Na perštýně 7
Tel: 224 211 916
Open: Mon–Sat 11.30am–11pm, Sun 11.30am–10pm. €
Founded in 1466, this traditional beer hall is friendly, bustling and noisy. Excellent Budvar beer washes down the menu of traditional Czech dishes, including garlic soup, pork with cabbage and dumplings and the ubiquitous fried cheese.

U vejvodů
Jilská 4
Tel: 224 219 999
Open: daily 10am–2am. €–€€
Like the Olympia in Smíchov and Kolkovna in

Josefov, this restaurant and beer hall is run by Pilsner Urquell. You get the same great beer and tasty, heavy Czech dishes as in the other two.

U zlatého tygra
Husova 17
Tel: 222 221 111
Open: daily 3–11pm. €
Well-known for the excellent quality of its beer (Pilsner Urquell), and as the hang-out of the late Bohumil Hrabal, a writer and observer of Prague's pub life. It now attracts many tourists but is still worth a quick visit for the superb beer.

PRICE CATEGORIES
Prices for three-course dinner per person with a glass of wine or beer:
€ = under 300 Kč
€€ = 300–600 Kč
€€€ = above 600 Kč

JOSEFOV

The Jews of Prague suffered persecution by the Christians from the Middle Ages, but found some freedom in their own ghetto, now preserved as the Jewish Quarter and a memorial to their tenacity

Map on page 138

The first Jewish community was founded in Prague in 1091. Throughout the centuries the Jews were alternately ostracised and accepted by the authorities and the Christian citizens. During the Age of Enlightenment in the late 18th century, the ghetto was renamed Josephstown (Josefov), in honour of the reforming Habsburg Emperor, Josef II. In the 1890s almost the entire area was demolished as the authorities deemed that its lack of sanitation made it a health hazard. Fortunately, the Jewish Town Hall, six synagogues and the old cemetery were spared, and are now administered by the Jewish Museum in Prague. The Nazis intended to create a "museum of the extinct Jewish race" here, but after the liberation it became the home of the largest collection of sacred Jewish artefacts in Europe.

The Prague ghetto is one of the oldest in Europe, dating back to at least the 11th century. It was established over several centuries, when laws segregating Jews kept the community within a designated part of the city. By the 17th century, despite periods of oppression, it was a flourishing community and a focal point for Jewish culture in Central Europe.

The Jewish community in the city was allowed to develop freely after 1848, when the laws segregating the Jews were finally repealed. Although the ghetto was largely demolished for health reasons in the 1890s (one consequence of the prejudice against the Jews was that the area had never been provided with adequate sanitation), the community remained active until the Nazi occupation of the country in 1939.

In the so-called Protectorate of Bohemia and Moravia the Jews suffered the same fate as those in Germany and elsewhere in occupied Europe. Immediately after the occu-

LEFT: the Torah shrine in the Old-New synagogue.
BELOW: the *fin de siècle* apartments of Pařížská.

The Jewish Museum comprises the Maisel, Spanish, Pinkas and Klausen synagogues, as well as the Old Jewish Cemetery and Ceremonial Hall. It is open Sun–Fri Nov–Mar 9am–4.30pm, Apr–Oct 9am–6pm; admission charge. The Ticket Reservation Centre is at U starého hřbitova 3a (tel: 222 317 191; www.jewishmusem.cz).

BELOW: the Old-New synagogue.

pation of Bohemia and Moravia by Hitler's army, the Nuremberg Laws, passed in 1935 "to protect the German race", were enforced retrospectively. These laws had deprived German Jews of their citizenship and turned them into "subjects of the state". The same now happened to Czechoslovak Jews. One persecution rapidly followed another – culminating in the mass deportations of 1941.

The first five transports, each with 1,000 people mainly from the Jewish intelligentsia – doctors, artists, lawyers – were deported to the so-called Litzmannstadt Ghetto in Lódê, which the Nazis themselves designated a starvation camp. A month later the old fortress of Terezín (Theresienstadt) in Bohemia was declared a Jewish ghetto, and received deportees from all over occupied Europe. Terezín was not itself an extermination camp, but from here the Jews were sent on for

so-called selection and thence to the gas chambers of Auschwitz.

Today Prague's Jewish community numbers around 3,000 (this figure includes foreigners who practise their faith here), in addition to about 1,500 people of Jewish descent. The quarter is a short walk from Staroměstská Metro along Valentinská Street, or down elegant and expensive **Pařížská ❶** which cuts through the old ghetto area. The sites in the quarter are very close together and can be seen in any order.

The Old-New Synagogue

The **Staronová synagóga ❷** (Old-New Synagogue; not part of the Jewish Museum but run by the Jewish Community of Prague; open Sun–Thur 9.30am–6pm, Fri 9.30am–5pm; admission charge, tickets available from High Synagogue; www.kehila prag.cz) is the oldest surviving synagogue in Europe, built in the late 13th century. First called the New

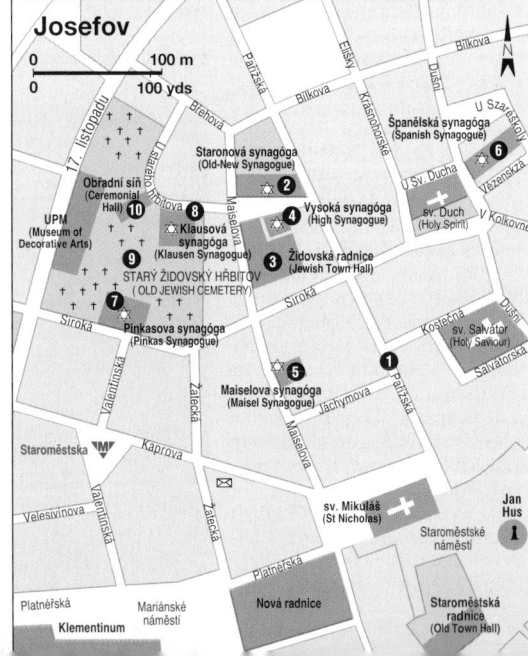

Josefov

0 — 100 m
0 — 100 yds

17. listopadu · Břehová · Pařížská · Bílkova · Bílkova · Elišky · Krásnohorské · Dušní · U Starého · hřbitova · Maislová · Široká · Valentinská · Kaprová · Žatecká · Vězeňská · U Sv. Ducha · V Kolkovně · Kostečná · Pařížská · Salvátorská · Maislová · Vachtnová · Platnéřská · Platňská

Staronová synagóga (Old-New Synagogue) ❷
Španělská synagóga (Spanish Synagogue) ❻
Vysoká synagóga (High Synagogue) ❹
Obřadní síň (Ceremonial Hall) ❿
Klausová synagóga (Klausen Synagogue) ❽
sv. Duch (Holy Spirit)
Židovská radnice (Jewish Town Hall) ❸
UPM (Museum of Decorative Arts)
STARÝ ŽIDOVSKÝ HŘBITOV (OLD JEWISH CEMETERY) ❾
Pinkasova synagóga (Pinkas Synagogue) ❼
Maiselova synagóga (Maisel Synagogue) ❺
sv. Salvátor (Holy Saviour)
❶
sv. Mikuláš (St Nicholas)
Jan Hus ❶
Staroměstská
Velesivinova
Nová radnice
Mariánské náměstí
Staroměstské náměstí
Staroměstská radnice (Old Town Hall)
Klementinum

Synagogue, it gained its present name when another synagogue – now destroyed – was built close by.

The building is an unparalleled example of a medieval two-aisled synagogue. The building has a plain, rectangular shape, a high saddle roof and a late-Gothic brick gable. The consoles, the capitals of the pillars and the vaulting are all richly decorated with relief ornamentation and plant motifs.

In the main aisle, between the two pillars, is the **Almemor** with its lectern for reading the Torah, separated from the rest of the interior by a decorated Gothic screen. In the middle of the east wall is the Torah shrine, called the Ark, formed of two Renaissance pillars on consoles, with a triangular tympanum. Next to the Ark is the **Chief Rabbi's Chair**, decorated with a Star of David. Men must cover their head when entering the synagogue (traditional Jewish skullcaps, *kippahs*, are handed out when buying an entrance ticket). Services in Hebrew are held weekdays at 8am, Fridays at sundown and Saturdays at 9am. (Casual visits may not take place during the services.)

The Jewish Town Hall

The **Židovská radnice** ❸ (Jewish Town Hall) on Maiselova was designed in 1586 in Renaissance style by Pankratius Roder for the mayor Mordecai Maisel, although the newest, southern part dates only from the beginning of the 20th century. It is an attractive pink-and-white building with an unusual wooden clock tower and green steeple. In keeping with the Hebrew practice of reading from right to left, the clock hands move in an anti-clockwise direction.

The **Vysoká synagóga** ❹ (High Synagogue) on Červená was originally part of the Jewish Town Hall, but in 1883 was given a separate

entrance. The central vaulting in the lower room with its rich stucco decoration, mirroring the profile effect of Gothic rib vaulting, shows how Renaissance forms adapted late-Gothic taste. Now, unfortunately, the synagogue is closed for viewing, but the ground floor contains a small, interesting gift shop of Judaica.

The synagogues of the Jewish Museum

The **Maiselova synagóga** ❺ (Maisel Synagogue) was founded in the 1590s, again by Mordecai Maisel, the wealthy leader of the community, as a place of worship for him and his family, and was the most richly decorated synagogue in the district. It was destroyed by a great fire a century later and replaced by the present building, which was given a Neo-Gothic appearance, at the end of the 19th century. A permanent exhibition tracing the history of Jews in Bohemia and Moravia from the first settlement to the emancipation is on view here, together with silver religious articles, textiles, manuscripts and prints.

Map on page 138

The holocaust memorial in the Pinkas Synagogue.

BELOW: the ornate Moorish interior of the Spanish Synagogue.

The Golem

Every city with a long history has its stories, in which real events are either embellished or shrouded in shadow. Prague, too, has many such legends.

The legend of the Golem, one of the strangest tales of them all, was engendered in the mysterious epoch of Rudolf II (1576–1611). It was this eccentric Roman Catholic emperor, living in the midst of a country of Protestants, who created a fantasy image of Prague as a city of alchemists and artists, astrologers and scholars, who were trying to lift the veil of divine secrets. It was a fitting world for the supposedly miracle-working Rabbi Löw and his monster.

They were strange times. The glory of the Renaissance was giving way to the power of the Baroque and curiosity of the Enlightenment. The Renaissance had freed humanity from the superstition of medieval times, but the world was not yet convinced of the power of reason.

Here, then, is the legend of the Golem, the creature of mud and clay created by the cabbalist, astronomer and magician Rabbi Löw. The *Sippurim,* a 19th-century collection of Jewish legends, relates that he breathed life into the Golem with a magic word, the *Shem*, in order to "send it out to protect his community, to discover crimes and to prevent them". One evening, Rabbi Löw forgot to remove the sign of life from the mouth of the Golem, which began a rampage of destruction in Löw's house. The spark of life was removed and the creature turned back into mud and clay, to lie forever under the roof of the Old-New Synagogue.

The origins of the legend itself are based on the cabbala, the mystical teachings and writings which are mentioned in the Talmud, but which say nothing about an artificially created human being. Not until the commentary of Eliezer of Worms in the 13th century does the word "Golem" in the sense of an artificial creation appear (along with exact instructions for making such a creature). In the medieval stories, the Golem is portrayed as a perfect servant, its only fault being that it interprets its master's instructions too literally. By the 16th century, it was seen as a figure that protected the Jews from persecution, but it had also acquired a sinister aspect.

Not until the middle of the 19th century do we find any connection in writing between these tales of the "creative" rabbi and the real-life figure of Rabbi Löw, alchemist, scholar and director of the Talmudic school. According to this version, Rabbi Löw, clothed in white, went one dark night to the banks of the Vltava and there, with the help of his son-in-law, he created the Golem from the four natural elements, earth, fire, air and water, while continually chanting spells.

This story forms the basis of the German novel *Der Golem* by Gustav Meyrink, from which most people know the story, in which the Golem rampages the streets of Prague once every 33 years. In the 1920s it was made into a film, which became a classic of German silent cinema. The Golem became the model for many other man-made monsters in literature and film, including the most famous one of all, Frankenstein. ❏

LEFT: Rabbi Löw's tomb, covered with messages and pebbles.

The restored **Španělská synagóga** (Spanish Synagogue) was built in the 1860s on the site of an earlier place of worship. It has a square ground plan, and a huge dome covers the central hall. The Moorish-style stucco decoration of the interior, an imitation of the style widely used in parts of Spain, including the Alhambra, earned the synagogue its name. It holds a continuation of the exhibition in the Maisel Synagogue, looking at Jewish life in this region from the 19th century through to the present day. On the first floor is a collection of synagogue silver from Bohemia and Moravia.

The **Pinkasova synagóga** ❼ (Pinkas Synagogue) is housed in a beautiful Renaissance building. It came into being in 1535 in a specially adapted private house belonging to the prominent Horowitz family. It was rebuilt in the early 17th century and extended by the addition of a women's gallery, a vestibule and a meeting hall.

Since 1958 the synagogue has become one of the most important sights in the Jewish Quarter, as it serves as a memorial to the 77,297 Czech and Slovak Jewish victims of the Holocaust. The inscriptions around the interior walls list the name, date of birth and date of deportation of each victim in horrifying succession. These names were obscured for some years, first because of damp and later through the reluctance of the Communist government to organise restoration, but between 1992 and 1996 the names were carefully rewritten in their original style. A few remnants of the original wall can be seen.

The synagogue now also serves as a moving memorial to more than 7,500 children who died in Nazi concentration camps, and to the woman who encouraged them to paint while they were awaiting deportation from the holding camp at Terezín (*see page 205*), in the Elbe Valley, about 60 km (38 miles) north of Prague. The children's pictures, with their names and the dates of their death, line the walls of the first-floor gallery.

The **Klausová synagóga** ❽ (Klausen Synagogue) at U starého hřbitova 3a is a Baroque building with a long hall and barrel vaulting. In 1694 it was built to replace the little "cells", three buildings which served as houses of prayer, classrooms and a ritual bath. The building has two rows of round arched windows in the south wall, facing the cemetery. The synagogue is now used to exhibit old Hebrew manuscripts, textiles, silver religious articles and a permanent exhibition entitled "Jewish Customs and Traditions", but religious services were held here until 1939.

The Old Jewish Cemetery

The **Starý židovský hřbitov** ❾ (Old Jewish Cemetery), with its entrance on U starého hřbitova, is both a moving and fascinating place. It came into being in the 15th century, when pieces of land on the

(*see page 205*)

The Hebrew name for the Old Jewish Cemetery – Bet Hayyim ("House of Life") – defies its purpose and its pitiable circumstances.

Map on page 138

BELOW: gravestones in the Old Jewish Cemetery.

Map on page 138

The star of David and Hebrew inscription above the door of the Ceremonial Hall.

BELOW: *Starting Work* by Fritz Taussig, in the Ceremonial Hall.

north-western edge of the Jewish ghetto were bought up. Burials continued to take place here until 1787. The number of graves is much greater than the 12,000 gravestones would suggest – the true figure is probably closer to 100,000. Because this was the only place where Jews could be buried, graves are layered one above the other, giving the ground its uneven appearance. It is a tragic testimony to the prejudice and restrictions that beset the Jews of Prague, even in death.

The majority of the inscriptions on the stones consist of poetic texts expressing grief and mourning. The reliefs portray the family name or the profession of the deceased. Some families had their own symbol, which can be seen on a number of tombs, while tradesmen's memorial stones depict the tools of the trade they followed, such as scissors for a tailor. The oldest monument in the cemetery is the tombstone of the poet Avigdor Kara, dating from 1439. Also buried here, in 1601, was the leader of the Jewish community, Mordecai Maisel, and Rabbi David

Oppenheim, Chief Rabbi of the city in the early 18th century. But the most famous tomb is that of Rabbi Löw (1520–1609), the scholar and supposed creator of the Golem. It is a Jewish custom to place small stones and written messages on the tombs of those they love or respect, and the graves of these eminent men are continually marked in this way.

The age and importance of the gravestones has meant that the cemetery is roped off to the public, but an organised path leads visitors past the most notable burial sites. The squawking crows overhead only add to the atmosphere.

The Neo-Romanesque **Obřadní šín ⑩** (Ceremonial Hall), built in 1911, stands at the entrance to the cemetery on U starého hřbitova 3a. It was built for the Prague Burial Society, which performed charitable duties as well as burials. It continues the permanent exhibition relating to Jewish customs and traditions in the Klausen Synagogue, detailing medicine, illness and death within the Jewish ghetto in Prague and other areas of Bohemia and Moravia.   ❏

RESTAURANTS & BARS

Restaurants

Barock
Pařížská 24
Tel: 222 329 221
Open: Mon–Fri
8.30am–1am, Sat
10am–2am, Sun
10am–1am. €€€
Like its partner Pravda,
this is a place for posing.
Well-made espressos
and calorie-laden break-
fasts are replaced by
international dishes at
lunch, before the space
turns into more of a bar
later in the evening.
Large pictures of mini-
mally dressed models
provide the decor.

King Solomon
Široká 8. Tel: 224 818 752.
Open: Sun–Thur
noon–11pm. €€€
This is the only strictly
kosher, if pricey, restaurant in Prague. The sur-
roundings are pleasant
but the food is really for
dedicated fans of Central
European Jewish cook-
ing. There is gefilte fish,
borscht, and a range of
(expensive) kosher
wines. If want to eat an
orthodox diet it is possible to arrange Shabat
meals beforehand and
have them delivered to
your hotel.

La Veranda
Elišky krásnohorské 2
Tel: 224 814 733
Open: Mon–Sat 11am–mid-
night, Sun noon–midnight.
€€€
Chic and expensive, La
Veranda has some of the
best fusion food in the
city. A bias towards East
Asian food – with noo-
dles, shitaké and oyster
mushrooms taking a
major place – is bal-
anced by some Mediter-
ranean dishes, all
beautifully cooked and
well-presented.

Les Moules
Pařížská 19
Tel: 222 315 022
Open: daily 9am–midnight.
€€–€€€
Tucked off to the side of
Pařížská, in sight of the
Old-New Synagogue, is
this Belgian bar and
restaurant. As well as a
wide variety of excellent
Belgian beer, bottled and
on tap, the food is both
delicious and filling, with
pride of place going to
the fresh mussels.

Pravda
Pařížská 17
Tel: 222 326 203
Open: daily noon–1am. €€€
A self-conciously cool
restaurant that isn't shy
of telling you which
famous faces have been
seen here. The "global"
cuisine is presented in
large portions with a
sometimes slightly fanci-

PRICE CATEGORIES

Prices for three-course
dinner per person with a
glass of wine or beer:
€ = under 300 Kč
€€ = 300–600 Kč
€€€ = above 600 Kč

ful nationality attached
to it on the menu. The
staff are friendly and
attentive and there are
good fish dishes and
tasty vegetarian options.

Bars

Alcohol Bar
Dušní 6
Tel: 241 430 762
Open: daily 7pm–3am.
One of a rash of swish
cocktail bars in this part
of town. Its name pretty
much gives the game
away; there is a stagger-
ing range of booze, all
beautifully mixed, and
the lovely at-table ser-
vice is useful as you
start to go cross-eyed.

Bugsy's
Pařížská 10
Tel: 224 810 287
Open: daily 7pm–2am.
The original Prague cock-
tail bar, and still up there
with the best. The drinks
are expensive but
extremely well-prepared
(taken from their exten-
sive "Blue Bible" drinks
list), and it continues to
pull in local celebrities.

Kolkovna
V Kolkovně 8
Tel: 224 819 701
Open: daily 11am–midnight.
€€
Like the Olympia in Malá
Strana, this pub-cum-
restaurant is run by Pil-
sner Urquell. As well as
the excellent beer, there
is a good menu of Czech
dishes, from fried

cheese and potato soup
to goulash and beef in
cream sauce. A friendly,
lively atmosphere adds
to its informal charm.

Ocean Drive
V Kolkovně 7
Tel: 224 819 089
Open: daily 4pm–2am.
This, and its partner Tretter's (below), both evoke
1930s America; in this
case South Beach,
Miami. Superb cocktails
– with a big emphasis on
coladas and daiquiris –
and a well-heeled, fash-
ionable crowd.

Tretter's
V Kolkovně 3
Tel: 224 811 165
Open: daily 7pm–3am.
A New York-style bar with
the best drinks in town.
Michael Tretter, the
owner, has won awards
for his mixing, and even
runs a Barmanská
akademie. The staff are
superb and the drinks
beautifully presented.

BELOW: the flags of
the King Solomon.

KAFKA'S PRAGUE

The identity of Prague's most famous literary son, Franz Kafka (1883–1924), is intimately tied up with that of the city

The author of some of the greatest works of 20th-century literature lived all but a few months of his life in Prague, yet his relationship with the city was ambivalent at best; he often expressed his wish to leave the town that he referred to as "the worst misfortune that had befallen" him and "a little mother with claws." However, apart from one early short work, *Description of a Struggle*, Kafka's stories were not set in Prague – or in any specific city. And yet, it's impossible not to see its influence in Kafka's fiction. "Kafka was Prague and Prague was Kafka," wrote one of his contemporaries, Johannes Urzidil. "Prague is contained … everywhere in his works." Perhaps it would be more correct to say that it was Kafka's unique

vision of Prague that was his real inspiration. Part of his perspective came from the fact that he lived almost his whole life with his parents and sisters (particularly Ottla, *pictured left*), until the sisters married, in relatively small apartments, forcing him into an intimacy with his family that allowed for little privacy. One of his first published works was a short piece printed in a newspaper complaining about how noisy his family was. His strained relationship with his father, Herman, eventually produced *Letter to His Father*, in which Franz catalogues all his complaints. He handed this to his mother with the request she deliver it to her husband. Wisely, she declined. Kafka's uneasy relationship with his family can also be seen as a major influence in his most famous story, *Metamorphosis*.

ABOVE: Looking out of the window of the Old Town Hall in Staré Město, the area in which Franz Kafka spent almost his entire life. On a walk across Old Town Square, you can see the houses where Kafka was born (U Radnice 5, now containing an exhibit dedicated to the writer); where he lived as a child (U Minuty House, Staroměstské náměstí 2); where he wrote most of *The Castle* (Oppelt House, Staroměstské náměstí 5); where he frequently attended a literary salon (House of the Unicorn, Staroměstské náměstí 18, which now bears a plaque to commemorate the luminaries who met there); and where he went to school (Staroměstské náměstí 12), the same building where his father had his haberdashery shop and which is now occupied by the Franz Kafka Bookstore. Kafka's university and several other family residences are only a stone's throw away from the square. It's no wonder that Kafka, looking out of his window down at the Old Town Square one day, drew several small rings with his finger and remarked to an acquaintance, "This little circle encompassed my entire life."

LIFE ELSEWHERE

Apart from his life around Old Town Square *(see opposite)*, Franz Kafka did manage to make it across the river to live in two other Prague locations. The house on Golden Lane (Zlatá ulička 22) was rented by his sister Ottla as a place to meet her boyfriend. Kafka saw its potential as a quiet place to write, and spent his evenings there penning the stories later collected as *A Country Doctor*. (It is now home to a small exhibition on the author, and a bookshop.) One of the few apartments that he rented for himself was in the Schönborn Palace in Malá Strana. The author of *Amerika* could not know that the building at Tržiště 15 would one day house the American Embassy.

LEFT: an illustration by Kafka, perhaps for *The Trial*. **RIGHT:** a sample of handwriting from Kafka's diary. Prague isn't mentioned in *The Trial* or *The Castle*, tortured tales of hapless people who struggle against a faceless, incomprehensible and malevolent bureaucracy. But no doubt Kafka's job at the Worker's Accident Insurance Company for the Kingdom of Bohemia in Prague, where attempting to negotiate the maze of Austro-Hungarian red tape was his daily routine, gave him food for thought.

NOVÉ MĚSTO

The name "New Town" is misleading – much of the area was built up in the 14th century. However, it is largely the New Town that witnessed the political upheavals of the 20th century

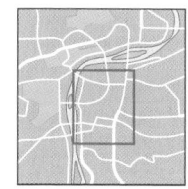

Nové Město is the New Town district of Prague. Despite its name, much of it dates from the early 14th century, commissioned by Charles IV, with a lot of 19th-century redevelopment. It does not have quite as many sights as the other central districts, but you should not miss taking a stroll through the area – even if you do have to cover considerable distances on foot – if only because it is this area that will give you a good impression of everyday life in Prague.

Wenceslas Square

Nearly a kilometre (two-thirds of a mile) long, **Václavské náměstí ❶** (Wenceslas Square) is not really a square at all, but a wide boulevard, reminiscent of Paris's Champs-Elysées. Nowadays, it is dominated by hotels, bars, restaurants, cafés, banks and department stores. It is a busy area, along which half the inhabitants of Prague seem to stroll in their leisure time, joined by masses of tourists. The square also has its sleazy side – most evident at night – with prostitutes soliciting for custom and men trying to lure visitors into suspect lap-dancing clubs. What you can't find here, it is said, won't be found anywhere in the Czech Republic.

The gently rising, gigantic former Horse Market is crowned by the martial-looking equestrian **Socha sv. Václava** (Statue of St Wenceslas), erected by Josef Myslbek in 1912 after taking 30 years to plan and design. The people of Prague always choose to congregate in the shadow of their patron saint in times of crisis. This is where proclamations have almost always been made and demonstrations have been started. Huge crowds assembled here in 1918 and again in 1939. In

Map on page 148

LEFT: the Wenceslas Statue and the National Museum.
BELOW: enjoying the fruits of a Wenceslas Square stall.

the television age, during the Prague Spring of 1968, and during the Velvet Revolution of 1989, pictures of Wenceslas Square were transmitted on news reports around the world.

On 16 January 1969, a philosophy student named Jan Palach hit headlines across the world when he protested against the crushing of the Prague Spring and the Soviet occupation by setting himself on fire in the square. Three days later he died. Palach was soon hailed as a national hero who had sacrificed himself for his people. His act inspired others, and about a month later, on 25 February, another student, Jan Zajíc, set himself alight. Twenty years later, Václav Havel was imprisoned yet again for attempting to lay flowers on the spot where the two young men had set themselves on fire. Today they are commemorated by a small stone memorial.

The two-storey Baroque houses that once lined the square have been replaced by six- and seven-storey buildings, of which only a few, such as the **Hotel Evropa** ❷ (Europa), still retain their Art Nouveau façades *(see page 62)*. The ground-floor interior of the hotel has also

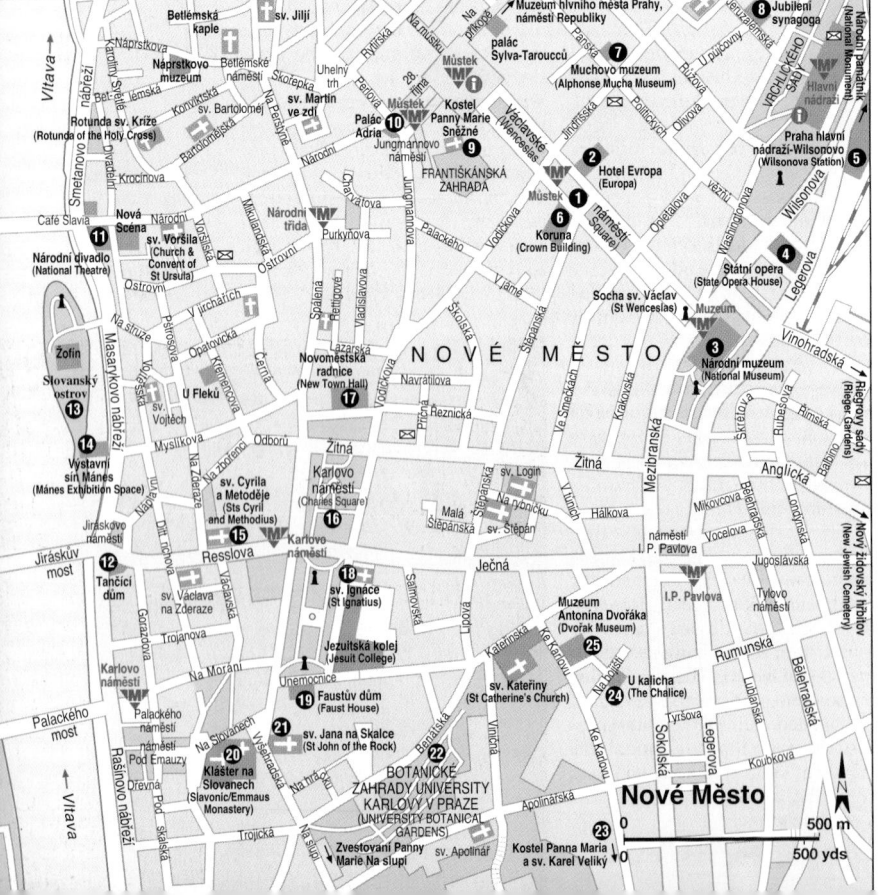

Nové Město

been preserved, albeit now a bit faded (which only adds to its rather decadent charm), adorned with flamboyant mirrors and chandeliers.

The National Museum

Behind the statue of St Wenceslas, so redolent of history, the square is enclosed by the **Národní muzeum** ❸ (National Museum; open daily, May–Sept 10am–6pm, Oct–Apr 9am–5pm; closed first Tues of the month; admission charge; www.nm. cz). A close contemporary of the National Theatre in Národní třída, it was built in 1885–90 by the Prague architect Josef Schulz. Although he was assistant to Josef Zítek, the architect who designed the National Theatre, Schulz did not display the same flair. The building that was intended to become the spiritual and intellectual centre of the Czech nation now seems rather unfortunate and clumsy. Inside, the effect is more impressive, the huge central stairwell is surrounded by busts of the rulers of Bohemia, from Vratislav II to Ferdinand V.

The broad stairways lead up to the "Pantheon" on the first floor. This is the "ideological centre of the entire building", used to host important state gatherings. Surrounded by busts of Czech worthies, and with nationalist paintings by Václav Brožník, František Ženíšek and Vojtěch Hynais, it makes for an arresting spectacle.

The galleries themselves are showing their age and the displays are, for the most part, a long series of lacklustre dark cabinets. However, the mineral galleries are impressive – case after case of ordered specimens – and include a large collection of meteorites. Of the other displays, the archaeological section has some fascinating exhibits (although the labelling is only in Czech), and there is the usual depressing array of stuffed animals.

Next door is the old **Stock Exchange Building**, transformed by Karel Prager, Jiří Kadeřábek and Jiří Albrecht in 1966–72 into a conspicuous glass structure to house the Federal Assembly. At present it is home to Radio Free Europe – beaming US propaganda to the citizens of countries further east – and surrounded by armed guards. Their lease on the building has been given a two-year extension while they search for "safer" premises outside the city centre.

Almost in its shadow, at Wilsonova 4, lies the **Státní opera** ❹ (State Opera House; www.opera. cz). It was built in 1888 as a successor to the wooden New Town Theatre which had stood on the same site, and was renovated in the 1980s. With one of the most beautiful auditoriums in Central Europe, it is well worth trying to catch a performance here. It used to be the New German Theatre, the second-largest German-language stage in Prague, and among the famous conductors and performers to have worked here are Gustav Mahler, Richard Strauss,

Map on page 148

The Art Nouveau Hotel Evropa on Wenceslas Square.

BELOW: the dome of the Wilsonova station.

Bohemia's most famous Art Nouveau artist was Alfons Mucha (1860–1939). He is chiefly known for his work in Paris, where he lived from 1887 to 1904. On his return to Bohemia in 1910 his work took on a more nationalist flavour, particularly in his later oil paintings.

RIGHT:
the Art Nouveau railway station has an atmospheric café.

Nellie Melba and Benjamino Gigli. The theatre's reputation was greatly enhanced under the stewardships of Alexander Zemlinsky (1911–27) and Georg Szell (1927–38), who staged contemporary works by composers such as Krenek, Hindemith and Schreker. After the war it passed into the hands of the Czechoslovak state and became part of the National Theatre, before being reconstituted as the Prague State Opera in 1992.

Just beyond the Opera is **Hlavní nádraží** ❺ (Wilsonova Station), Prague's main railway terminus on the eastern edge of the New Town, which has become quite sleazy in atmosphere of late, but its architecture is well worth a look. An Art Nouveau structure, it does have more nondescript additions, but the ornate façade and the domed and decorative entrance hall remain very attractive.

Na příkopě

Walking down Wenceslas Square, the main shopping area of Prague begins around Jindřišská and Vodičkova streets with a series of early-20th-century shopping arcades *(pasáže)*. One of the more interesting – between Štěpánská and Vodičkova – is in the **Lucerna Building**, built in 1907–21 by Václav Havel's grandfather. Inside, along with shops and a cinema, is David Černy's take on the Wenceslas monument, featuring the hapless king on an upside-down horse.

On the corner at the bottom of the square is the **Koruna Building** ❻ (1912–14), designed by Antonín Pfeiffer, with its distinctive tower. Underneath is the entrance to the Metro and the city's largest music shop. The name of the Metro station, Můstek, is a reminder that a little bridge *(most or můstek)* which led to the Old Town once stood on this site. Remains of the bridge can be seen in the station.

The pedestrian precinct of **Na příkopě** ("on the moat") follows the course of the old fortifications towards the Powder Tower *(see page 125)*. Some of the most interesting buildings in this street, now given over almost exclusively to shopping, are No. 12, the **palác**

Coffee Houses

At one time Prague café society was equal to that of Paris and Vienna. Many of the famous inter-war coffee houses *(kavárny)* have now closed; gone, for example, are the National and the Arco, the meeting place of the "Arconauts", who included Franz Kafka, Max Brod and Franz Werfel. But some of Prague's other illustrious cafés are still humming with a vibrant mix that includes students, entrepreneurs with their mobile phones, ladies of a certain age, and the inevitable tourists. Prague's coffee houses are excellent places for people-watching, and an afternoon can be pleasantly spent observing the comings and goings from a windowside table while sipping a cup of espresso or glass of herbaceous Becherovka, the national liqueur. In most places the staff won't mind if you linger writing in your diary or glancing through the newspapers or magazines made available to customers. Coffee is usually drunk black, although a Viennese variation, topped with whipped cream, is also popular, and tourists have brought with them the cappuccino. You can also nibble a pastry as an accompaniment or indulge in a light meal, or occasionally something more substantial.

Sylva-Taroucců (Sylva-Tarouca Palace), built in 1670 and extensively altered in 1748, and No. 22, which dates from the 18th century and is now called the **Slovanský dům** (Slavonic House). A sign of the times, it now serves as an upmarket shopping centre, with cafés, restaurants and a multiplex cinema.

The passage from Na příkopě 11 is an attractive street to wander down, while on Panská, which also leads off Na příkopě, is the small **Muchovo muzeum** ❼ (Alfons Mucha Museum; open daily 10am–6pm; admission charge; www.mucha.cz). Here you can see examples of the artist's posters of the actor Sarah Bernhardt, and a number of his less-well-known oil paintings.

Further east on Jeruzalémská (towards the Hlavní nádraží) is the **Jubilejní synagoga** ❽ (Jubilee Synagogue), a confection built in similar style to the Spanish Synagogue *(see page 140)*

Florenc and the City of Prague Museum

Immediately opposite the Slovanský dům, on náměstí Republiky – where the Old Town meets the New – is the Art Nouveau Obecní dům, or Municipal House *(see page 126)*. Running off náměstí Republiky is V celnici which brings you to Havlíčkova, site of the famous **Café Imperial**. Also here is **Masarykovo nádraží** (Masaryk Station), another rather sleazy railway terminus.

Things get little better further east where, beyond Wilsonova, is Prague's main bus station at **Florenc**. However, just before the bus station, at Na Poříčí 51 is the **Muzeum hlavního města Prahy** (Museum of the City of Prague; open Tues–Sun 9am–6pm; admission charge; www.muzeumprahy.cz). Despite the unpromising location, this is a fascinating musem set in an imposing building. Much of the

labelling is in Czech only, so ask to borrow the English booklet from the front desk.

The galleries take you through the history of the city in great depth, from prehistory and the medieval period on the ground floor, to the Renaissance and Baroque upstairs. The gallery on the Renaissance is particularly interesting, dealing with the reign of Rudolf II and his team of alchemists; it has also been given a very attractive painted and beamed ceiling.

However, the museum's prize exhibit is undoubtably Antonín Langweil's enormous paper model of the city made in 1826–37. This shows the streets and buildings in phenomenal detail, making it possible to trace your present-day wanderings along the early-19th-century street pattern. Also here is Josef Mánes's original design for the astrological face of the Old Town Hall Clock *(see page 124).*

Our Lady of the Snows

Back at Wenceslas Square, on the other side of Na můstku, 28. října leads to the Jungmannovo náměstí,

Map on page 148

Legend has it that in the 4th century the Virgin Mary appeared before the Pope and asked him to build a church on the site on which snow fell in August. The Church of Our Lady of the Snows is named in honour of this tale.

BELOW: mosaic from Our Lady of the Snows.

where there is a memorial to the Czech linguist Josef Jungmann (1773–1847). Here, aside from Emil Králíček's **Cubist Lamppost** (1913, *see page 164*), is the gate of the Franciscan rectory through which is the Gothic **Kostel Panny Marie sněžné**  (Church of Our Lady of the Snows), planned as a huge building in the 14th century.

Today, all that is visible is the choir. Our Lady of the Snows was planned as a coronation church by Charles IV in 1347. The designs envisaged a three-aisled Gothic cathedral church, comparable to St Vitus's Cathedral, which was to be the tallest building in Prague. However, shortage of money and the start of the Hussite Wars saw to it that the plans were never fulfilled. This is why the proportions of the church look rather odd. Inside, the 16th-century altar and the font dating from 1459 are worth special attention. You can get a good view of the church from the peaceful little park **Františkánská zahrada**, which leads to an arcade and on to Wenceslas Square.

The market by Národní třída Metro is a good place to buy fresh fruit and vegetables.

BELOW: the imposing Národní divadlo.

Národní třída

Národní třída (National Avenue) leads off Jungmannovo náměstí and on to the Vltava and the most Legií (Legions' Bridge). En-route are a number of interesting buildings.

On the corner of Jungmannovo náměstí and Národní třída is the striking **palác Adria** ❿. Built in 1922–5 for the Riunione Adriatica Insurance Company by Pavel Janák and Josef Zasche, it is an outstanding example of Rondocubism. The basement theatre was the headquarters of the Civic Forum during the heady days of 1989. About halfway down at No. 26 (by Národní třída Metro) is the Tesco supermarket. This is one of the city's more successful examples of 1970s architecture – it originally contained the Máj department store – and was fittingly, given its present owners, was influenced by trends in contemporary British architecture.

In the square behind the supermarket is a market selling fresh fruit and vegetables. A little further on is the Baroque Ursuline Convent and **Kostel sv. Voršily** (St Ursula's Church), dating from 1672. The church has been restored, and in front of it is a group of statues. Best-known is St John Nepomuk surrounded by cherubs, by Ignaz Platzer, dating from 1746–7.

At the end of the avenue is the **Národní divadlo** (National Theatre; www.narodni-divadlo.cz), a symbol of the Czech nation. In 1845 the Estates, with their German majority, turned down the request for a Czech theatre. In response, money was collected on a voluntary basis, and the building of a Czech theatre declared a national duty. In 1852 the site was bought, and the foundation stone was laid in 1868. The building, designed by Josef Zítek in a style reminiscent of the Italian Renaissance. The theatre was completed by 1881 but then destroyed in a fire just before it was due to open. Under Josef Schulz's direction, using many notable artists including Vojtěch Hynais, and more public subscriptions, it was rebuilt and opened in 1883 with a performance of Smetana's *Libuše*.

Next door to the National Theatre is the controversial modern glass construction of **Nová Scéna** (1983), designed by Karel Prager and now the permanent home of Laterna Magika. Behind this, and also part of the 1980s development, is the box office where you can buy tickets for here and the Estates Theatre.

On the opposite side of Národní třída (on the corner with Smetanovo nábřeží) is the **Café Slavia**, once the haunt of Prague's writers and intellectuals *(see page 134)*.

Masarykovo nábřeží

Running in the opposite direction from the Legions' Bridge (the second-oldest bridge in Prague) is Masarykovo nábřeží, an elegant riverfront avenue overlooked by *fin de siècle* apartment blocks. On the corner of Na struze is the Goethe Institute, easily recognisable by the large eagle on its façade, which was previously the East German embassy (on reunification, the German embassy became that of the old Federal Republic in Malá Strana).

Masarykovo nábřeží runs up to the next bridge, Jiráskův most, opposite which is Frank Gehry and Vlado Milunič's Nationale Nederlanden Administrative Building, aka the **Tančící dům** . Also nicknamed the "Fred and Ginger" building on account of its supposed likeness to a dancing couple, it was built in 1992–6, and, now the novelty has worn off its faults have become apparent; it isn't well finished and the quirky design now seems like Postmodern grandstanding.

Opposite the Goethe Institute is a small bridge leading over to **Slovanský ostrov** (Slavonic Island). Pleasant and wooded and with a small children's playground, it is also home to the **Žofín** (Sophie) cultural centre (www.zofin.cz). This concert hall received its Neo-Renaissance appearance in 1885–7.

At the far end of the island is the **Výstavní síň Mánes** (Mánes

Map on page 148

The Žofín has seen performances by numerous famous musicians, including Berlioz, Liszt and Wagner.

BELOW: the Žofín.

Exhibition Space), an excellent example of Functionalist architecture built for the Mánes Association of Fine Artists in 1927–30 and designed by Otakar Novotný. It is now run by the Foundation Czech Art Fund and is used to hold temporary exhibitions of contemporary art (open Tues–Sun 10am–6pm; admission charge; www.nadace-cfu.cz).

SS Cyril and Methodius

The memorial outside SS Cyril and Methodius.

Resslova, which runs uphill from Jiráskův most, is the location of the Orthodox **Kostel sv. Cyrila a Metoděje** (Church of SS Cyril and Methodius), now best known for its part in the tragic history of World War II resistance. The church itself is usually closed but you can see through the windows in the porch into the ornate Baroque interior. Below, in the crypt is the **National Memorial to the Heroes of the Heydrich Terror** (open Tues–Sun Apr–Oct 10am–5pm, Nov–Mar 10am–4pm; admission charge). A number of photographs, documents and a plaque are on display telling the story of the seven

BELOW: golden light on Masarykovo nábřeží.

men who held out here after the assassination of *Reichsprotektor* Richard Heydrich *(see opposite)*.

Close by on Křemencova, either take Myslikova up from the Mánes building or follow Na zderaze from Resslova, at No. 11 you'll find one of the oldest and most famous of Prague's beer halls, **U fleků**, now overrun by tourists but stilll worth a visit to try its famous dark beer brewed on the premises.

Charles Square

Resslova runs in to **Karlovo náměstí** (Charles Square). This, too, was part of Charles IV's building project for the New Town, and was laid out in 1348. Charles Square was the biggest market in the city and, until 1848, was known as the Cattle Market. Its present appearance as attractive, landscaped parkland is due to 19th-century rebuilding. The monuments in the park portray numerous famous Czech scientists, scholars and literary figures.

More interesting than the square itself is the **Novoměstská radnice** (New Town Hall) situated at the northern end. It was built in several stages between 1348 and 1418, after the founding of the New Town. Alterations to the south wing followed about 100 years later, in 1520, and the tower was rebuilt in 1722. The extensive renovations carried out in 1906 restored the building to its original splendour. This is the site of the first defenestration of Prague, which took place in 1419, initiating the Hussite Wars, which lasted for the next 15 years *(see page 22)*. Today the building is used for social functions and is closed to the public.

In the middle of Charles Square, on the eastern side, is the Baroque **Kostel sv. Ignáce** (Church of St Ignatius). This is where the Jesuits built their second college after the Klementinum in 1659 *(see page 130)*. The college was dissolved in

1770 and since then the large complex has served as a hospital. The church, which was built between 1665 and 1670 by Carlo Lurago, was extended in 1679–99, with a pillared hall and arcade designed by Paul Ignaz Bayer. Inside, among other works of art, is a beautiful altarpiece depicting Christ in prison by Karel Škréta (1610–74).

The present-day pharmacy, which achieved fame as the **Faustův dům** ❶⓽ (Faust House), has been well renovated, but unfortunately the interior is not open to the public. An occult priest once lived on this site in the 14th century.

Then, in this Renaissance-style building at the bottom end of Charles Square, alchemists Edward Kelley, in the 16th century, and Ferdinand Antonín Mladota, in the 18th century, conducted their experiments. The latter also entertained his guests with a series of conjuring tricks and magic-lantern shows. In Prague, a city sensitive to such activities, that provided reason enough to give the house its peculiar name. Two centuries earlier, Kelley,

an Englishman whose ears had been cut off in his own country as a punishment for fraud, was no more a serious scholar than Mladota. However, he was given the task of discovering the Philosopher's Stone for Emperor Rudolf II, and of trying to turn metal into gold.

The search for the stone probably lasted too long for Rudolf's liking, and he had Kelley thrown into a cell, where he died of poisoning after two attempts at escape.

Emmaus Monastery

Just on from the Faustův dům, along Vyšehradská, is the **Klášter na Slovanech** ❷⓿ (Slavonic Monastery; open Mon–Fri 9am–4pm; admission charge), also called the **Emmaus Monastery**. This establishment was founded by Charles IV in 1347 for Croatian Benedictines, and it became most famous as a medieval scriptorium producing Slavonic manuscripts. Like many churches in Prague, it was given Baroque towers in 1635, but in 1880 was stripped of these Baroque elements and returned to something approaching

Map on page 148

The Faust legend, made famous by Goethe's plays, concerns a man who sells his soul to Mephistopheles for knowledge and riches; neither of which prevent him from coming to a sticky end.

LEFT:
the New Town Hall.

Reinhard Heydrich

On 17 May 1942 two Czech men who had been plotting in England assassinated Reinhard Heydrich by throwing a bomb at his open-top car. Heydrich, the brutal Nazi governor *(Reichsprotektor)* of Bohemia and Moravia, had been on his way to his office in Hradčany. After the murder, the assassins and five other members of the resistance movement barricaded themselves into the crypt of SS Cyril and Methodius. Their hiding place was discovered on 18 June, and they shot themselves rather than surrender to the SS. The plan had been hatched without the approval of the Czech resistance movement in Prague and proved disastrous. The Nazis exacted cruel revenge for the assassination: after Heydrich was given a grand funeral, the cortège pointedly moving down Wenceslas Square, his successor ordered the village of Lidice, some 25 km (16 miles) from Prague, to be burnt to the ground *(see page 202)*. This was done on 10 June 1942. All the men in the village were shot. The women were deported to concentration camps where many of them ultimately died in the gas chambers. Some of the children were dispersed around Germany to be raised as Germans, while others also perished in the camps.

its original Gothic appearance. However, this was not to last for long, as much of the building was destroyed by an Allied bombing raid in 1945.

Reconstruction and restoration began in the 1950s and, while much of it is now finished, is still ongoing. To replace the towers, two concrete sail-shaped buttresses were added in 1965–8, designed by František Černý. One of the most striking examples of modern architecture in the city, the towers are only 40 cm (16 in.) thick.

In the cloisters is a remarkable series of Gothic frescos dating from the 14th century. Many of them are damaged (from the bombing), but what remains is still colourful. Notable among these are the *Flight into Egypt* and the series of saints climbing a ladder to heaven. Just off the cloisters is the beautifully restored and highly ornate **Imperial Chapel**, while close by is the entrance to the light and airy space of the reconstructed church, which still retains elements of its original decoration.

The elegant new towers of the Emmaus Monastery.

BELOW: the Church of St John on the Rock.

Almost directly opposite the entrance to the monastery is the towering façade of **Kostel sv. Jana na skalce** (Church of St John on the Rock; closed except for services). This beautiful Baroque church was designed by Kilián Ignaz Dientzenhofer and built 1729–39. The restricted access is unfortunate, as inside there are some notable works of art, including a wonderful ceiling fresco of St John Nepomuk (1745), and a wooden statue by Jan Brokoff.

The Botanical Gardens

At the bottom of the hill is the **Botanické Zahrady University Karlovy v Praze** (University Botanical Gardens; open daily Jan–Mar 10am–5pm, Mar–Oct 10am–6pm, Nov–Dec 10am–4pm; admission charge for the glasshouse; trams 18 and 24). First set out in 1897, and one of the few stretches of greenery in the area, they are delightful; all the specimens are well labelled and the gardens are dotted with modern sculptures. The winding paths, rockeries and pools mean there are lots of quiet nooks and crannies to explore. The highlight is a beautiful series of restored pre-war greenhouses, dripping with tropical vegetation and including a delicious lily pond.

Along Na slupi, you come to another important (but often locked) church, **Zvestovaní Panny Marie na slupi**. This former convent church of the nuns of the Elizabethan is a rare example of a Gothic church supported by a central pillar. Close by, on Svobodova, is the old Praha-Vyšehrad railway station, now closed and decrepit but ornate and grand in its day.

Turning left up Horská and climbing the steps brings you to a building that's well worth seeing, **Kostel Panna Maria a sv. Karel Veliký** (Church of the Virgin Mary and Charlemagne; open Sun

Map on page 148

2–5pm). The former Augustinian Karlov monastery is surrounded by university buildings, and you enter it through a plain gate. It is evident just by looking at the exterior that it is an unusual building, having an octagonal ground plan and a central dome. Founded in 1350 by Charles IV and dedicated to Charlemagne in 1377, it is reminiscent of the imposing Imperial Chapel in Aachen in Germany. Although the basic plan is much earlier, the spectacular roof of the nave dates from the 16th century, while below, in the crypt, is a fake grotto dating from the 18th century. Beside the church is the uninspiring **Muzeum policie Čr** (Police Museum; open Tues–Sun 10am–5pm; admission charge; www.mvcr.cz).

The church lies right on the edge of the descent into the Nusle valley, and only a few yards away from its surrounding wall the Nuselský most (Nusle Bridge) arches across the valley, over the apartment houses that lie beneath it. At 500 metres (1,640 ft) it is the second-longest bridge in Prague. There are two modern glass palaces at the end of the bridge. One is the Hotel Forum skyscraper, completed in 1988, and on the other side, the huge **Kongresové centrum Praha**, the former Palác kultury (Palace of Culture), was opened in 1981 and is an important venue for Prague's trade fairs and the occasional large-scale concert.

Villa Amerika

The quiet backstreets around Ke Karlovu that leads back into town are home to many university buildings. Off to the right, on Na bojišti, is **U kalicha** ㉔ (The Chalice). This pub is where the Prague author Jaroslav Hašek frequently used to drink, and it is his novel *The Good Soldier Švejk* which has made The Chalice famous; "When the war's over, come and visit me. You'll find

me in The Chalice every evening at six," Švejk says to a friend. This connection has been shamelessly exploited, and the restaurant is now packed with tour groups.

At the bottom of Ke Karlovu, opposite the Church of the Virgin Mary and Charlemagne, is the Villa Amerika, now housing the **Muzeum Antonína Dvořáka** ㉕ (Dvořák Museum; open Tues–Fri 10am–1.30pm, 2–5pm; admission charge; www.nm.cz), dedicated to one of the Czech Republic's greatest composers *(see page 49)*. This charming little building, named after a 19th-century inn and designed by Kilián Ignaz Dientzenhofer, was constructed in 1717–20 as a summer palace for the Michna family. Inside, the museum contains various Dvořák memorabilia, including his Bösendorfer piano and viola, as well as displays of photographs and facsimiles of letters, tickets and manuscripts. On the first floor is a beautifully decorated little concert hall where recitals are sometimes given. Although the labelling is in Czech, a guide in English can be borrowed from the front desk. ❏

The Kostel sv. Kateřiny (St Catherine's Church), on Kateřinská, goes back to a foundation laid by Charles IV in 1355, but was largely destroyed during the Hussite Wars in the 15th century. The octagonal Gothic tower is all that remains of the original medieval building. The present-day church is the result of work undertaken in 1737.

BELOW: inside the Dvořák museum.

RESTAURANTS, CAFÉS AND PUBS

Restaurants

Albio
Truhlářská 20
Tel: 222 325 414
Open: Mon–Sat
11am–10pm. €€
This is an excellent vegetarian restaurant, with tasty and inventive dishes, many cooked with organic ingredients. The menu (printed on recycled cardboard) gives lots of nutritional information, and the dishes range from salad with grilled goat's cheese and walnut oil to tasty noodle dishes. The ginger beer is definitely worth a try, as are the very good unpasteurised Bernard dark and light ales. Next door they run a well-stocked organic supermarket.

Alcron
Radisson SAS Alcron Hotel,
Štěpánská 40
Tel: 222 820 038
Open: Mon–Sat 6–10.30pm.
€€€
Dating from the 1930s, the Radisson Hotel has great period decor and this top fish restaurant. A varied menu, from South-East Asian to French dishes, uses very fresh ingredients. Don't miss out on the wonderful desserts either.

Café Imperial
Na poříčí 15
Tel: 222 316 012
Open: daily 9am–midnight.
€
One of the grand old cafés of Prague. It is worth a visit just for the outstanding Art-Nouveau interior with wonderful tiling, but it is also has a friendly, laid-back atmosphere.

Café and Galerie Louvre
Národní třída 20
Tel: 224 930 949
Open: daily 8am–11.30pm.
€
An elegant Art Nouveau café, much loved in the past by Prague's intellectuals, this is a great place to sit and browse through the papers. Below the café proper is a lovely café-gallery featuring contemporary art, while upstairs you can get good-value breakfasts and light meals throughout the day.

Cicala
Žitna 43
Tel: 222 210 375
Open: Mon–Sat
11.30am–10.30pm. €€
Very pleasant, very helpful and very Italian, Cicala serves the most authentic, and some of the tastiest, Italian food in the city. Set in a basement off a busy street, the menu has a splendid range of antipasti, pasta and meat dishes, interesting daily specials and lovely desserts. There is also an extensive list of Italian wines.

The Globe Bookstore and Coffeehouse
Pštrossova 6
Tel: 224 934 203
Open: daily 10am–midnight.
€
Well-known as a centre of ex-pat intellectual life. As well as the friendly café, with good coffee and light meals (pasta, salads and bur-gers), the bookshop has occasional live music, lectures and book readings and signings. It is also one of the most pleasant, and cheapest, places to check your e-mail.

La Perle de Prague
Rašínovo nábřeží 8
Tel: 221 984 160
Open: Mon 7–10.30pm,
Tues–Sat noon–2pm,
7–10.30pm. €€€
A formal restaurant on top of the Tančící dům ("Fred and Ginger" building), with a menu of French and international dishes. The food is good, but the real attraction is fabulous view over the city and river.

Le Bistrot de Marlène
Plavecká 4
Tel: 224 921 853
Open: Mon–Fri
noon–2.30pm, 7–10.30pm,
Sat 7–10.30pm. €€€
A delightful French restaurant serving absolutely classic cuisine. The wonderful dishes, among many, include foie gras with figs, snails, confit de canard and crêpes Suzette, all backed up by a staunchly French wine list.

Posezení u čiriny
Navrátilova 6
Tel: 222 231 709
Open: Mon–Sat

11am–11pm. €€
A small but very good Czech restaurant, tucked out of the way close to Karlovo náměstí. The menu covers a good range of traditional dishes, including palačinky (pancakes), roast pork and beef with a variety of sauces.

Ultramarin
Ostrovní 32
Tel: 224 932 249
Open: 11.30am–4am. €€
Like the Celnice, this too is above one of Prague's best bars and clubs. The food here, however, is very different. Tasty grills, Thai and Mexican dishes, and big Mediterranean salads are order of the day here.

Universal
V Jirchářích 6
Tel: 224 934 416
Open: Mon–Sat 11.30am–12.30am, Sun 11am–midnight. €€
A reasonably priced and comfortable French bistro with straightforward but lovely food. Once settled in the slick interior, you can choose from dishes such as salade niçoise, lamb chops and steaks, and some classic desserts.

Zahrada v Opeře
Legerova 75
Tel: 224 239 685
Open: daily 11.30am–1am. €€–€€€
The outside of this restaurant initially looks a bit threatening, given the armed guards (there

to protect Radio Free Europe in the same building). However, this is a good place to treat yourself. The chic interior and smooth service put you at ease, while the food is excellent: tasty soups, garlicky grilled calamari, and some of the best desserts in Prague.

Zvonice
Jindřišská věž, Jindřišská
Tel: 224 220 004
Open: daily 11.30am–midnight. €€€
This Gothic tower, dating back to 1347 and restored in the 19th century, now houses a restaurant. The food comprises straightforward Czech and international dishes, but the surroundings are fascinating, all Gothic wooden beams, giving the place a definite romantic charm.

Celnice
V celnice 4
Tel: 224 212 240
Open: daily 11.30am–midnight. €–€€
Yet another Pilsner Urquell-owned beer hall, with all the advantages they bring of excellent beer and gut-busting Bohemian food. This one has the added advantage on being on top of one of Prague's best clubs where you can dance off the dumplings.

Pivovarský dům
Ječná/Lípová 15
Tel: 296 216 666
Open: daily 11am–11.30pm. €
This microbrewery and restaurant is noted for its wide and varied range of beers brewed on the premises (even including coffee and banana beer). The hearty Czech food (such as roast pork and stuffed dumplings) is tasty and helps to soak up the drink. Among the other offerings are a wheat beer, mead and a delicious dark beer.

U fleků
Křemencova 11
Tel: 224 934 019
Open: daily 9am–11pm. €–€€
An ancient and well-known brewery with an illustrious past. Its present is not so admirable, filled as it is with hordes

of tourists who bash tables, scoff down the goulash and quaff beer. However, the dark beer, brewed on site, is just as wonderful as ever. Avoid the "free" Becherovka.

U kalicha
Na bojišti
Tel: 224 912 557
Open: daily 11am–11pm. €€
The same warnings apply to "The Chalice" as to U fleků; it is over-priced and packed with tourists. The sole attraction of the restaurant is its mention in *The Good Soldier Švejk*, now exploited beyond belief.

LEFT: elegant surroundings in the Café Imperial.
RIGHT: posh dining at the Perle de Prague.

VYŠEHRAD

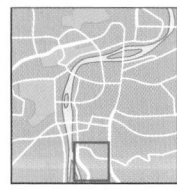

The first royal region of Prague, Vyšehrad has now been given over to parkland, preserving its ancient sites. Also here is a cemetery devoted to the Czech Republic's finest artists and writers

The River Vltava flows down from the Bohemian forest and reaches Prague by the rock fortress of Vyšehrad (literally meaning "High Castle"). This is where, according to legend, the rule of the wise women skilled in magic was replaced by the rule of men. The marriage of Princess Libuše to the ploughman Přemysl brought this change about, and their successors ruled over the Czech people until the year 1306, when Wenceslas III, the last of the Přemyslid dynasty,

BELOW: a ruined medieval watch tower, popularly called the "Baths of Libuše".

was assassinated during his Polish campaign *(see page 18)*. It was here on this rock, where the couple are supposed to have lived in a magnificent palace, that Princess Libuše experienced the vision in which she prophesied the future greatness and glory of the new capital, when "two olive trees will grow in this city… they will shine throughout the world through signs and wonders".

Not until the 19th century did the Vyšehrad legend re-enter the newly revived national consciousness. Then it was imaginatively embroidered and Vyšehrad became once more the seat of Libuše and the cradle of Czech history. Many poets and painters, musicians and sculptors, historians and architects worked on the Vyšehrad site, creating a memorial which says much about this nation living in the centre of Europe – Slavs, surrounded by German tribes, involved in complex relationships with their neighbours, yet very different in character and language.

Near the **Táborská brána** ❶ (Tábor Gate; actually at the Špička, or Peak, Gate), on the southern side of the hill (walk up Na bučance from Vyšehrad Metro) is the **Information Centre** of the Vyšehrad Národní Kulturní Památka (Vyšehrad National Cultural Monument). Here you can pick up information on the site (tel: 261 225 304; www.praha-vysehard.cz).

Vyšehrad's churches

The oldest building in Vyšehrad is **Rotunda sv. Martina** (St Martin's Rotunda; only open for mass) ❷, a tiny Romanesque church dating from the 11th century, sensitively restored in the 1870s, and one of the oldest churches in the country. There are other Romanesque churches in various parts of Prague, such as St George's Basilica in Hradčany *(see page 86)*, the Holy Rood Rotunda in the Old Town and St Longinus in the New. They are all that remains today of cores of old individual settlements.

Much more is known about the vast, twin-spired **Kostel sv. Petra a Pavla** ❸ (Church of SS Peter and Paul; open Fri 9am–noon, Sat–Mon, Wed–Thur 9am–noon, 1–5pm), which can be seen in its present Neo-Gothic form, dating from the mid-1880s. Archaeologists have been kept busy examining the walls of its predecessor on the same site, as there has been a church here since the 11th century, which was destroyed by fire in the 13th century. Vyšehrad used to be a place of pilgrimage, and here, in this sandstone church, the votive tablet popularly known as the Madonna of the Rains was kept, along with the tomb of St Longinus.

On the corner of K rotundě is a structure called the **Devil's Column**, said to have been put there by Satan after he lost a bet with a priest. This is just one of the myths concerning this ancient area of Prague.

Vyšehrad Cemetery

The redundant fortress on Vyšehrad Rock was finally demolished in the 19th century, for it had long lost its strategic importance. But in 1870, the **Vyšehradský hřbitov** ❹ (Vyšehrad Cemetery; open daily,

One of the most pleasant ways to reach Vyšehrad is to walk along the Vltava embankment and take the path up through the woods by the Cubist Triple House (see page 163).

BELOW:
St Martin's Rotunda.

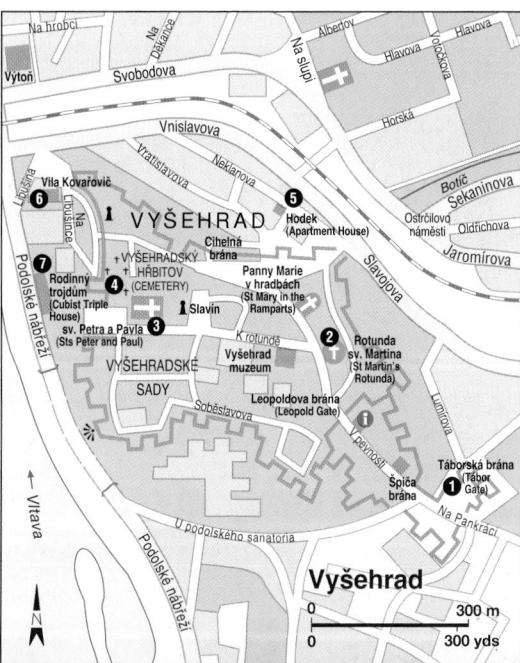

The grave of composer Bedřich Smetana.

BELOW: colourful doors with the Czech eagle and lion on SS Peter and Paul.

Nov–Feb 9am–4pm, Mar–Apr and Oct 8am–6pm, May–Sept 8am–7pm) was created solely to be the final resting place for the country's most revered musicians, writers and artists. Dominating the cemetery is one of its last additions, dating from 1890, the tomb of honour known as the **Slavín Monument**, at the end of the main avenue. This communal grave of artists such as Mucha and Gočár is topped by a statue representing Genius.

Many of the graves within the cemetery are still regularly decorated with flowers, for the works of these artists live on in the memory of the nation. The most visited graves are those of the two best-known Czech composers, Bedřich Smetana and Antonín Dvořák. Smetana's *Bartered Bride* has been performed in Prague more than 5,000 times alone, and the performance of his opera *Libuše* at the newly opened National Theatre in 1883 symbolised the fervent nationalist aspirations of the Czech people in the 19th century. Dvořák's grave is among the most extravagant in the complex. But these two composers are not the only musicians buried here. There are also great performers, members of the Prague Conservatory, such as the violinist Jan Kubelík (1880–1940).

Also buried here is the 19th-century author of tales of life in Malá Strana, Jan Neruda. His stories chronicle the world of the lower middle classes living in Malá Strana in the shadow of the great palaces. They feature old women and their books of dreams, moonstruck students, grumbling caretakers, and a number of curious characters who inhabit the yards and alleyways.

Other writers of Neruda's generation who are buried here include Svatopluk Čech, Jaroslav Vrchlický and Karel Hynek Mácha, whose romantic poem "Máj" (May) is known to every Bohemian. It was at Mácha's grave that the November 1989 demonstration that sparked the revolution began. A little more recently, the Czech poet, journalist and dramatist Karel Čapek (1890–1938) joined his famous compatriots here in death.

Visual artists and painters are represented by the sculptor Josef Myslbek (1848–1929), who created the impressive group of statues, including those of Přemysl and Libuše, which now stand in the western part of Vyšehrad, but he is perhaps best known as sculptor of the Wenceslas Monument in Wenceslas Square; and by Alfons Mucha, who is best known outside the Czech Republic for his Art Nouveau posters, some of which featured the French actress Sarah Bernhardt.

Cubist Housing

Below the citadel, on the western and eastern sides, are three of the best examples of Cubist architecture to be found in Prague; all of them are by the architect and designer Josef Chochol (1880–1956).

Descending to the east will bring you down to Neklanova. At No. 30 is the **Hodek apartment house ❺** (1913–14). The best-known of Chochol's Cubist buildings, this corner building is very bold in the way it projects forward (helped by its position on the side of the hill) and,

interestingly, displays the influence of Classicism in its cornice.

On the other side of the hill are two other examples of his work: the **Vila Kovařovič ❻**, and the **Rodinný trojdům ❼** (Cubist Triple House). The former, built in 1912–13 and so the earliest of Chochol's Cubist constructions, is at Libušina 3 close to the railway bridge. Also built on a corner site, but less dramatic, the façade it presents to the road is graceful and beautifully proportioned. Around the corner, at Rašínovo nábřeží 6–10, is the Triple House. These three domestic spaces, joined as one, were built in 1913–14.

Getting to Vyšehrad

Vyšehrad can be reached easily from the Metro station of the same name, passing the gigantic **Congress Centre**. However, you can also get to it on foot along a pleasant path from Čiklova or from the Vltava embankment through the wooded park to the castle. From the remains of the old fortifications there is a beautiful view over the city and the Vltava running below. ❏

Map on page 161

Josef Chochol, a committed socialist, studied with Otto Wagner in Vienna before adopting the Cubist style on his return to Prague. In 1914, immediately after these three houses had been built, he abandoned Cubism and started working in a Constructivist style.

BELOW: Chochol's Cubist Triple House.

CZECH MODERNISM

Although generally perceived as a Gothic and Baroque city, Prague has some of the finest examples of 20th-century architecture in Europe

With its intellectual links to the old imperial capital Vienna, its geographical location at the centre of Europe and a strong homegrown architectual tradition, it is not surprising that Prague came to be one of the great centres of early-20th century architecture. Rising nationalist conciousness at the end of the 19th century coincided with the flowering of Art Nouveau in the city, seen to greatest effect in the Obecní dům *(see page 126)*. This outpouring of decoration received its antithesis with the development of architectural Cubism, a movement unique to Czechoslovakia. Taking its cue from the angular planes in the work of Picasso and Braque, these – and a general geometric approach to design – were applied to building; and even, in the case of Emil Králíček's lamppost *(inset)*, street furniture.

After the First World War, and with the independence of the Czechoslovak state, a more nationalist style emerged, incorporating folk motifs, which became known as Rondocubism. This, however, was short-lived and soon ideas from elsewhere – specifically the rigorously modern Functionalism – came to dominate Czech architecture. A few architects, such as Janák and Gočár, who had first made their mark as Cubist designers went on to dominate the new style.

Although the great architect Adolf Loos (1870–1933) was born in Czechoslovakia, few of his buildings are to be found in the Czech Republic (the majority are in Vienna where he established his practice). However, the building many consider to be his crowning achievement – the Müllerova vila *(picture inset; see also pages 179–80)* – is in the Prague suburb of

Střešovice. Fittingly, given Loos' opposition to extraneous decoration (given somewhat bizarre justification in his essay *Ornament and Crime*), the exterior is austere, indeed rather bleak, only enlivened by the strong primary yellow of the window frames. This, however, belies the ingenuity and masterful handling of space of the inside. The use of high-quality, luxurious materials, and the seemingly complex layout of the interior on a number of different levels, gives an almost fantastical atmophere to the house. Much of the original furniture survived in storage throughout the Communist years and the building has now been restored to its initial state.

THE BABA ESTATE

One of the jewels in the crown of Czech modernism, the Baba Estate of the Czechoslovak Werkbund, is on a high bluff overlooking the northern district of Dejvice. Built between 1928 and 1940, the estate displays a unity at odds with the way it developed. After the basic infrastructure and ground plan of the area (by Pavel Janák) had been set out, each house was commissioned separately and the individual plans were discussed between the architect and client. With the exception of the Dutch architect Mart Stam, the others were all drawn from the Czechoslovak Werkbund, which included some of the finest architects of its day: Janák, Josef Gočár and Ladislav Žák. Although none of the houses are open to the public, it is still worth wandering around to see the elegant designs. Notable buildings include: the Čeněk Villa (*pictured left*; Na Babě 11, by Ladislav Žák, 1932); the Janák House (Nad Paťankou 16, 1931–2); and the Palička House (Na Babě 9, by Mart Stam and Jiří Palička, 1929–32).

BELOW: the Veletržní palác, now used as part of the National Gallery *(see pages 171–5)*, is one of the great Functionalist buildings of Prague. Functionalism as a movement was inspired by the ideas of Le Corbusier and Mies van der Rohe and arose after the First World War. Its central thesis was that buildings should be designed with decoration subordinate to function (hence Le Corbusier's famous quote about a house being "a machine for living in"). The Veletržní palác was the first large-scale experiment along these lines; below you can see its large, light-filled central atrium.

ABOVE: the streamlined Baarová Villa (Ladislav Žák, 1937) is at Neherovská 8 in the district of Dejvice. This classic 1930s building was the home of the Czech actor Lída Baarová (who was controversial for an affair with Hitler's henchman, Josef Goebbels).

HOLEŠOVICE TO BÍLÁ HORA

The northern and western reaches of the city, often ignored by tourists, contain some of Prague's most important and interesting sights: from the exceptional modern art collections of the Veletržní palác and elegant modernist architecture, to the site of Bílá Hora

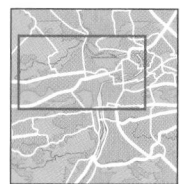

Northern and western Prague (known by their postcodes as Prague 6 and 7 respectively) comprise the districts of Holešovice, Troja, Dejvice and Bílá Hora, each with a number of sights that are well worth a visit.

The František Bílek villa

To the north of the Palace Gardens, by the Chotkovy sady tram stop, is a striking building housing a museum of the works of Czech Symbolist and Art Nouveau sculptor **František Bílek** ❶ (open 1 May– 15 Oct Tue–Sun 10am–6pm, 16 Oct–30 Apr Sat–Sun 10am–5pm; admission charge; www.citygalleryprague.cz; trams 18, 22 and 57). The house, which dates from 1911, was designed by the artist to create, in his own words, "a workshop and a temple". A large room on the ground-floor interior has good examples of the sculptor's work; much of it religious in inspiration with a strong emphasis on struggle and suffering (for example, *Grief*, 1908– 9).

The interior of the villa makes much use of rough-hewn stone, arches and niches. Unfortunately, little of the original furniture remains but that which does is very attractive, especially the Cubist sideboard of 1910. The first floor has his large plaster model for the

National Monument for the White Mountain, which was planned for 300th anniversary of the battle in 1920. Bílek submitted a design after an initial proposal from Stanislav Sucharda was poorly received. This would have been his largest project, and very spectacular. However, in the end the project was not realised, ostensibly due to lack of funding, and the commemoration had to make do with the small mound and plaque that can still be seen at the site *(see page 180)*.

Map on page 168

LEFT: the Müller Villa.
BELOW: the Baba Estate looks out over the city.

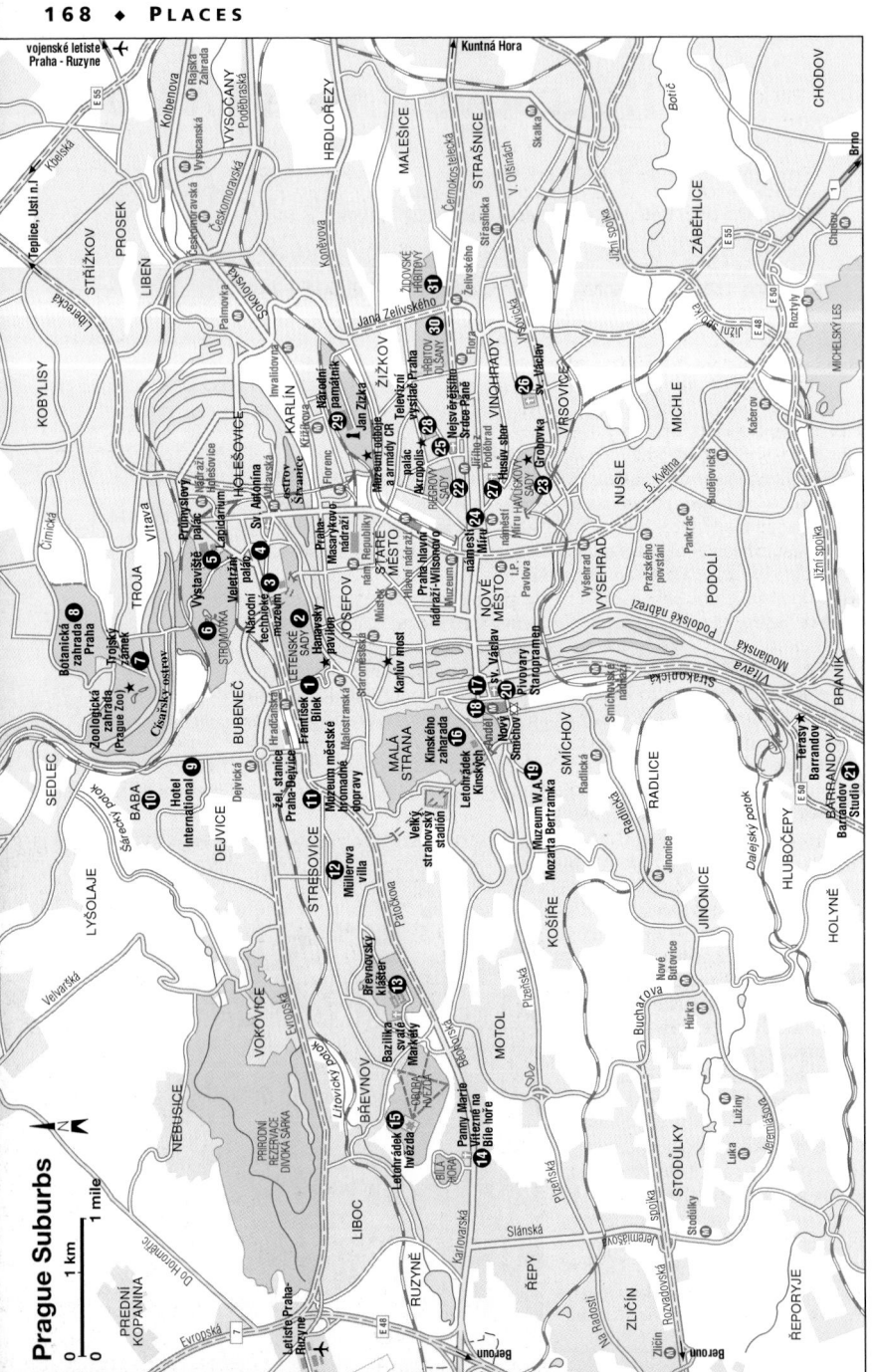

vojenské letiste
Praha - Ruzyne

◀ Kuntná Hora

CHODOV

Prague Suburbs

N

0   1 km
0   1 mile

Letná Park

Across the road from the villa is the beginning of **Letenské sady** ❷ (Letná Park), a spread of green between Hradčany and Holešovice. It was laid out in the mid-19th century, and the views across the city from its southern edge are wonderful.

It was on the edge of this escarpment that an enormous statue to Stalin was erected in 1953–5. Huge and solid (it weighed around 14,000 tons), this became an embarrassment to the regime during the period of de-Stalinisation following his denunciation by Khrushchev in 1956. The statue was demolished in 1962 and now all that remains is its pyramidal granite base, topped with a large metronome by the artist David Černý. The park was also the scene of the largest demonstration of the Velvet Revolution – an irony given that it was also the venue for the Communist May Day parades – but is now given over to people cycling, walking dogs and jogging.

On the edge of the park, overlooking the escarpment, are two buildings of interest. The first, at the Hradčany end, is the **Hanavský pavilon**. This ornate, early Art Nouveau, building was, like Výstaviště *(see page 175)*, built for the 1891 Exhibition, and was relocated to this spot, where it is now a restaurant.

Further along, almost at the end of the park, is another building designed for an exhibition; in this case the **Czechoslovak Pavilion** for the Brussels Expo 1958. After winning the gold medal in Brussels (this form of Modernism became known as the "Brussels style") it was shipped home and reassembled here. Unfortunately the original interior was destroyed by a fire in 1991.

National Technical Museum

On the northern edge of Letná Park is the **Národní technické muzeum** ❸ (National Technical Museum; open Tues–Fri 9am–5pm, Sat–Sun 10am–6pm; admission charge; www.ntm.cz; trams 1, 8, 25 and 26 to Letenské náměstí). At present some parts are closed for renovation (including, unfortunately, the full-sized model of a coal mine in the basement); however, you can visit most of the museum, which is quite fascinating. Helpfully, many of the exhibits are labelled in English.

The most fun is probably to be had in the main **Transport Hall**. The floor space is devoted to rail and road transport, while overhead a number of aircraft are suspended from the ceiling. The loveliest exhibits are the two Art Nouveau saloon coaches (1891 and 1900) decorated by Jiří Stibral, one of which is from the court train of Emperor Franz Josef I. Although most of the steam locomotives are Austrian- and German-built, the largest is the "Hunchback" (so-called because of its distinctive shape), built in Prague in 1911. The workmanship on the engines and carriages is wonderful. Other interesting items include the first factory-

Map on page 168

During the Velvet Revolution of 1989 a demonstration in Letná Park attracted close to one million people.

BELOW:
the Hanavský pavilon.

*Close to the National Technical Museum is the **Národní zemědělské muzeum** (National Museum of Agriculture; open Tues–Sun 9am–midday, 12.30–5pm; admission charge; www.pruvodce.com/ nzm) with displays of agricultural machinery and tools used in baking, brewing and distilling.*

BELOW: the Stalin monument used to tower over Letná Park.

built car to be brought to the Czech Republic (a Benz Viktoria made in 1893), and beautifully made – as well as large and glamorous – cars from the 1930s.

The aviation exhibits include a variety of aeroplanes and helicopters, including the tiny Nebeská Blecha plane from 1937: it is hard to believe that it ever got off the ground. However, perhaps the most intriguing pieces are the two balloon baskets, one from 1904 only one cubic metre in volume, the other from the 1930s and powered by an propeller. The galleries around the hall (from which you can see the airborne exhibits) have displays of bicycles and motorcycles, as well as a large number of model ships.

Also on the ground floor is a gallery of **clocks and clockmaking** and the rooms devoted to **photography and cinema**, both areas in which the Czechs have excelled (think of the astronomical clock in Staroměstské náměstí). The latter runs the full gamut from box brownies to huge movie projectors, though the most unlikely exhibits are Char-

lie Chaplin's bowler hat, cane and gloves, donated to the museum by his brother in 1949.

On the first floor is a gallery devoted to **acoustics**, with an array of wax-cylinder phonographs, music boxes, gramophones and pianolas. Better still are the models that demonstrate wave forms, resonance, sound proofing and decibel levels, all with lots of buttons to press. Upstairs are the **astronomy** displays, mostly a collection of instruments such as telescopes, globes and sextants, as well as some very fine 16th-century ivory compass boxes.

Holešovice

The district of Holešovice is a 19th-century suburb (incorporated into the city in 1884), now a little run down but with elegant and decorated late-19th-century apartment buildings. Also here, on Strossmayerovo náměstí, is the church of **Sv. Antonína** built in 1908–14 (open Mon–Fri noon–7pm, Sat 7am–noon, Sun 7am–noon 5–7pm). The towers are clearly derived from those on the Týn Church in Staré Město.

Inside is an imposing altar, surrounded by a well-executed frieze, and elegant plain columns along the nave that sprout into the Neo-Gothic vaulting. As well as some good *fin de siècle* stained glass, there is also an interesting fake grotto, dripping with stalactites.

Veletržní palác

The **Veletržní palác** ❹ (Trade Fair Palace) at Dukelských hrdinů 47 is one of the earliest large-scale Functionalist buildings. Intended for exhibitions to show off Czech industrial expertise, it was used for this until 1951, and then for foreign trade until 1974 when it was badly damaged in a fire. It was decided that it should be rebuilt and used as an impressive, and fitting, space for the National Gallery's **Collection of 19th, 20th and 21st Century Art** (open Tues–Sun 10am–6pm; admission charge; www.ngprague.cz; trams 5, 12 and 17).

The first floor is used for temporary exhibitions (on the left as you enter is a café, on the right an excellent art bookshop with useful, in-depth guides to the exhibitions), and the huge atrium space has been left clear to give you an idea of how the size and space of the building works. A glass lift takes you up to the fifth floor (also used for temporary exhibitions), giving a vertigo-inducing view of the hall. It is best to go right to the top and work your way down through the floors, though there's enough to justify a couple of visits (you are allowed to buy tickets for combinations of, and individual, floors). Some of the highlights are described below.

19th-century art

The permanent exhibitions start on the fourth floor with Czech 19th century painting and sculpture. It opens with several sculptures by **Josef Václav Myslbek** (1848– 1922) who was responsible for the St Wenceslas statue in front of the National Museum. Notable here are the standing female figure with a harp entitled *Music* (1907–12) and the busts of 19th-century worthies. Of the early works, perhaps the most interesting are the architectural paintings of

Map on page 168

Designed by Oldřiich Tyl and Josef Fuchs, the Veletržní palác was built in 1924–8 and was admired by Le Corbusier. He saw in it how his own large-scale projects might be realised, while qualifying his enthusiasm by saying, "It's an interesting building but it's not yet architecture."

BELOW: inside the Technical Museum.

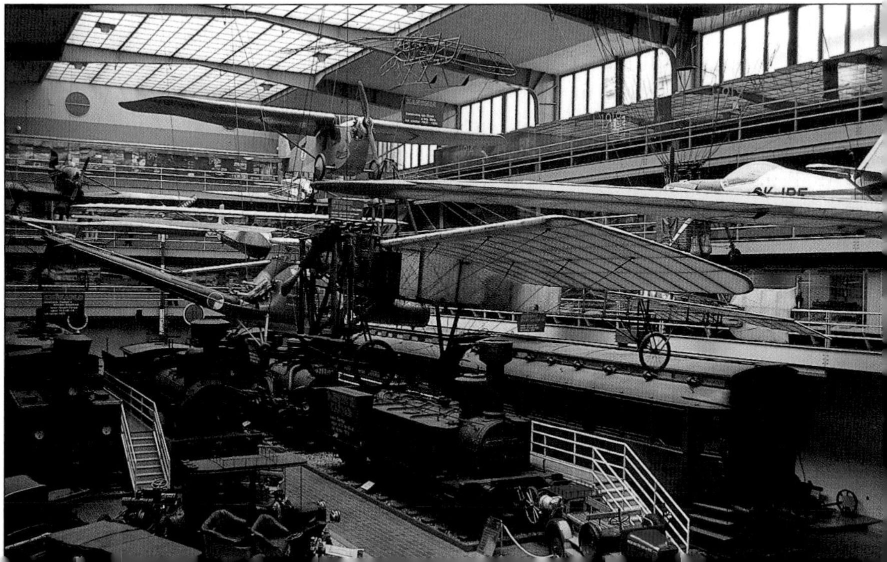

Ludvik Kohl (1746–1821), especially *The Interior of St Vitus Cathedral* (1814) and *The Vladislav Hall* (1810–20).

Some of the most outstanding paintings are the mid-19th-century landscapes by **Antonín Mánes** (1784– 1843), particularly the castle of *Křivoklát* (1842), **Josef Navrátil's** (1798–1865) highly Romantic *The Mumlava Waterfall in the Giant Mountains* (1850–3); and the dark and dreamy *Moonlight Night* (1860) or the brighter, and earlier, *Mountain Country* (1840s) by **August Piepenhagen** (1791–1868).

Later landscape painters include **Alois Bubák**, **Bedřich Havránek** – see especially his *Near Rajice in Moravia* (1850) – and **Maximilian Haushofer**, who worked outdoors to paint *Weissensee near Lermons in Tyrol* (1863). **Adolf Kosárek** (1830–59) died of TB at the age of 29 but was highly prolific; particularly good are *Forest Scenery* (1856) and *Summer Country with Chapel* (1859), with its shimmering heat. The collection even includes a small painting by **Casper David-**

As well as the displays of painting and sculpture, each floor ends with extensive galleries devoted to applied art, architecture and theatrical design (see also pages 128–9).

BELOW: modern sculpture outside the Trade Fair Palace.

Friedrich, *The North Sea by Moonlight* (1823–4).

The Realist paintings show the influence of French art, as do the *plein air* works, notably *On the River* by **Vilém Riedel** (1832–76). Of the Realist works look for *Portrait of the Blacksmith* (1860) by **Karel Purkyně** (1834–68), which depicts the working man reading a newspaper.

Landscape painting continued with the large woodland scenes of **Julius Edvard Mařák** (1832–99), while a lighter, and charming, touch is given by **Vojtěch Hynais** (1854–1925), especially his delightful, and rather flirtatious, *Company in the Country* (1889).

The landscapes of **Antonín Chittussi** (1847–91) were inspired by the time he spent in France, his wonderful paintings including the impressive *In the Bohemian-Moravian Highlands* (1882). Almost startlingly different are those by the, later **Jakub Schikaneder** (1855–1924), in particular *Honeymoon* (1919–20) with its delicate handling of light. Other striking exhibits are

Poor Country (1900) by **Max Švabinsky** and two verdant pictures by **Josef Schusser** (1864–1941). **Miloš Jiránek**'s two full-length portraits of women are also interesting, especially the Whistler-inspired *Study in White* (1910).

After a display of sculptures by František Bílek *(see page 167)* come the decidedly Jugendstil *Beeches* (1904) by **Alois Kalvoda** and *Evening Silence* (1900) by **Antonín Hudeček**. Also impressive are the large landscapes of **Antonín Slavíček** (1870–1910), the leading light in Czech Impressionism.

Art 1900–1930

Entering the galleries on the third floor, the first space is given over to **František Kupka** (1871–1957), from early Symbolist works (see *The Path of Silence I*, 1903), to Fauvist paintings, such as *Family Portrait* (1910), via the excellent *Two-Colour Fugue – Amorpha* (1912), to his later outright abstraction, as in *Vertical Planes III* (1912–13) and the De Stijl-like *Series CVI* (1935–6).

The experimental photographic works of **František Drtikol** (1883–1961), with their Art Deco feel are worth a look. The Cubism of **Emil Filla** (see *Salome*, 1911–12) shows Czech art at the forefront of European art, while another luminary of the Czech avant-garde, **Bohumil Kubišta**, seems – strangely given his name – more Futurist than Cubist (see *Meditation*, 1915).

However, in terms of Cubism, the furniture and ceramics of **Josef Gočar** (1880–1945) and **Pavel Janák** (1882–1956) are unsurpassed. In contrast, the works of **Gutfreund**, **Čapek** and **Špála** seem less convincing and dated by the time they were produced. Things tend to degenerate from here on, but the sculptures of **Karel Dvořák** (1893–1950) display a sense of social purpose. See especially the charming *To America* (1925) of an emigrating couple asleep on a bench.

French art

The highlight of the collections for many people will be the galleries of French art. Hardly any major painter

Map on page 168

To see more works by František Kupka and Otto Gutfreund visit the permanent exhibition at Museum Kampa (see page 110).

BELOW: *View of Prague from Ladvi by Antonín Slavíček.*

from the mid-19th to early-20th century is not represented here. After some busts by **Rodin**, the displays start with three small pictures by **Delacroix** and a couple of paintings by **Corot** (*Young Shepherds among the Rocks*, 1842, and *Farm Dwelling in the Woods*, 1873). The gallery also contains some fine examples of the work of **Courbet**, notably *Woman in a Straw Hat with Flowers* (1857) and *Forest Grotto* (c. 1865).

The French collections of the gallery came about through a piece of inspired buying by the newly-founded Czechoslovak state in 1923, at a time when many of the artists represented in the galleries were not fashionable.

The Impressionists are particularly well represented, especially by **Pissarro** (*In the Kitchen Garden*, 1881, and *Garden at Val Hermeil*, 1880) and **Sisley** (*The Bridge at Sèvres*, 1877, and *Bourgogne Lock at Moret*, 1882). There are also a couple of early works by **Monet**, *Orchard Trees in Blossom* (1879) and *Women among Flowers* (1875). The academic side of **Degas** can be seen in his *Portrait of Lorenzo Pagans* (1882), and there is a rather sentimental picture by **Renoir**, *The Lovers* (1875).

Toulouse-Lautrec's picture of two women dancing together, *At the Moulin Rouge* (1892), is excellent,

as is the collection of pictures by **Gaugin**, especially his *Flight* (1902). *Green Wheat* by **Van Gogh** (1889) is a spectacular work, but perhaps the most impressive part of the collection are the 19 works by **Picasso**, from the early *Seated Female Nude* (1906) to a wide range of his Cubist paintings.

The gallery has three fabulous works by **Cézanne**: *Portrait of Joachim Gasquet* (1896–7), *House in Aix-en-Provence* (1885–7), and *Fruits* (1879–82). There are also pictures by **Rousseau** and **Seurat** (see especially his *Port of Honfleur*, 1881), **Braque** and **Derain** (including the wonderful *Cadaquès*, 1910, and *Montreuil-sur-Mer*, also 1910).

Also represented are **Despiau**, **Dufy**, **Chagall** and **Bourdelle**. As well as a series of his lithographs, there is a lovely painting by **Matisse** (*Joaquine*, 1910). At the end of the collection is a beautiful chalk drawing (*Female Nude*, 1902) by Maillol.

Czech art from 1930 and 20th century foreign art

The collections on the second floor are hard to pick your way through without specialist knowledge, and a lot of what is there merely serves emphasise how good the previous two floors are.

The graphic designs of **Ladislav Sutnar** (1897–1976) are convincing and exciting, as are the clean lines of his glass and porcelain designs. However, by far the best, and most exciting, exhibits are those from the small display of **Socialist Realism**.

The Socialist Realist works in the gallery begin with an excellent monumental bronze, *Fraternisation* (1945–50), by **Karel Pokorný**, and a plaster model of a girl reading (*Young Female Pioneer*) by **Jaroslav Záhoř**. Also look out for the wonderful poster designs *We Produce More, We Live Better* by

BELOW: ornate Holešovice architecture.

Alena Čermáková and *Farmer, Count Well!* by **Karel Skála**. Particularly interesting are the Czechoslovak items sent to the **Brussels Expo of 1958**, including glass, ceramics and furniture.

On the first floor is another impressive collection, starting with an excellent display of Expressionist works. Look out for *Operation* (1912) by **Max Oppenheimer**, *Pregnant Woman and Death* (1911) by **Egon Schiele** and **Kokoschka**'s *Portrait of the Poet Albert Ehrenstein* (1913–14). Also interesting are the townscapes of Prague painted by Kokoschka in 1934–5.

As well as two Secessionist works by **Gustav Klimt** (*Virgin*, 1913, and *Castle with Moat*, 1908–09), there are two fabulous large paintings by **Lentulov**, *A Ballet Theme* (1912) and *Landscape near Kislovodsk* (1913).

The two early works by **Edvard Munch** (*Dancing on a Shore*, 1900, and *Seashore Landscape near Lübeck*, 1907) are interesting, as is *Tropical Forest* (1915) by **Paul Klee**.

Výstaviště and the Lapidarium

Beyond the Veletržní palác, and past the Communist-era Parkhotel, is the **Výstaviště ❺** exhibition ground (trams 5, 12 and 17). The huge and ornate **Průmyslový palác**, designed by František Prášil and Bedřich Münzberger, was constructed for the Exhibition of 1891. One of the first Art Nouveau buildings in Prague, it is still used for trade fairs and exhibitions – which vary from Erotica Sex to Móda Praha – but when there is no show on it can appear a little strange and bleak.

To the right of the Průmyslový palác, in one of the side pavilions, is the National Museums's **Lapidarium** (open Tues–Fri noon–6pm; Sat–Sun 10am–6pm; admission charge; WWW.nm.cz). This, the Bohemian stone-sculpture collection of the 11th to 19th centuries, contains the most important statues that at one time decorated the city.

Rooms 1 and 2 have exhibits in the Romanesque and Gothic styles. The first has, by way of an exception, the original of the bronze

Map on page 168

The Průmyslový palác is sometimes used as a venue for large rock and pop concerts; check with ticket agents for upcoming events (see page 221).

BELOW: the main exhibition hall at Výstaviště.

equestrian statue of **St George**, which originally stood outside St Vitus (now replaced by a copy, *see page 84*). Also here is the original tympanum from the Týn Church (1380–90). Room 2 has Petr Parléř's exceptional figures from the Old Town Bridge Tower, as well as the original pillar and statue of the Bruncvík *(see page 110)*.

The Renaissance room (3) is dominated by the Krocín fountain that used to stand in Staroměstské náměstí. However, some of the finest exhibits are next door at the start of the Baroque collection. This room contains seven of the original statues from the Karlův most *(see page 117)*: St Ignatius Loyola and St Francis Xavier by Ferdinand Maximilian Brokoff; St Wenceslas; the Baptism of Christ; the Virgin with SS Dominic and Thomas Aquinas; and St Ivo by Mathias Bernhard Braun.

Other Baroque pieces include the original (earlier) **Equestrian Statue of St Wenceslas** from Václavské náměstí as well as a series of interesting gilded and brightly painted statues.

Stromovka is popular with cyclists.

BELOW: waterlilies in Stromovka.

The remainder of the collection is given over to works from the 19th century. Notable amongst these are the two tombs made by Václav Prachner, and the four allegorical groups designed for the cupola of the National Museum by Bohuslav Schnirch.

Also in the grounds of Výstaviště, behind the main exhibition hall, is the newly restored **Panorama** (open daily 10am–5pm; admission charge). This huge 19th-century, circular painting by Luděk Marold (1865–98) depicts *The Battle of Lipany, 1434.*

Stromovka and Troja

To the left of the main entrance to Výstaviště is the way into **Stromovka ❻**. Previously a royal hunting ground, this wooded park became a public space at the beginning of the 19th century and is one of the most extensive open spaces in the city. A signposted foot- and cycle-path leads through the park towards the Troja château. A turn off to the right takes you under the railway line and over a footbridge to

Císařský ostrov (Emperor's Island). The path continues straight across the island to an elegant modern footbridge. On the other side turn left along the river.

A short walk brings you to the **Trojský zámek** ❼ (Troja château; open Apr–Oct Tues–Sun 10am–6pm, Nov–Mar Sat–Sun 10am–5pm; admission charge; www.city galleryprague.cz; also bus 112 from Nádraží Holešovice Metro). The main entrance is on U trojského zámku, although you may be able to get in on the southern side via the large formal gardens, part of which is a large apple orchard.

Built in 1679–85 by Jean-Baptiste Mathey for Václav Vojtěch of Sternberg, this large Baroque mansion has an ornate interior covered in frescos on classical themes (not greatly enhanced by a bodged restoration). The château and gardens suffered greatly in the 2002 floods but much of the damage has now been repaired. Approaching through the gardens does give you a view of the southern façade, with its staircase decorated by monumental sculpture representing the battle between the gods and Titans.

When you enter the building you will be given a pair of overshoes, designed to protect the floors. The château is home to a collection of Czech 19th-century painting, the best of which are probably the landscapes on display in the first few rooms. Many of the same artists are represented as in the Veletržní palác; of particular interest are: Ludvík Kohl's highly Romantic *Gothic Hall with a Meeting of a Secret Brotherhood* (1812); two lovely landscapes of mountain waterfalls by Charlotta Peipenhagenová (1880s); a *Forest Scene* (1853) by Josef Mánes; and the virtuoso *Path in a Deciduous Forest* by Bedřich Havránek (1878).

The rooms upstairs have particularly fine decoration, the most impressive being the Grand Hall, completely covered in frescos by Abraham Godyn (1663–1724).

Botanical Gardens

Just outside the Troja château is the bus stand for the 112, behind which is the entrance to the Zoologická

Map on page 168

The Troja château occasionally holds classical music concerts in its Grand Hall. Check the City Gallery website for details.

BELOW: the Troja château.

zahrada (Prague Zoo). This is not one of the world's most humane institutions – many of the animals are kept in cramped and squalid conditions – and is best avoided.

However, just up the hill is another sight well worth a visit (follow the signs from the bus stop), **Botanická zahrada Praha**  (Prague Botanical Garden; open Tues–Sun, Nov–Mar 9am–4pm, Apr 9am–6pm, May–Sept 9am–7pm, Oct 9am–5pm; admission charge; www.botanicka.cz). Following the road up to the left brings you to the new curving **Fata Morgana** glasshouse. Divided into three main sections – semi-desert, tropical rainforest and cloud forest – the plants are still being established but the results so far are impressive. From the dry zone a subterranean passage leads through a divided pool, one side for the Americas, the other for Africa and Asia, before emerging into the hot and steamy tropics; very green and beautiful. However, perhaps even more interesting is the cooler cloud-forest room, where jets provide a constant mist of water.

A Socialist Realist relief on the Hotel International.

BELOW: the humid tropics hall in the Fata Morgana glasshouse.

Above the glasshouse footpaths lead through an attractive woodland with picnic and play areas. The main outdoor areas of the gardens are below the glasshouse, and here there are extensive plantings showing, among other things, a Mediterranean and Japanese garden, medicinal and poisonous plants, as well as a perennial flower bed. Also attached to the garden, cascading down the hill towards the château, is the St Clara vineyard. The view from the top of the hill by the St Clara chapel is lovely.

Bubeneč to Břevnov

To the west of Holešovice are the districts of Bubeneč and Dejvice, and to the south of these are Střešovice and Břevnov stretching out towards the airport at Ruzyně.

Bubeneč, to the north of Hradčanská Metro, is a district of large villas and *fin de siècle* bourgeois apartments. As such – and like Střešovice – it is home to diplomats, embassies and high-ranking civil servants. The district covers the western end of Stromovka, and merges further west into the estates that surround Vitězné náměstí (Dejvická Metro). North of the huge square, along Jugoslávských partyzánu, is the **Hotel International** (now the Crowne Plaza; take tram 20 or 25 to its terminus). Built in 1951–6 and designed by František Jeřábek, this is one of the great Stalinist monuments of the city *(see page 187)*. Similar in style to Socialist Realist architecture in Warsaw and Moscow, there is a distinct Art Deco influence to the hotel and the building, and its interior are beautifully finished.

The Baba Estate

On the hillside above the hotel is one of the great examples of Czech modernist architecure, the **Baba Estate of the Czechoslovak Werkbund** ❿ (take bus 131 from Zelená, just to the south of the Hotel International, and alight at Matějská). Built between 1928 and 1940, these are some of the most interesting examples of modernist housing to be found anywhere. Although none of the buildings are open to the public, it is still interesting to wander around the quiet streets of the estate *(see also page 165)*.

Prague Transport Museum

Behind Hradčany is Střešovice, similar in feel to the upmarket parts of Bubeneč. Here, at Patočkova 4, is the **Muzeum městské hromadné dopravy** ⓫ (City Transport Museum; open 30 Mar–18 Nov, Sat–Sun 9am–5pm; admission charge; trams 1, 2, 8 and 18). This collection of trams and trolleybuses demonstrates the history of public transport in the city, from a horse-drawn tram car dating from 1886 to a bus dating from 1985. Some of the early trams are beautifully made and decorated in Art Nouveau style, and there is an interesting exhibition showing the building of the city Metro.

The Müllerova vila

Not far away, at Nad hradním vodojemem 14, is the **Müllerova vila** ⓬ (open Tues, Thur, Sat–Sun, Apr–Oct tours at 9 and 11am, 1, 3 and 5pm, Nov–Mar tours at 10am, noon, 2 and 4pm; admission charge; only by

On Saturdays and Sundays between April and November an old tram, no. 91, runs from Vozovna Střešovice (by the Transport Museum) to Výstaviště. It leaves every hour from midday to 6pm, from both ends, and the trip takes in many of the sights in the historic centre.

BELOW: the J. Palička House on the Baba Estate.

The severe exterior of the Müller Villa.

prior arrangement, tel: 224 312 012; www.mullerovavila.cz; trams 1, 2 and 18). The only example of the work of Brno-born architect Adolf Loos in Prague, it was designed and built in 1928–30 for the wealthy couple František and Milada Müller. As befits an iconic Modernist building, the exterior is plain and severe, but the beautifully designed interiors are luxurious.

Now the villa has been restored to its former glory it is possible to see just how well laid-out the building is and how colour is used as an element in the organisation of the overall design. Particularly appealing elements are the open-plan living room with its large windows and a dining space above, the "boudoir', a cosy space which acted as a private retreat, and the elegant lady's dressing room.

The Břevnovský klášter

To the west, in the district of Břevnov, is the **Břevnovský klášter** ⑬ (guided tours Sat–Sun 10am, 2 and 4pm, in Czech only; trams 8 and 22). This is the oldest monas-

BELOW: Our Lady of Victory at Bílá Hora.

tery in Prague, founded in 993 by Boleslav II and St Adalbert; its present Baroque appearance dates from the early 18th century. The most interesting part of the complex is the **Bazilika svaté Markéty** (Church of St Margaret; open Mon–Sat 7am– 6pm).

This beautifully renovated church was remodelled in 1708–45 by Christoph Dienzenhofer and Kilián Ignaz. Most of the altar paintings are by Petr Brandl, while the ceiling was painted in 1719–21 by Jan Jakub Steinfels. Under the choir is an 11th-century pre-Romanesque crypt. Note the early carving preserved on the outside of the Church.

Bílá Hora

The site of the Battle of the White Mountain (Bílá Hora) is at the terminus of tramlines 8 and 22. Here, on 8 November 1620, the Protestant forces of Frederick V were defeated by the Imperial Catholic armies led by Johann Tserclaes Graf von Tilly. From this point until 1918 Bohemia became part of the Habsburg Empire and entered a period of

Catholic domination, disasterous for the Czech Protestant population but a blessing for Baroque architecture.

Just by the tram terminus is the attractive church of **Panny Marie Vítežné na Bílé hoře** ⑭ (Church of Our Lady of Victory). This early-18th-century Baroque building – erected in 1713 to commemorate the Catholic victory in 1620 – was designed by the Czech architect Jan Blažej Santini. If you can get inside (it is often closed), the dome frescos by Cosmas Damian Asam, Johann Adam Schöpf and Wenzl Lorenz Reiner are worth a look.

The site itself (take the road on the right just after the church and follow it uphill) is marked by a small monument in the middle of a field, reached by a footpath from either Nad višňovkou or Řepská. Although there is little to see, the view is extensive and the site can appear suitably desolate in bad weather. Looking north from the monument you can see the wall of the Obora hvězda (park) surrounding the star-shaped Letohrádek hvězda (*see below*).

Obora hvězda

Taking the tram back into town and alighting at the Vypich stop brings you to the edge of the park. Either walk diagonally across the green to the small gateway, or walk along Na vypichu to the main gate, just where it turns into Libocká (also close to the Petřiny tram terminus).

The park, with its tree-lined avenues, was laid out around one of the most interesting Renaissance buildings in the city, the **Letohrádek hvězda** ⑮ (open Tues–Sun, May–Sept 10am–6pm, Oct–Apr 10am–5pm; admission charge). The six-pointed structure was designed by Hans Tyrol and Bonifac Wohlmut in 1555 for Archduke Ferdinand of Tyrol. On the ground floor, as well as some beautiful stucco work on the ceilings, there are exhibits describing the palace and its restoration by Pavel Janák. In the basement is a huge model of the Battle of Bílá Hora, while on the first floor is a fascinating exhibition on the mystical significance of the star; unfortunately, like all the exhibits, only labelled in Czech. ❑

Map on page 168

To the north of Ruzyně and Břevnov is Divoká Šárka. This wild expanse of parkland was, like many other Prague parks, originally a hunting ground but is now a place to walk, cycle, and swim in the lakes.

LEFT: eating in Letná Park.

RESTAURANTS & BARS

Fraktal
Šmeralova 1
Tel: 732 156 096
Open: daily 11am–midnight. €
This somewhat run-down little bar-cum-music venue is a bit out of the way. However, it is friendly and welcoming, and a popular meeting place.

Hanavský Pavilon
Letenské sady 6
Tel: 233 323 641
Open: daily 11am–1am. €€€
An eccentric Neo-Baroque building, dating from the 1891 exposition, perched on the edge of the Letná Park escarpment, with a fabulous view. The traditional Czech menu comprises duck, pigeon and game dishes, along with a good selection of Moravian wines.

Letenský zámeček
Letenské sady 341
Tel: 233 378 200
Open: daily 11am–11pm. €–€€€
At the other end of the park from the Pavilon, this mansion has two expensive restaurants, but its main draw is the large beer garden.

● ● ● ● ● ● ● ● ● ● ● ● ● ●

Price includes a three-course dinner and a glass of wine or beer. €€€ *over 600 Kč,* €€ *300–600 Kč,* € *under 300 Kč.*

SMÍCHOV AND BARRANDOV

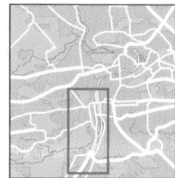

To the south of Malá Strana, these two previously industrial districts are home to a number of diverse attractions, from parkland and villas to film studios, a brewery and a huge new shopping centre.

To the south of Malá Strana is the district of Smíchov (Prague 5), a traditional working-class area that now shows off the spoils of capitalism in shiny office blocks and shopping centres *(see below)*. Industrialisation began early in the 19th century and gathered pace after the arrival of the railway, changing the district from one of scattered farmsteasd and fields to one of apartment blocks and factories. Notable industries still in place include the Staropramen brewery.

BELOW: the glass-clad Nový Smíchov shopping centre.

Kinsky Gardens and Villa

The short walk south from Malá Strana along Ujezd (also trams 6, 9 and 12) brings you to náměstí Kinských (Kinsky Square). This was previously called náměstí Sovětských tankistů after the Soviet tank (one of those that liberated Prague in 1945) that stood on display here. With the fall of Communism the tank became surplus to requirements and, after a period during which it was painted pink by David Černý, was removed.

Retail is detail

The Nový Smíchov shopping centre, designed by the French architect Jean Nouvel, is by far the largest and brashest mall in Prague. A world away from the small corner shops that traditionally served this part of town, this is 150,000 sq. metres (1,614,580 sq. ft) of modern retail heaven. The shops are generally those of high-street fame, with little to attract visitors who can find the same items in their home towns and cities. However, there is a large multiplex cinema, and a quick walk around will give you a much better idea of how young, contemporary Prague is faring than a few days spent on Hradčany.

To the west of the square lies the entrance to the **Kinského zahrada** ⑯ (Kinsky Gardens), part of the open space that spreads over Petřín Hill. This is one of the loveliest parks in Prague, quieter, wilder and with less people than other parts of Petřín. The steep, wooded hillside with numerous small paths rises above the villa gardens *(see below)*. The walk from here, over the top of the hill and down to the Strahovský klášter *(see page 97),* is very pleasant, giving excellent views over the river and city.

The **Letohrádek Kinských** (Kinsky Villa), a 19th-century mansion, has been carefully restored and is due to be reopened as an annexe of the National Museum to hold part of its enormous ethnographic collections (check with www.nm.cz for details). The villa is beautifully sited, looking down over the well-maintained lawns of the Kinsky Gardens.

Sv. Václav

South of here, along Štefánikova, is the late-19th-century church of **Sv.** Václav ⑰ (1881–5), rather dark and gloomy, designed by Antonín Barvitius. Behind the church is the small park of náměstí Října. On the northern side of the square, beside the church, is the **Portheimka**. This small mansion was built in the 18th century by Kilián Ignaz Dientzenhofer (one of the architects of Chrám sv. Mikuláše in nearby Malá Strana) as his town house. Some of the interior decoration was carried out by Václav Reiner.

Anděl

Štefánikova ends at **Anděl Metro,** ⑱ above which is the huge Nový Smíchov shopping centre *(see box opposite).* The Metro used to be known as Moskevská (Moscow) as a gesture of friendship towards the Soviet Union, and had a number of large murals showing triumphant workers striding into the future: ironic given what is now overhead.

Opposite the platforms are eight bronze reliefs, one showing two cosmonauts, another with a young girl waving flags marked Moskva and Praha.

Map on page 168

A bronze relief in Anděl metro station.

BELOW: the Bertramka Villa.

Just up from the Metro, on the corner of Plzeňská and Stroupež-nického, is the **Smíchovská Synagoga** (Smíchov Synagogue). It was founded in 1863, given a Modernist make-over in 1931 by L. Ehrmanna, and completely renovated and re-opened in 2004. The building also contains an interesting second-hand bookshop, Antikvariat Korouš.

Bertramka

Following Plzeňská up from Anděl you come to the glossy Mövenpick business hotel; on the hill above is the small but charming **Muzeum W.A. Mozarta Bertramka**  (open daily 9.30am–6pm; admission fee; www.bertramka.cz; trams 4, 7, 9 and 34). Previously the country villa of František Dušek and his wife, the singer Josefa Dušková, this was where Mozart stayed on his visits to Prague in 1787 and 1791. It was here he composed the aria *Bella mia fiamma, addio* from *Don Giovanni* for Josefa, and is allegedly where he completed the opera before its premiere in Prague. The villa was largely destroyed in a fire on New

Year's Eve 1872–3 and in 1941 was eventually reconstructed as before. The many famous musical visitors include Tchaikovsky, Vincent d'Indy and Leoš Janáček.

Inside, the villa has been turned into a museum, well displayed and all labelled in English. The first room has a cabinet of instruments, including an early clarinet and basset horn, which Mozart was chiefly responsible for introducing into the orchestra. In the next room is a real piece of Mozartiana, an elegant fortepiano by Ignatz Kober (Vienna, 1785–6), one of only three surviving instruments. Legend has it that Mozart played on this instrument in Prague in January 1787. Close by is a hammer piano (1807–10) used in the filming of *Amadeus*.

To complete the trio of keyboard instruments, towards the end of the exhibition is a large harpsichord (1722, the only surviving example example by Johann Heinrich Gräbner of Dresden); the connection with Mozart is a little tenuous, as it is claimed he might have played it during the autumn of 1787.

The Staropramen Brewery at Nádražní 84 has a bar and restaurant, and also offers a tour from its visitors centre that includes a beer tasting session (daily by prior arrangement; tel: 257 191 402; www.pivovary-staropramen.cz).

BELOW: meeting up in Barrandov.

There are numerous illustrations and documents lining the walls, all of which build up an interesting picture of Prague during Mozart's visits. On the more kitsch side is a small glass tablet in which a lock of Mozart's hair is encased.

Above the villa is a delightful garden, complete with a fish pond and a bust of Mozart. In the courtyard in front of the house is a small café, useful for a quick meal. The villa regularly holds concerts of Mozart's music (see the website for details), and the café opens late on those evenings.

Staropramen

On the other side of Anděl metro, down towards the river, is the enormous **Pivovary Staropramen** ⓴ (Staropramen Brewery), the largest in the city. Attached to the brewery is a pub and restaurant serving, of course, extremely good beer. It is also possible to go on a tour of the brewery *(see margin)*.

In the south of the district is **Smíchovské nádraží** (Smíchov Station), one of the first to be built in the city,

dating back to 1854. It was modernised in 1947 to designs by Jan Zázvorka and Jan Žák, and now has an imposing Socialist Realist façade.

Barrandov

Beyond Smíchov, on the edge of the city, is the Czech Hollywood, **Barrandov** (named after the 19th-century geologist Joachim Barrande). The huge **Barrandov Studio** ㉑ (www.barrandov.cz; bus 105 from Smíchovské nádraží to Lumiérů), perched on top of Barrandov Hill, were crucial for the development of the Czech film industry *(see page 57)*. They were designed by architect, director and cameraman Max Urban and built between 1931–4.

Close by, at the end of Barrandovská, is the **Terasy Barrandov** (Barandov Restaurant). Now abandoned and half derelict, this was once a glamorous restaurant and swimming complex tucked into the curve of the hill, overlooking the river. It was also designed by Max Urban and built in 1929–30 (the baths with their elegant diving boards were by Václav Kolátor). ❑

Maintaining the Betramka gardens.

LEFT:
the Terasy Barrandov restaurant building.

Map on page 168

RESTAURANTS

Il Giardino
Mövenpick Hotel, Mozartova 1
Tel: 257 154 262
Open: daily 5.30–11am, noon–11pm. €€€
This hotel is conveniently just below the Mozart Museum. Although the restaurant serves extremely well-regarded Mediterranean food, the experience is greatly heightened by the short cable-car ride it takes to get there (entry on the left of the lobby). The views over the southern part of the city are wonderful.

Olympia
Vítězná 7
Tel: 251 511 080
Open: daily 11am–midnight.
€–€€
A long-standing café given a make-over by the brewers Pilsner Urquell. On offer is a wide selection of traditional Czech dishes – including the inevitable duck and dumplings but with some more unusual dishes – and, of course, excellent Urquel from the tap.

● ● ● ● ● ● ● ● ● ● ● ● ● ●

Price includes a three-course dinner and a glass of wine or beer. €€€ *over 600 Kč,* €€ *300–600 Kč,* € *under 300 Kč.*

COMMUNIST PRAGUE

Prague was spared devastation during World War II, and little touched during the subsequent regime; here are some of the few architectural legacies of Communist rule

When the Communist Party took the reigns of power in 1948 there was little need to embark on a large-scale rebuilding of the city, as was necessary elsewhere in Europe. So, wisely, they left much untouched, if subsequently uncared for. Where they did make their mark was on the outskirts, with large-scale public housing projects of little architectural worth.

One of the central projects for which the Communist authorities can claim credit, however, was the rebuilding of the **Emmaus Monastery** *(see page 155)* with its elegant, curving concrete towers. Another spectacular project, if not one universally loved, was the **Žižkov Television Tower** *(inset; see page 191)* which does have a certain space-age appeal. The two department stores **Máj** (now Tesco) and **Kotva** are also quite successful buildings. However, not all projects were so well judged, the huge **Congress Centre** in Nusle is rightly considered an eyesore.

BELOW: Although the National Monument on Žižkov Hill was first built in 1929–30 it was remodelled under the Communists as a Tomb of the Unknown Soldier and as a mausoleum for Communist leaders; in doing so they gave it with a splendid series of bronze reliefs depicting valiant revolutionaries and workers.

THE METRO AND CITY INFRASTRUCTURE

One of the most noticeable legacies of the Communist era, at least as far as visitors are concerned, is the city's clean and efficient Metro. Much of Prague's integrated public transport system was already laid out by the time the Communist Party came to power in 1948. However, in the early 1960s it was decided to expand the network and in 1967 the government formally agreed to develop an underground rail system. The first line (C) was opened in 1974, coinciding with a major overhaul of the city trams, and the rest of the system was finished by 1985 (although there have been extensions to the three lines since). As a showcase of Czechoslovak engineering the system was finished with a great deal of care; it was given a bold modern design and some of the stations are worth a look in their own right (try Anděl on line B for its Communist era bronze plaques). The skill with which it was built is still evident today in its smooth operation.

BELOW: The Hotel International (now the Crowne Plaza) is perhaps the most striking example of Stalinist architecture in the city. Its monolithic structure, crowned with a spire and red star, is decorated with Socialist Realist friezes. The impressive, if somewhat heavy, interior is beautifully finished.

ABOVE: From the "schemes" of Glasgow to the *banlieue* of Paris, the 1960s and 70s saw governments of all political hues look to high-rise, mass produced blocks of flats as a universal panacea to the problem of providing social housing. Prague was no exception and the outskirts of the city have large swathes of unbeloved *paneláky* (prefab concrete blocks). To see them, take a visit to Prague 11 to the southeast (Metro line C to Hajé).

VINOHRADY AND ŽIŽKOV

The two eastern suburbs of Vinohrady and Zizkov
form one of the most diverse parts of the city,
from elegant *fin de siècle* apartments to
local pubs, and from ivy-covered cemeteries
to the imposing National Monument

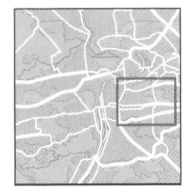

The eastern districts of the city are fascinating, and quite a change from the Gothic- and Baroque-dominated areas in the centre of the city. They also vary in feel from an ex-pat, arty chic to gritty working-class sleaze. Impressive monuments are not lacking either, the east being home to two of the most imposing in the city, the National Monument, with its huge statue of Jan Žižka, and the Žižkov Television Tower.

Vinohrady

The district of Vinohrady gets its name from the vineyards that once thrived here. Today it is a pleasant, lively area, full of young, upwardly mobile Czechs, who live in the *fin de siècle* apartment blocks that make up much of the area.

The district is bordered by two parks, both within walking distance of náměstí Míru Metro, one in the north, the other to the south. The **Riegrovy sady** ㉒ (Reiger Gardens) to the north is a large, well laid-out park along the slopes of the hill, which offers a beautiful view across the whole city right up to Hradčany and the castle. Numerous local pubs with good basic food and beer can be found alongside the park.

To the south is the **Havlíčkovy sady** ㉓ (Havlíček Gardens), an-

other pleasant green space with views across the city. Also here is the **Gröbova vila**, a 19th-century villa by the architect Antonín Barvitius.

Sv. Ludmila and náměstí Míru

At the heart of Vinohrady is the large square of **náměstí Míru** ㉔ (Metro of the same name, also trams 4, 16, 22 and 34). Lined with late-19th-century apartments, and also with the newly restored Art Nouveau **divadlo Na vinohradech**

Map on page 168

LEFT: stained glass in sv. Ludmila.
BELOW: the palác Akropolis.

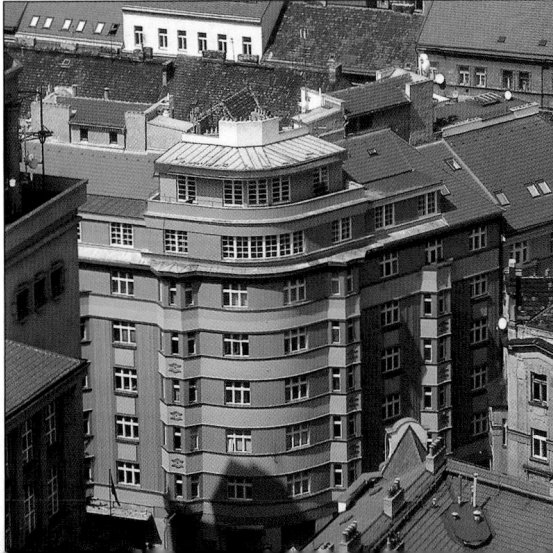

(Vinohrady Theatre). At the centre of the square is the large Neo-Gothic church of **Svatá Ludmila**. Built in 1888–93 and designed by Josef Mocker, it has some interesting stained glass (as with a number of other Prague churches it is not often open but you can see the interior through the glass in the porch).

Sv. Ludmila towers over náměstí Míru.

Church of the Holy Heart

On náměstí Jiřího z Poděbrad (by the Metro station of the same name) is the most unusual Modernist building in Prague, **Nejsvětějšího Srdce Páně** N (Church of the Holy Heart; open for mass). Designed by the architect Josip Plečnik (who was responsible for the restoration of St Vitus, *see page 82*), it was built in 1928–32, early considering its eclectic style that looks forward to the later developments of Postmodernism. The monolithic structure uses elements of Classical and Egyptian styles on what is a rather uncompromising exterior, impressive but in some ways hard to like. However, it is enlivened by the huge glass clock on the narrow tower flanked by obelisks.

BELOW: the Church of the Holy Heart.

The interior (unfortunately often closed to visitors) is, unlike the forbidding façade, high and spacious with a coffered ceiling. The tower is climbed via a ramp to the clock – double-sided so the light streams through from one side of the tower to the other – and peering out through the glass faces gives a spectacular view over the city.

Modernist Churches

For those in search of more Modernist churches two other treats lie in the east of the city: Josef Gočár and Alois Wachsman's **Sv. Václav** N, and Pavel Janák's **Husův sbor** N.

The closest of the two is Janák's Hussite congregational building, reached from náměstí Míru along Korunní and then by turning right down Kladská. The building, built 1931–3, is designed with both living quarters and a prayer hall. Perhaps of most interest to visitors will be the monument on the northern side that commemorates the use of the tower by Czech resistance fighters as the site of a radio transmitter during World War II.

The church of Sv. Václav (1929–30) is actually in the district of Vršovice, to the south. On náměstí Svatopluka Čecha (trams 4, 22 and 34), the striking building is set into the contour of the hill. The high central tower makes a dramatic statement, while the interior is light and airy, cleverly lit by a series of stained-glass windows on a series of terraced roofs.

Žižkov

A sometimes seedy district of run-down apartment blocks, Žižkov (Prague 3) lies to the north of Vinohrady and stretches out to the eastern edge of the city. Its working-class credentials are well established and it was at one time a hotbed of sedition. It is also famous for its huge number of basic local pubs (more than any other district of Prague), not all of which are welcoming or salubrious; one notable exception, however, is U vystře-lenýho oka (The Shot-Out Eye), named after the Hussite leader – Jan Žižka *(see box below)* – whose statue towers above.

The Television Tower

On Mahlerovy sady (Mahler Park), dominating the entire district – and much of the city – is the **Televizní vysílač Praha ㉘** (Prague Television Tower; open daily 10am–11pm; admission charge; www.tower.cz). At 216 metres (708 ft) and with a boldly modern (almost science-fiction-inspired) design based on three interlocked towers, this is the most adventurous piece of architecture (by Václav Aulický and Jiří Kozák) of the Communist era. Inspired by the similar tower on Alexanderplatz in Berlin, in an unpopular move it was built on the site of an old Jewish cemetery (used between 1786 and 1890).

Work began on construction in 1985 and the finishing touches were only made in 1991 after the fall of the Communist regime; although before then it had been allegedly used for blocking foreign broadcasts from the West. Since then the tower has acquired a number of mutant, rather alien, babies crawling up the steel tubes, courtesy of David Černý *(see also pages 150, 169 and 182).*

Map on page 168

Local artist David Černý has acquired a degree of notoriety with his, often humorous and scatalogical, works. For more examples take a look at his amusing website (www.david cerny.cz).

BELOW: mutant babies on the TV Tower.

The Hussite Hero

The heroic Jan Žižka, after whom the district of Žižkov was named in 1877, had extensive military experience, including fighting for the English at the battle of Agincourt in 1415. He was the chosen leader of the popular movement after the Hussite uprising on 30 July 1419. Having conquered Emperor Sigismund's army and captured Prague after the battle of Vítkov Hill (present-day Žižkov) in 1421, he erected the fortress at Tábor, from which the radical Táborites get their name. Despite losing both eyes in battle, Žižka did go on to secure religious liberty for the Hussites.

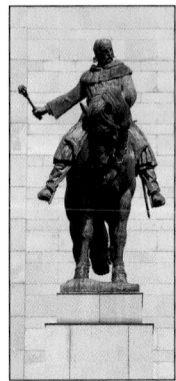

The enormous statue of Jan Žižka in front of the National Monument.

It is possible to take the lift up the viewing platform at 93 metres (305 ft), from where there is an awe-inspiring view over the entire city. The cube-like rooms suspended on the towers each have an annotated map pointing out what you can see, as well as an interesting series of photographs on the wall showing the construction of the tower. Below the viewing platform is a decent restaurant with the same astounding views *(see page 195)*.

Akropolis

Easily visible from the tower (looking north) is a colourful apartment block on the nearby corner of Kubelíkova and Víta nejedléno. This is the **palác Akropolis** (www.palacakropolis.cz), an arts centre set in the pre-war Akropolis theatre. The centre has a concert hall, cinema, theatre and exhibition space. Notable for putting on an eclectic selection of groups and acts, especially World Music performers, this is one of Prague's more exciting music venues. There is also a café, bar and the Akropolis Restaurant with decent, cheap food. You might also want to check out www.radioakropolis.cz for online streamed music.

National Monument

Also to the north and dominating Žižkov Hill above Husitská is the **Národní památník** ㉙ (National Monument; if coming from elsewhere in Žižkov, walk down Husitská and just before the railway bridge take U památníku on the right, which will take you up the hill, otherwise bus 133 from Florenc will take you to the same spot). The National Monument is an immense granite-faced cube containing the Tomb of the Unknown Soldier (closed to the public). In front of it stands one of the biggest equestrian statues in the world, the monument to the Hussite leader Jan Žižka.

On the way up the hill you will pass the rather lacklustre **Army Museum** (open Tues–Sun 10am–6pm; admission charge; www.militarymuseum.cz). The exhibits tell the story of the Czechoslovak army from its inception in 1918 up to World War II.

BELOW: the revolutionary bronze doors of the National Memorial.

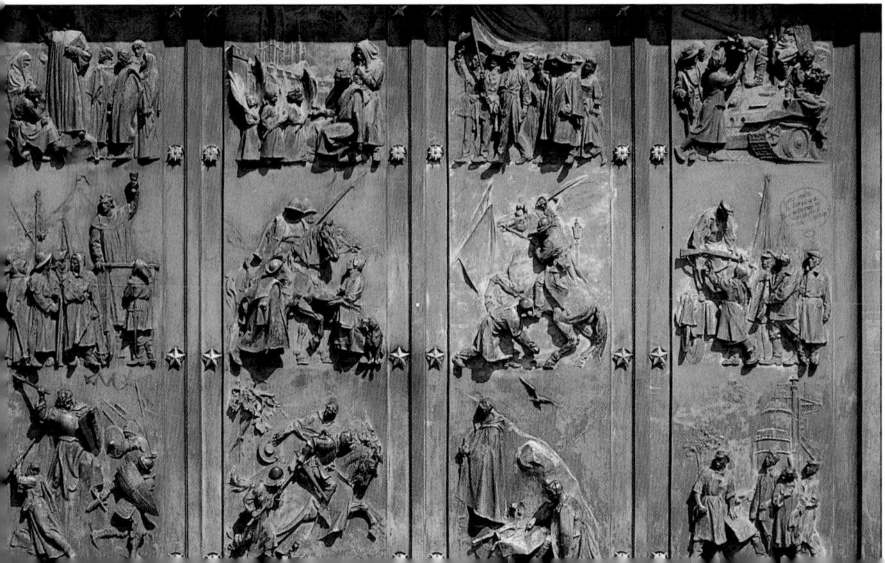

Keep on climbing through the wooded park and you will come to a series of steps that lead up to a wide esplanade, at the head of which is the Žižka statue, and behind that the National Monument. The enormous equestrian statue (given greater height by being placed on a granite platform), by Bohumil Kafka, was commissioned after a competition in 1925 (one of a series that had created bad feeling and controversy about how to commemorate Žižka's victory). Only the Stalin monument, which had dominated Letná Hill until it was demolished in 1963, was bigger than that of Žižka.

The granite monolith of the National Monument itself was initially designed by Jan Zázvorka and built in 1929–30. However, after World War II the building was redesigned and used as both a Tomb of the Unknown Soldier and as a final resting place of worthies of the Communist Party, including Klement Gottwald, whose body was preserved in a similar way to that of Lenin in Red Square in Moscow.

Gottwald is now in Olšany Cemetery *(see below)* and visitors can no longer get into the building. However, the legacy of the Communist redesign can be seen in the numerous reliefs and statues of heroic workers and revolutionary soldiers that adorn the bronze doors.

The complex now has a rather neglected air, and there are few other places in Prague where the ghost of the Communist years can be so easily felt *(see also pages 186–7)*. However, the walk up through the park is pleasant and the views from the top of the hill are wonderful.

Cemeteries

The other sites of interest in Žižkov lie further out, but are easily accessible by either tram or Metro. The first of these is **Hřbitov Olšany ③⓪** (Olšany Cemetery; open Nov–Feb 8am–5pm, Mar–Apr and Oct 8am–6pm, May–Sept 8am–7pm; Flora Metro or trams 11, 16 and 26). This huge necropolis has been the preferred burial spot of many famous Czechs (particularly if they have not managed to get a spot in Vyšehrad,

Map on page 168

After Klement Gottwald's body had been placed in the National Memorial things did not go entirely to plan. Despite the best efforts of scientists the corpse started to decompose and it eventually had to be cremated.

BELOW:
Kafka's grave in the New Jewish Cemetery.

Dr FRANZ KAFKA

1883–1924

יום ג' ר"ח סיון תרפ"ד לב"ע
הל הבחור המפואר מור אנשיל ע"ה
בן הנעלה כ"ר העניך קאפקא נ"י
ושם אמו יטל
ת נ צ ב ה

Map on page 168

Háje metro station (close to some of the most extensive areas of paneláky) was previously called, in a Moscow-pleasing move, Kosmonautů to honour Soviet space heroes.

BELOW:
high-rise *paneláky*.

see page 161). Wonderfully Gothic in parts with higgledy piggledy graves, all slightly overgrown. Among the famous people buried here are Josef Mánes, František Bílek and Josef Lada. However, perhaps the most venerated grave is that of Jan Palach *(see page 148),* whose body was moved here 1990. Palach is buried near the main entrance on Vinohradská. Also here is what must be one of the most overblown tombs, that of Rodina Hrdličkova; a sculptural group with a woman pleading with a man in uniform not to follow an angel up to heaven.

Just beyond this cemetery is the **Židovské Hřbitovy** ③ (New Jewish Cemetery; open Mon–Thur and Sun, Oct–Mar 9am–4pm, Apr–Sept 9am–5pm, Fri 9am–2pm; male visitors must wear yarmulkes, skullcaps, which are available from the gatehouse; Želivského Metro or trams 11, 16 and 26). It is just as impressive as the Olšany Cemetery, perhaps even more so with its attractive, tree-lined avenues of graves overgrown with ivy. Looking at the headstones, you realise just how wealthy and important the local Jewish community was before World War II, from owners of industry to doctors and lawyers, and that, ironically, many of them were German-speakers (most of the inscriptions are in either Hebrew or German).

Many people visit to see the grave of Franz Kafka, usually covered in flowers and notes (follow the signs leading you to block 21). However, the plain Cubist headstone is not the most impressive; look, for instance, for the striking Art Nouveau peacock on the headstone of painter Max Horb (block 19).

Paneláky

To the east and south-east of Vinohrady and Žižkov there is little of specific interest to visitors. The areas from Prague 4 (Podolí and Hodkovičky) across to Prague 11 (Chodov) are dominated by *paneláky*, prefabricated concrete tower blocks that were put up in the 1960s and 70s as a solution to a chronic housing shortage and now merely form a characterless and uniform urban sprawl *(see also page 187).* ❑

RESTAURANTS, CAFÉS AND PUBS

Il Conte Deminka
Škrétova 1
Tel: 224 224 915
Open: Mon–Fri 8am–midnight, Sat 11am–midnight, Sun 11am–11pm. €€–€€€
This grand, if rather faded, *fin de siècle* dining room is home to a reasonable Italian restaurant. The large menu has a wide variety of pasta, and an extensive list of Italian wine.

Pizzeria Grosseto
Francouzská 2/náměstí Míru
Tel: 224 252 778
Open: daily 11.30am–11pm. €–€€
A friendly, welcoming place on the corner of náměstí Míru. It serves some of the best pizza in Prague (all freshly cooked in a wood-burning oven) and is very popular with local residents and office workers. If you enjoy this one you might want to look out for their branches in Dejvice (Jugoslávských partyzánů 8) and Průhonice (Květnové náměstí 11).

Radost FX
Bělehradská 120
Tel: 224 254 776
Open: Mon–Fri 8am–3am, Sat–Sun 10am–4am. €€
Connected to the popular club of the same name is this great vegetarian restaurant (hence the late opening times). A globally ranging menu offers delicious food from the Mediterranean

to Mexico via China. A real bonus for vegetarians visiting Prague.

Restaurace Akropolis
Kubelíkova 27
Tel: 296 330 990
Open: Mon–Fri 10am–midnight, Sat–Sun 4pm–midnight. €
Part of the Akropolis arts venue in Žižkov, this newly reopened restaurant was designed by František Skála. A good selection of straightforward food, from pancakes to steaks, and some good vegetarian dishes; they even have a menu for dogs.

Restaurace a salónek
Žižkovská televizní věž, Mahlerovy sady1
Tel: 267 005 778
Open: daily 11am–11.30pm. €€–€€€
This restaurant is 66 metres up the Žižkov Television Tower. The food is decent – a selection of international dishes – and the draught beer is remarkably cheap, but what really sells it is the extraordinary view you get over the city.

Restaurant Atelier
Na Kovárně 8

Tel: 271 721 866
Open: Mon–Sat midday–midnight. €€–€€€
Just to the east of Havlickovy sady is this lovely modern restaurant serving French and Mediterranean dishes, all cooked to a very high standard. As well as a summer terrace for dining outside, there is an impressive list of French wines.

Restaurant Myslivna
Jagellonská 21
Tel: 222 723 252
Open: 11.30am–11.30pm. €€
Not far from the TV Tower is this restaurant for carnivores. Specialising in game and hung with hunting trophies, if it is furry and lives in the Bohemian forest there is a good chance you can eat it here. Specialities include boar and venison – different bits cooked in various ways with different sauces – and there is an excellent selection of classic Czech dishes.

Shakespeare and Sons
Krymská 12
Tel: 271 740 839
Open: daily midday–midnight. €
An excellent English-language bookshop with a pleasant café-bar attached. Laid back with good coffee and tasty beer, they also hold occasional book readings.

Taj Mahal
Škrétova 10

Tel: 224 225 566
Open: Mon–Fri 11.30am–11.30pm, Sat–Sun 1–11.30pm. €€
If you are desperate for a taste of Indian food as cooked back home (Brick Lane or Bradford that is), head for the Taj Mahal. Here are all the usual favourites, from chicken *tikka* to lamb *korma* and *alu gobi* to *mattar panir*, as well as *nan*, *paratha* and *kulfi*.

U vystřelenýho oka
U božích bojouníků 3
Tel: 222 540 465
Open: Mon–Sat 4.30pm–1am. €
The Shot-Out Eye is one of the best pubs in Žižkov, and there is a lot of competition. Excellent beer is served up in bizarre and tatty surroundings, all authentically smoky and generally with loud music playing.

BELOW: dining at the Restaurace a salónek.

AROUND PRAGUE

The area around Prague has long been important historically as a link between the capital and the rest of Bohemia. In this countryside of deep river valleys, sweeping plateaux and vast forests, there are any number of towns, villages and architectural wonders that are certainly worth a day trip after you have had your fill of the city

One of the most impressive sights near Prague is that of **Karlštejn Castle ❶** (open Nov–Jan and Mar Tues–Sun 9am–midday, 1–3pm; Apr and Oct 9am–midday, 1–4pm; May–Jun and Sept 9am–midday, 12.30–5pm; Jul–Aug 9am– midday, 12.30–6pm; admission charge; www.hradkarlstejn.cz). Some 30 km (19 miles) south-west of Prague, it is stormed by thousands of visitors every year. They achieve what their predecessors never managed, for the great fortress, protected by its massive walls and a series of protruding cliffs, was impregnable to attackers. But Karlštejn's builder, Emperor Charles IV, did not intend the castle to be a military stronghold; strategically speaking it would have served no useful purpose. It was planned solely to safeguard the holy relics and coronation insignia of the kingdom.

In medieval times these relics were of immense significance: they included what are said to be two thorns from Jesus's crown, a fragment of the sponge soaked in vinegar offered to Him on the Cross, a tooth of St John the Baptist, and the arm of St Anne. To possess such treasures was seen as a sign of God's favour, a blessing for the Emperor and his subjects. The collection of relics was presented twice a year for public worship: on the Friday after Easter, the Day of the Holy Relics, and on 29 November, the anniversary of Charles IV's death. Mass is still celebrated in the Chapel of the Cross where the precious items are conserved.

The castle is reached by road along the attractive wooded valley of the River Berounka, a route also followed by the main Prague-Pilzeň railway line; local trains from Prague's Smíchov station (Metro line B) call at Karlštejn station.

Map on page 200

PRECEDING PAGES: Karlštejn castle.
LEFT: the Cathedral of St Barbara, Kutná Hora.
BELOW: the Chapel of St Catharine, Karlštejn.

After so much splendour, it is almost a relief to gaze out from the superb vantage point of the castle over the lovely Bohemian countryside all around. The limestone (karst) landscape in which Karlštejn is set is characterised by forests rich in wildlife, numerous lakes, and fissures and caverns: 12km (7 miles) to the west, the caves at Koněprusy were used as workshops by medieval counterfeiters.

From Karlštejn village the way to the castle leads steeply uphill for 1.5 km (1 mile). Horse-drawn carriages make the climb easier.

Visitors to the castle must join a guided tour, available in a number of languages. Tour 1 concentrates on the Imperial Palace, Tour 2 on churches and chapels, including the Chapel of the Cross. Taking a tour may restrict your freedom but will teach you much about the castle's history and significance. Karlštejn was built in the 14th century, possibly under the direction of Matthew of Arras, architect of St Vitus's Cathedral; it was modified in Renaissance times and then fell into near decay. Much of what we see today is a zealous late-19th-century reconstruction by the conservation architect Josef Mocker, who attempted to return the castle to its original Gothic appearance.

Tour 1 explores the interiors of the Imperial Palace and the Marian Tower. They include the Great Hall,

the Audience Chamber and the private apartments of the Emperor and his wife, and are lavishly appointed with furnishings from the 14th to the 19th century.

Tour 2, which needs to be booked in advance, takes in the castle towers, the lapidary museum, the library with its exhibition on Karlštejn's reconstruction, as well as the relics and the magnificent interiors in which they are housed, the ornamentation of which is almost beyond imagination. In the **Church of Our Lady**, Charles's court painter, Nikolaus Wurmser, portrayed the Emperor with the relics of the Passion beneath a heaven filled with an angelic host.

The **Chapel of St Catherine**, adorned with semi-precious stones, is where Charles IV spent time in meditation. Above the door is a portrait of the Emperor with the second of his four wives, Anna von Schwednitz. The Chapel of the Cross

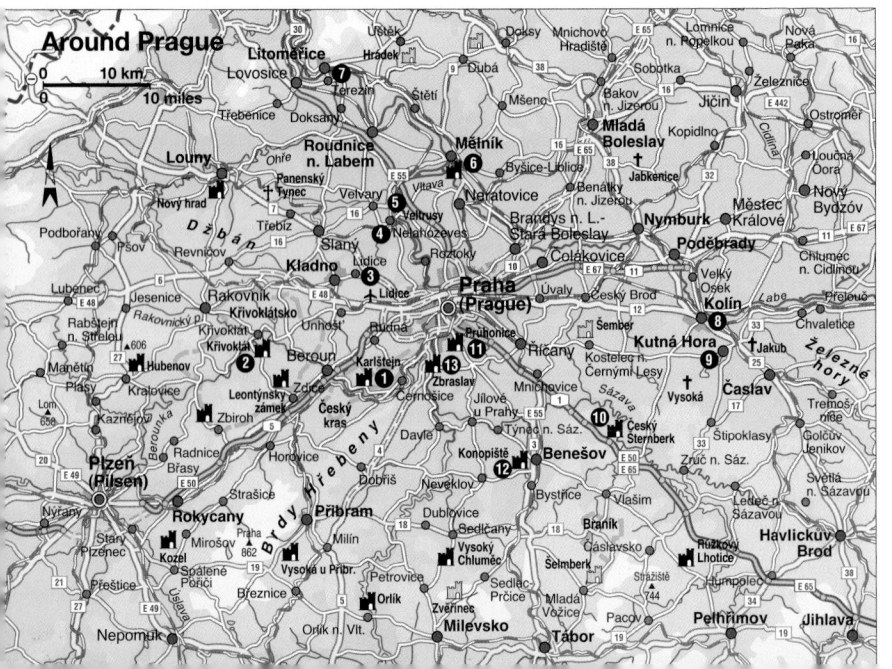

itself – renovated and once again open to the public – is decorated with over 2,000 semi-precious stones. It is divided into two sections by a golden railing; the precious relics were preserved in the sanctuary, which only the Emperor and the priests were allowed to enter.

The walls are covered with over 100 paintings by Master Theodoric, dating from the mid-14th century; more relics are set in the picture frames. The themes include the heavenly host of apostles and saints.

Křivoklát Castle

Set among seemingly endless forests, which were once the favourite hunting grounds of kings and emperors, is **Křivoklát Castle** ❷ (open Jan–Feb by appointment; Mar–Apr, Oct–Dec Sat–Sun 9am–midday, 1–3pm; Jun–Aug Tues–Sun 9am–midday, 1–5pm; May and Sept 9am–midday, 1–4pm; admission charge; www.krivoklat.cz). It is everything a medieval fortress should be, with sturdy walls, proud towers, an arcaded courtyard, Gothic interiors, dungeons and a torture chamber.

Occupying a fine defensive site some 60 km (37 miles) from Prague, high above the meanders of the River Berounka, Křivoklát is one of the oldest and most important castles in Bohemia, and although much restored in the late 19th and early 20th century, it remains full of the atmosphere of ancient times, more so than the far more famous and popular castle at Karlštejn further down the Berounka.

The castle's origins go back to the very beginnings of the Bohemian state, to the 9th century, when the early Přemyslid princes built a lodge here as a base for their hunting expeditions. The lodge developed into a timber fortress, then in the 13th century into a stone castle, famous for the lavishness of its festivities. Charles IV spent his early childhood in Křivoklát, returning here with his French wife, Blanche of Valois. When she was about to give birth to their daughter Margaret, he had hundreds of nightingales released into the surrounding woods to cheer her with their song.

No such distraction was provided to the prisoners languishing in the castle dungeons; among their number was the English alchemist Edward Kelley, locked up for failing to turn base metal into gold, and who broke a leg in an unsuccessful attempt at escape.

The castle tour reveals much of interest; the outstanding feature is perhaps the lovely Gothic chapel, the work of a master architect from Frankfurt. In addition there is a Knights' Hall, a royal palace, a richly stocked library and a torture chamber named after the unfortunate Bishop Jan Augusta whose beliefs were cruelly put to the test here. The quarters lived in by the last owners, the princely Fürstenberg family, are particularly fascinating, and the views from the ramparts are superb.

In the Church of Our Lady at Karlštejn.

BELOW:
Křivoklát Castle.

Lidice

Twenty-five km (16 miles) north-west of Prague is the former mining village of **Lidice**  (open daily, Feb–Mar, Oct–Dec 9am-4pm, Apr–Sept 9am–6pm; admission charge; www.lidice-memorial.cz), the site of a World War II massacre carried out by the SS in retaliation for the assassination of *Reichsprotektor* Reinhard Heydrich by Czechoslovak parachutists sent from Britain. Lidice was wrongly thought by the Germans to have harboured the assassins; on the night of 9 June 1942 the inhabitants were rounded up, the 192 adult men shot at dawn, the women and children sent to concentration camps. Burnt to the ground, its remains bulldozed, Lidice was declared by the Nazis to have been erased from history.

The effect, however, was quite different, with the village becoming a worldwide symbol of Nazi terror and Czech torment. After the war a new Lidice was built next to the ruins of the old, an extensive rose garden was planted and the site became a memorial to the dead. A small museum shows poignant films of the destruction and rebuilding of the village.

At the end of World War II, many countries around the world renamed villages Lidice as a symbol of resistance to Nazi destruction. Towns as far afield as Mexico bear this Czech name.

BELOW: the memorial at Lidice.

Nelahozeves

The unpretentious, and to most foreigners, near-unpronounceable village of **Nelahozeves**  on the banks of the Vltava some 27 km (17 miles) north of Prague, boasts not one but two major attractions; on a bluff overlooking the river stands a splendid Renaissance castle, while on the village green below the castle is the humble home where Antonín Dvořák, perhaps the most famous of all Czech composers, was born.

In the early 19th century, the **Rodiště Antonína Dvořáka** (Dvořák birthplace) was the residence of a Mr Dvořák, the local butcher and innkeeper and a prominent member of the village band. The eldest of his nine children, young Antonín was expected to take over his father's business, but luckily the musical talent he had presumably inherited from his parent was recognised by the village schoolmaster and he was sent to the organ school in Prague. The house contains memorabilia of the great composer, whose other interests were pigeon-fancying and trainspotting, the latter facilitated by the proximity of the main Prague–Dresden railway line running parallel to the river.

The Zámek

The **Zámek** (open Tues–Sun 9am–midday, 1–5pm; admission charge; www.lobkowicz.org) at Nelahozeves is more of a great country house than a castle. It was begun in 1552 by Florián Griespek of Griespak, an ambitious courtier who duties included supervision of all royal building work in Bohemia. He was thus well placed to employ the kingdom's best builders and craftsman, and his residence, though never fully completed (one wing remained unbuilt), is an outstanding example of Bohemian Renaissance architecture, with bold sgraffito work and a partly arcaded courtyard. In the 17th century it passed into the hands of a branch of the princely Lobkowicz family, though they mostly used it as the headquarters of their local estates rather than as a principal residence. Confiscated by the state in the late 1940s, it was restored at a painfully slow pace until its restitution to Lobkowicz ownership after 1989.

The family have striven to make Nelahozeves an example of how the run-down and neglected architectural heritage of Bohemia can be restored to its former glory; the castle is now not only a glittering architectural gem in its own right, but a splendid container of the family's extraordinarily rich collections of furniture, sculpture, ceramics, porcelain, glass, arms and armour, and, above all, paintings.

These treasures are displayed in no fewer than 25 exhibition rooms, some of which are of outstanding quality themselves; two storeys high, the **Knights' Hall** features a superb Renaissance fireplace, a stucco ceiling of great exuberance, and fascinating traces of wall-paintings. The array of Old Master paintings is the equal of many a national collection, and in fact some of the pictures now on show here were the pride and joy of the National Gallery in Prague, notably *Haymaking*, the only one of Pieter Brueghel the Elder's cycle of the months of the year which is in private ownership. This alone would make a visit to Nelahozeves worthwhile, but there is much else besides, including works by Cranach, Veronese, Rubens, Velázquez and Canaletto. Portraits of kings, queens and emperors emphasise the close connections with royalty enjoyed by the Lobkowicz family.

Many family members were musical; their court orchestra had a high reputation, and one of their number, Prince Josef Franz Maximilian, was a friend and patron of Beethoven, who dedicated numerous works to him. The castle's music room exhibits a rich collection of

Map on page 200

Among the gems in the Zámek's music collection are Mozart's annotated score of Handel's Messiah, and two 'cellos, one by Stadivari and the other by Guarneri.

BELOW:
Nelahozeves Zámek.

musical instruments and memorabilia, including many original scores.

In the Czech Republic, the offerings in the souvenir shops attached to visitor attractions such as castles can be very disappointing. The shop at Nelahozeves is a notable exception, with a tempting range of tasteful products inspired by the castle's treasures.

Veltrusy

Among the riverside meadows on the far bank of the River Vltava from Nelahozeves stands a very different sort of structure from the grand palace erected by Florián Griespek. **Veltrusy** ❺ is of much later date, a Baroque country house built by the Choteks, an old Bohemian family whose line goes back much further than that of the upstart Griespek. In more recent times, a Count Chotek was responsible for much of the beautification of 19th-century Prague, while his granddaughter Sophie married the Habsburg Archduke Franz Ferdinand and was assassinated with him in Sarajevo in 1914. Veltrusy is laid

Looking up at the tower of Mělník castle.

BELOW: Mělník, high above the river.

out on an intriguing star-shaped plan, centred on a domed rotunda which is pierced by a *sala terrena* allowing the landscape to flow right through the building; on one side is an English-style informal park with grand old trees, on the other an open Baroque courtyard with stairways and fine sculpture. Along with many other riverside properties, Veltrusy fell victim to the terrible floods of 2002, and restoration work is likely to last for several years before visitors can be readmitted.

Mělník

Visible from far away, the little hilltop town of **Mělník** ❻ overlooks the confluence of the rivers Vltava and Elbe some 39 km (24 miles) due north of Prague. This prominent site was fortified as early as the 9th century by the Slav tribe known as the Pšovs, who were great rivals to the Přemyslid dynasty in Prague. But harmony was assured when the Pšov princess Ludmila married the Přemyslid prince Bořivoj and their territories were united. Thereafter the castle at Mělník served as a dowager residence for the princesses of Bohemia.

The settlement flourished as a trading centre and also became known for its viticulture, especially after 1365, when Charles IV ordered vines to be brought from Burgundy and planted here. Not only was the red Burgundy-type wine popular at the Imperial court, it brought considerable revenue to the town. Mělník continued to flourish, particularly during the mid-15th-century, when it was favoured by the minor nobleman George of Poděbrady, who rose to become King of Bohemia. It then fell into decline; the castle changed owners more than once, and was rebuilt and altered on several occasions.

During the Baroque era it acquired its present character as a *zámek*, or princely residence. The prestige that

Mělník enjoyed in the Middle Ages never returned, however, as its new owners, the Lobkowicz family, preferred to live in Prague. The town's growth stagnated, though viticulture continued to prosper.

The architecture of the **castle** (open daily 10am–5pm, by tour only; admission charge; www.melnik-lobkowicz.cz) reflects its historical development, each of the three main wings being characterised by a different style. In the west wing the Gothic influence is dominant, in the north the Renaissance is evident in the arcaded walks and ornamental facades, while in the south the opulent Baroque style unfolds.

The old town centre is quite picturesque. Framed by a curving line of arcaded town houses, the market square has an attractive fountain celebrating the grape harvest. The clock tower of the twin-gabled town hall and the **Church of the Fourteen Auxiliary Saints** complete the harmonious picture. On the far side of the square, a busy street leads down to the Prague Gate and the remains of the town fortifications.

Terezín

The Baroque fortress town of **Terezín** ➐ (www.pamatnik-terezin.cz), 60 km (37 miles) north-west of Prague, stands guard over the northern approaches to the capital. With elaborate moated defences, a chequerboard pattern of intersecting streets lined with cheerless barrack-like buildings, it was established in 1780 by Austrian Emperor Josef II to defend Bohemia against attack from Prussia, and given the German name Theresienstadt in honour of his mother Empress Maria Theresa.

Soon redundant as a fortress, and simply bypassed by the Prussian army when it did attack almost a century later in 1866, Terezín achieved notoriety when it was used by the Nazis during World War II as a detention centre for Jews, first from Germany, then from Bohemia and Moravia. Although Terezín was not an extermination camp as such, most of those who did not die here of disease or starvation (and many did) were doomed to be sent off to more lethal camps such as Auschwitz.

In one of the cells at Terezín.

BELOW: the infamous gates at Terezín camp.

Some 140,000 people passed through Terezín, which also had the bizarre distinction of being proclaimed a "model camp" by the Nazis; a widely shown propaganda film was called *The Führer Gives the Jews a Town* and even Red Cross inspectors were misled about the place's real purpose.

Despite the grim conditions, the presence here of numerous intellectuals and creative people of all kinds meant that the town had an extraordinarily vibrant cultural life, with classical concerts, opera performances, and even a jazz band known as the Ghetto Swingers. The children's opera *Brundibar* was staged dozens of times, though another opera, *The Emperor of Atlantis*, was forbidden because it was too obviously a satire on Hitler.

Visitors today can see numerous exhibits documenting Terezín's past. Especially illuminating is the **Muzeum Ghetta** (Ghetto Museum; open daily, Apr–Sept 9am–6pm; Oct–Mar 9am–5.30pm; admission charge) just off the main square. Equally chilling is a tour of the

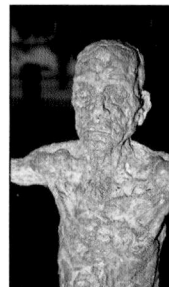

A Sculpture at the Terezín memorial.

BELOW: the wonderful roof in the Cathedral of St Barbara.

Malá pevnost (Small Fortress; open daily, Apr–Sept 8am–6pm, Oct–Mar 8am–4.30pm; admission charge) just south of the town. This grim prison was used by the Austrians to incarcerate political opponents of the Habsburg regime; Gavrilo Princip, the assassin of Archduke Franz Ferdinand was imprisoned here, his death from tuberculosis no doubt hastened by damp walls and poor food. However severe the conditions in Austrian times, they were as nothing compared to those imposed by the Gestapo during the occupation, when the fortress harboured members of the Czech resistance. In the immediate postwar period, it was the turn of Czechoslovak Germans to suffer, several thousand of whom were interned here.

Kolín

Just under 60km (37 miles) due east of Prague, **Kolín** is a rather nondescript industrial town on the banks of the River Labe. However, it makes a convenient stopping point on the way to or from Kutná Hora, and has a fine main square with a Renaissance town hall as well as the splendid Gothic Church of **St Bartholomew**, the glorious choir of which was the work of Petr Parléř.

The name of the town's most famous son is held in high esteem by brass-band fans all around the world; Czech bandmasters had a virtual monopoly on Austria-Hungary's military bands, and supreme among them was František Kmoch, born here in 1848. His memory is honoured every year in June, when oompah enthusiasts from around the world converge on Kolín and the air is filled of the cheerful sound of trumpets, trombones, and tubas.

Kutná Hora

Nowadays a quiet little place, **Kutná Hora** , 70 km (45 miles) east of Prague, was one of the

busiest and most prosperous cities of medieval Bohemia, thanks to its extraordinarily productive silver deposits. From the 13th century on, miners trekked here from all over Europe, particularly from Germany, hoping to make their fortune. A royal mint was set up, and at the height of its prosperity the town was one of the continent's most populous cities, able to fund the construction of fine buildings to rival those of the capital.

The Hussite Wars brought this era to an end, and many of the German miners fled. Silver was still mined, but then richer seams were found elsewhere, both in Europe and in the New World. Kutná Hora became something of a ghost town, with less than a third of its former population. However, many fine edifices from the glory days remain, and the combination of this rich building heritage with the town's unique history has resulted in its designation as a UNESCO World Heritage Site.

Chrám sv. Barbory

Kutná Hora's pride is the mammoth **Chrám sv. Barbory** (Cathedral of St Barbara; open Tues–Sun, Dec–Mar 9am–midday, 2–4pm, Apr and Oct 9am–midday, 1–4pm, May–Sept 9am–6pm; admission charge), a jewel of Bohemian Gothic architecture; it was designed by Jan Parler, son of Petr Parléř (*see page 82*), who began work on it in 1388. The magnificently complex mid-16th-century nave vaulting is a triumph of inventiveness by the designer of the equally extraordinary vault of Prague Castle's Old Royal Palace, Benedikt Ried. A stroll around the interior reveals coats of arms and wall-paintings paying tribute to the town's miners, under whose patronage the great edifice was constructed.

Kutná Hora's winding lanes invite leisurely exploration, and reveal a number of other fascinating ecclesiastical and civic buildings as well as views out over the valley of the little River Vrchlice. You can enjoy intriguing glimpses into the town's past by visiting the 15th-century edifice known as the **Hrádek** (open Tues-Sun, Apr and Oct 9am–5pm, May–Jun and Sept 9am–6pm, Jul–Aug 10am–6pm; admission charge), where after donning miner's gear you can descend into the shafts of an old silver mine.

However, Kutná Hora's other great attraction is a short distance away in the suburb of **Sedlec** (3 km/2 miles north-east). The cemetery here boasts a funeral chapel which is now a *kostnice*, or ossuary (open daily, Nov–Mar 9am–midday, 1–4pm, Apr–Sept 8am–6pm, Oct 9am–midday, 1–5pm; admission charge). This example of a "bone church" is definitely not for the squeamish; it features grotesque "sculptures" fabricated from 40,000 bones removed from a nearby graveyard and arranged to form elaborate chandeliers or even eye-catching coats of arms; a truly macabre sight.

Map on page 200

Kutná Hora's medieval but much restored Vlašský dvůr (Italian Court) is so called because it was here that experts from Florence instructed locals in the art of minting coins. Among their products was the famous Prague groschen or groat, a coin used all over Europe until well into the modern age. You can see examples of the minters' work in a small museum.

BELOW:
the ossuary at Sedlec.

Český Šternberk

In the courtyard of Český Šternberk visitors may come across a number of birds of prey. They are here to raise money for a local wildlife rescue and preservation centre who rescue the birds, nurse them back to health and release them back into the wild.

Crowning a narrow rock spur dividing the River Sázava from one of its tributaries some 53 km (33 miles) south-east of Prague, **Český Šternberk ⑩** (open Apr and Oct Sat–Sun, May and Sept Tues–Sun 9am–5pm, Jun–Aug Tues–Sun 9am–6pm, Nov–Apr by prior arrangement; admission charge) is one of the most romantically sited castles in Bohemia. It is also one of the country's most venerable strongholds, its foundation dating to 1241, when one Zdeslav of the Divisov family decided to build himself an impregnable fortress.

At the time it was fashionable to take on a German-sounding name; inspired by their coat of arms featuring an eight-pointed star, the Divisovs became the Šternbergs (*Stern* meaning "star" in German). The Šternbergs went on to become one of the country's great aristocratic dynasties, helping in the 19th century to found both the National Gallery and the National Museum in Prague. Their public spirit did not spare them from expropriation by

BELOW: the castle of Český Šternberk.

the Communist regime in 1949, but Český Šternberk was given back to to them during the restitution programme that followed the Velvet Revolution.

The castle is approached up a steep stairway, which does not seem to deter its many visitors (though far fewer than those drawn to Karlštejn Castle). Much rebuilt over the centuries, the castle is basically Baroque in style, though there was little room on its cramped ridge-top site to indulge in the Baroque love of elaborate spatial effects, and many of the interiors are oddly shaped. They are filled with fascinating furnishings and fittings in styles ranging from Renaissance to Baroque and Empire. There are portraits of eminent members of the family, hunting trophies, splendid tiled stoves, chandeliers, and artefacts from the Thirty Years War, when the castle withstood a couple of sieges .

The winding, wooded course of the lovely valley of the Sázava is a favourite with weekenders from Prague, many of whom have a chalet here.

Průhonice

Just off the motorway leading southeast from Prague, a mere 16 km (10 miles) from the capital, the village of **Průhonice** ⓫ is famous for its castle and vast landscape park. The castle (not normally open to the public) is occupied by the Botanical Institute of the National Academy of Science, whose botanists have a wonderful array of trees, shrubs and other plants at their disposal in the vast park where they work.

Průhonice Castle dates to the Middle Ages, but the present building is a romantic structure in Czech neo-Renaissance style. It was built in the late 19th century by Count Ernst Silva-Taroucca, who was also responsible for laying out the **park** (open daily, Nov–Mar 8am–5pm, Apr–Oct 7am–7pm), a major achievement of landscape design, with lakes, vistas, walks, an alpine garden and, above all, countless trees, both native and exotic. Only 16 km (10 miles) from the city centre, it makes a welcome retreat from metropolitan noise, bustle, and summer heat.

Konopiště

About 40 km (25 miles) south-east of Prague is **Konopiště Castle** ⓬ (open, Apr and Oct Tues–Fri 9am–midday, 1–3pm, Sat–Sun 9am 4pm, May–Aug Tues–Sun 9am– midday, 1–5pm, Sept Tues–Fri 9am–midday, 1–4pm, Sat–Sun 9am –5pm, Nov Sat–Sun 9am–midday, 1–3pm; admission charge; www. zamek-konopiste.cz). It was first built in the 13th century, subsequently remodelled on many occasions, then given its final, mock-medieval character in the late 19th century by Habsburg Archduke Franz Ferdinand, heir to the throne of Austria-Hungary.

The most prominent genuinely medieval feature is the high round tower rising from one corner, while the castle is entered through an imposing Baroque gateway adorned with fine statuary.

Franz Ferdinand is best known for his death at the hands of an assassin in Sarajevo in June 1914, the event that precipitated the First World War, but a tour of lavishly furnished Konopiště, his favourite residence, reveals him as a many-sided, not altogether attractive character, as well as a devoted family man. He was obsessed by arms and armour, and the castle **Armoury** is almost without equal for the range and beauty of its collections.

The Archduke was also a zealous huntsman, reckoned to have dispatched an animal or bird for every hour of his life, and Konopiště is full of trophies of the chase, as well as the many and varied works of art he assembled. In the political field, Franz Ferdinand was a moderniser, hoping to preserve the Habsburg inheritance by giving greater rights to its many and varied ethnic minorities, particularly its Slav communities such as the Czechs, whose language he spoke, and one of whose aristocrats, Sophie Chotek,

Map on page 200

The attractive stable block at Konopiště.

BELOW: statues in the gardens at Konopiště.

Map
on page
200

*While Franz
Ferdinand perished
in far-off Sarajevo,
his assassin, the
young Bosnian Serb
nationalist Gavrilo
Princip, was to die
not far from Prague.
Too young to be
executed, he was
brought to Bohemia
to serve a life
sentence in the grim
fortress prison at
Terezín, where he
succumbed to
tuberculosis.*

BELOW:
the Zámek Zbraslav.

he married. Konopiště was more successfully modernised than the decaying Empire; the Archduke installed central heating, hot and cold running water, and even a lift. The grounds were transformed too, with statuary, specimen trees, and a splendid rose garden set in an English-style landscape park.

Konopiště became the property of the Czechoslovak state, then during the occupation was confiscated by the Nazis, who turned it into accommodation for the SS. These gentlemen seem to have spent their leisure hours shooting the bears whose skins adorn the floor of the Archduke's smoking room.

Zbraslav

On the River Vltava just 12 km (7 miles) south of the city centre, **Zbraslav** ⑬ has something of the air of a country town, despite having formed part of the metropolitan area of Prague for many years. It was once a popular destination for day-trippers from the city, who would swarm off the paddlesteamers that had brought them here to enjoy the rural atmosphere and be entertained by the typical Bohemian brass bands playing in pubs and riverside cafes.

One of the most productive Czech composers of waltzes and polkas for brass bands, Jaromir Vejvoda, was a Zbraslav man. His catchy tune entitled "Škoda lásky" ("What a shame about love") was one of the great hits of the mid-20th century, though it is far better known abroad by its English or German titles ("Roll Out the Barrel" or "Rosamunde"). A restaurant on the town square is a kind of shrine to Vejvoda and his music.

Nowadays most visitors to Zbraslav come here for the National Gallery's **Collection of Asian Art** (open Tues–Sun 10am–6pm; admission charge; www.ngprague.cz). Of very high quality indeed, this is housed in **Zámek Zbraslav**, a spacious and splendid 18th-century Baroque palace set in a lovely park just off the square. The palace was built to replace a medieval Cistercian monastery destroyed by the Hussites.

The emphasis of the collections is on Japanese and Chinese arts and crafts, but there are also many items from other Asian regions ranging from Turkey to Tibet. The Japanese collections on the ground floor include superb examples of arms and armour, ceramics, metalwork, enamels, fans and screens, as well as painting and graphic works by such masters as Hokusai and Hiroshige.

The exhibits from China shown on the first floor demonstrate the extraordinary achievements of that country's artists and craftspeople from the earliest times, with items from the Neolithic period as well as more familiar ceramic works from the various dynasties. The section on Buddhist art is especially rich.

Among the treasures from other regions on the second floor are rare paintings of sacred subjects from Tibet. ❏

RESTAURANTS

Karlštejn

Restaurace u janů
Karlštejn 13
Tel: 311 681 210
Open: Tues–Sun
11am–10pm. €
Reasonably priced basic establishment serving standard Czech menu supplemented by venison specialities. There's a pleasantly shaded terrace for dining outside. Live music at the weekend.

Konopiště

Restaurace stará myslivna
Tel: 317 721 148. €€
The castle at Konopiště caters for its many visitors with its own wine cellar and bistro, but while here you should take the opportunity to sample the many and varied game specialities served in the characterful "Old Huntsman" restaurant. Good desserts too.

Křivoklát

U jelena
Hradní 53
Tel: 313 558 235. €€
"At the Sign of the Stag" occupies a fine location beneath the castle at Křivoklát. Once the residence of the local forestry superintendent, it is now a stylish restaurant and pension with ambitions to please. You can dine outside, accom-panied by live music of an appropriate kind.

Kutná Hora

Hotel u růže
Zámecká 52
Tel: 327 523 524. €€
Recover from the macabre sights of the charnel house in Sedlec in the pleasant setting of the Rose Hotel. Fish and game specialities and a garden section for sunny days.

Mělník

Zámecká restaurace
Svatováclavská 19
Tel: 315 622 121
Open: Tues–Sun
11am–6pm. €€
The restaurant belonging to the castle at Mělník is the place to dine in town, with plenty of room, inside and out, and with the classic view down over the vines to the confluence of the rivers Vltava and Elbe.

Nelahozeves

Castle restaurant
Zámek Nelahozeves
Tel: 315 709 111. €€€
Impeccable gourmet restaurant on the first floor of Nelahozeves castle overlooking the River Vltava, serving Czech and international specialities accompanied by wines from the Lobkowicz estate and beers from the family brewery.

Průhonice

U bezoušků
Květnové náměstí 5
Tel: 267 750 551. €–€€
This newly opened and well-run establishment boasts its own microbrewery, the smallest of its kind in Bohemia, which forms the centrepiece of its dining room. You can also eat in the garden or in the Bezouška's own "Mexican" restaurant.

Hliněná bašta
Újezdská 619
Tel: 272 690 700. €–€€
The characterful "Earthern Bastion" sports among its amenities a half-timbered tower, while its reliable offerings include home-made duck paté, succulent goose liver, and even a "Dish for the Hungry Man". Reasonable range of salads and vegetarian dishes. The wine list features bottles from selected Czech vineyards.

Zbraslav

Barabizna
Pod Špitálem 363
Tel: 257 921 362. €€
Among its range of exoitic dishes, the "hut" offers a selection of formidable-sounding Mexican steaks, including "Desperado" (with mushrooms).

Pizza-Restaurant Antonio
U Národní galerie 471
Tel: 257 921 449. €
Welcoming pizzeria with wood oven and menu in English. Reliable pizzas and a range of other dishes. Famous Krusovice beer on draught.

Restaurace Škoda lásky
Zbraslavské náměstí 453
Tel: 257 924 407. €–€€
A compulsory call for all admirers of Czech polkas and waltzes, this otherwise conventional establishment on the main square in Zbraslav features an array of memorabilia celebrating master bandsman Jaromir Vejvoda, composer of that timeless hit "Škoda lásky" ("Roll Out The Barrel").

BELOW:
delicious Krusovice beer.

TRANSPORT

GETTING THERE AND GETTING AROUND

GETTING THERE

By Air

Prague's expanded, modernised Ruzyně airport lies about 20 km (13 miles) north-west of the city. For flight information tel: 220 113 314 or check www.csl.cz

It is possible to book a flight to Prague from most European capitals and from New York, Montreal and Toronto. The flight from London takes about 2 hours.

The national airline is ČSA (České Aeroline; www.csa.cz), with several offices abroad:

Australia
Suite 809 level 8, Australia Square Tower, 264 George Street, Sydney
Tel: 9247 7706

Canada
2020 rue Université, Montréal, Québec H3A 2A5
Tel: 844 6376
401 Bay Street, Suite 1510, Toronto, Ontario M5H 2Y4
Tel: 363 3174

Ireland
Link Building, Level 2, Dublin Airport
Tel: 818 200 014

United Kingdom
Sovereign House, 361 King Street, London W6 9NA
Tel: 0870 444 3747

United States
1350 Avenue of the Americas, Suite 601, New York
Tel: 800 223 2365

Numerous budget airlines now fly to Prague. From the UK these include: easyJet, flying from Gatwick and Stansted (www.easyjet.com); bmibaby from Birmingham, East Midlands and Manchester (www.bmibaby.com); and EUjet, who fly from Kent Airport at Manston (www.eujet.com). The Czech-based Smart Wings fly from elsewhere in Europe (www.smartwings.net).

Airline Offices

Air France
Václavské náměstí 10, Prague 1
Tel: 221 662 609
www.airfrance.com

British Airways
Ruzyně Airport, Prague 6
Tel: 239 000 299
www.ba.com

ČSA
V celnici 5, Prague 1
Tel: 239 007 007
Airport tel: 220 111 111
www.csa.cz

KLM
Ruzyně Airport, Prague 6
Tel: 220 114 148
www.klm.com

Lufthansa
Aviatická 12, Prague 6
Tel: 220 114 456
www.lufthansa.com

Train

There are direct train connections to Prague from many places in Germany and Austria. From Stuttgart and Munich the journey takes approximately 8 hours, from Frankfurt 10 hours, Berlin 6 hours, Hamburg 14 hours and Vienna 6 hours. Most trains from southern Germany and Austria arrive at the main Wilsonova Station (Hlavní nádraží). Trains from the west stop at Prague-Holešovice Station and many proceed on to Wilsonova. Other destinations in the Czech Republic can be reached via Prague.

The most direct way to reach Prague from London by train is via Paris and Frankfurt, which takes around 18 hours (for details and booking check with www.raileurope.co.uk). Some of these trains arrive at Smíchov.

Travellers who do not have a ticket from the capital to their destination may purchase one at any of the railway stations in Prague. Domestic and international tickets can be purchased in Czech crowns, western currency or with credit cards at Čedok, Na Příkopě 18, Prague 1, or from the railway stations in crowns. Further information about rail schedules can be found on the **Czech Railways** (České dráhy) site at www.cd.cz

Hlavní nádraží (the main station at Wilsonova) is clearly laid out on two floors. The lower end contains the counters for domestic tickets as well as the **PIS (Prague Information Service)** office, and a number of shops. International tickets are purchased in the upper hall, which also has room-booking agencies and exchange bureaux.

Two digital boards in the upper and lower halls show departures and arrivals. Toilets and left luggage are located beneath the main hall, together with the luggage lockers.

Bus & Coach

There is a wide choice of cheap and efficient coach journeys from many European cities. Check with operators in your country for information. The main operator is **Eurolines** (www.eurolines.com).
In the United Kingdom
52 Grosvenor Gardens, London
SW1 0AU
Tel: 08705 143 219
www.eurolines.co.uk

In Prague
Bohemia Euroexpress International
Autobusové nádraží Florenc,
Křižíkova 6
Tel: 224 218 680
www.bei.cz

Kingscourt Express operates buses between London and Prague, one-way and round trip. Departures in both directions are four times a week in low season, and six times in high season.
In the United Kingdom
15 Balham High Road, London
SW12 9AJ
Tel: 020 8673 7500
In Prague
Havelská 8, Prague 1
Tel: 224 234 583
You can also book online and consult the timetables at
www.kce.cz

CSAD is the national bus company. The terminus for most routes is the Prague-Florenc bus station. Information on national connections can be obtained on tel: 475 212 066 (6am–6pm Mon–Sat, 7am–noon Sun) or by visiting www.csadbus.cz

GETTING AROUND

To/From the Airport

The cheapest way into the city from the airport (or vice versa) is by city transport. There are public bus services to the Metro at Dejvická (buses 119 and 254), probably the most useful for the majority of visitors, the Metro at Zličín (bus 100), and the Metro at Nové Butovice (buses 179 and 225). The journey by bus 119 or 179 takes about 30–45 minutes (15 minutes by bus 100) and tickets (12 Kč) are available from either the DPP counter in the arrivals hall or from machines by the bus stop just outside the terminal building. The ticket is valid for 60 minutes between 5am and 8pm, 90 minutes at other times and at weekends, and can also be used on the tram or metro within that time limit. If you arrive late at night a night bus (510) will take you to the tram stop at Divoká Šárka, where you can pick up the night tram (51) into town.

A private minibus shuttle service, Čedaz (tel: 220 114 296; www.aas.cz/cedaz), operates between the airport and náměstí Republiky with a stop at Dejvická Metro station, every half-hour between 5.30am and 9.30pm, and charges 90 Kč. The journey between the airport and náměstí Republiky terminus or vice versa takes 30–45 minutes depending on traffic. Čedaz also has a number of minibuses that will take you directly to your hotel for a fee. However, the rates are almost as high as by taxi.

Taxis from the airport are controlled by a monopoly, Bellinda. After a period of overcharging and dangerous competition between firms, Bellinda was granted exclusive rights by the city to carry passengers out of the airport. (All other taxi services may bring passengers to the airport, however.) Bellinda taxis do not have meters; go to

BELOW: the national carrier.

their booth at the airport arrivals area, where the clerk will write the fee for your destination on a piece of paper, which you then show to the driver. Taxis are lined up outside the arrivals exit. Rates are relatively high, however; a ride to the centre will cost around 500 Kč.

City Transport

The various means of public transport in Prague are cheap, clean, efficient and well integrated. Run by the DPP (Prague City Transport; www.dpp.cz), the network includes trams and buses, the Metro and the funicular up Petřín Hill.

Tickets can be purchased in shops, at the kiosks of Prague City Transport, and at hotel receptions, as well as from the automatic ticket machines at some tram stops and in all Metro stations. It can be useful to stock up on tickets for the weekend if you don't have the necessary change to use in the machines, as not all Metro stations have attendants on duty at weekends. On all Prague public transport, an 8 Kč ticket is valid on trams and buses for 15 minutes with no transfer (up to four stops on the Metro), a 12 Kč ticket is fully transferable between buses, trams and the Metro and allows you to travel for 60 minutes 5am–8pm Monday to

Friday, and for 90 minutes after 8pm and at weekends.

Long-term tickets are very good value and useful if you plan on seeing a number of different sites, or are staying more than a couple of days. A 24-hour ticket costs 70 Kč, a three-day ticket 200 Kč, a weekly ticket 250 Kč, and a fortnightly ticket 280 Kč. These, and longer-term tickets, are available from Ticket Information Centres and certain newsagents.

Remember that bus and tram drivers do not sell tickets. Transport operates on an honesty system; each traveller must get his or her ticket punched by a machine on the upper platform at

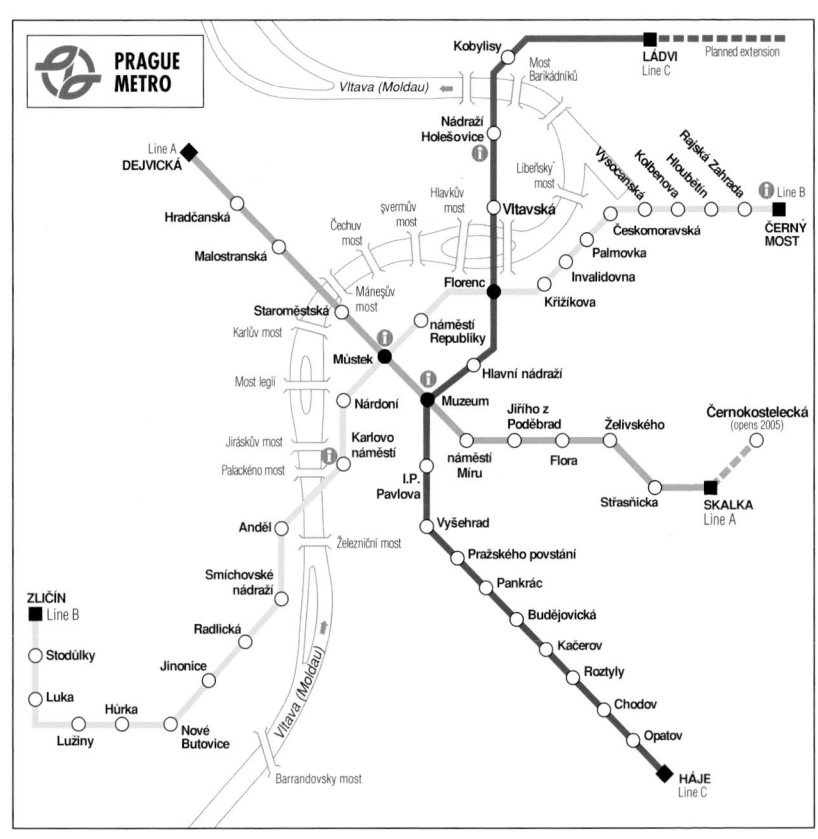

TRANSPORT

the Metro stations, or on the tram or bus (passengers may enter any door of trams and buses). Plain-clothes controllers carrying small identity badges make periodic checks; if you can't show that your ticket has been punched recently you could be faced with a large fine, to be paid on the spot.

The Metro

The modern underground Metro system links the city centre with the suburbs, and provides for convenient travel inside the city. It is a remarkably clean and fast means of public transport. The three lines have been developed with an eye towards expediency, and by transferring it is possible to reach just about all the important tourist attractions located within the city.

The lines intersect at three main stations. From Můstek station at the bottom of Václavské náměstí you can take the green **line A** over to Malá Strana and Hradčany. The yellow **line B** runs south to Karlovo náměstí and to the Smíchovské nádraží station. The Florenc bus station and the north-east can be reached by travelling in the opposite direction. Line A intersects with the red **line C** at the Muzeum station at the upper end of Václavské náměstí. The latter runs north to the main station, then to the Florenc bus station where it intersects with line B before continuing to the terminus Nádraží Holešovice, the station for many of the trains on the Berlin–Budapest route. To the south it leads to Vyšehrad.

Because of the frequency of the trains (every 3–10 minutes), you don't need to plan for more than about 30 minutes even for journeys into the suburbs. The Metro operates 5am–midnight.

Metro signs outside the stations are small and square and decidedly inconspicuous, with a white M on a green, yellow or red background, depending on which line the station is on. But inside, the stations, often beautifully designed, are clean and clearly laid out. Network plans are prominently located at all entrances and above the platforms; the station you are at is highlighted; the stations you can change at are marked with the colour of the intersecting line.

Trams and Buses

Among the many tram and bus routes within Prague, line 22 is one of the most interesting for visitors, although all will have their uses. It runs from náměstí Míru through Karlovo náměstí and along Národní třída. It crosses the Vltava and then runs along Karmelitská in Malá Strana to Malostranské náměstí. From there it winds its way up to Hradčany and on along the Keplerova to the starting point for the Strahov and Petřín Hill. On line 22 it is possible to have an almost complete tour of the city for the price of a single ride. Do, however, look out for pickpockets, who target this route for tourists' wallets and purses.

Prague has a comprehensive bus network: buses *(autobus)* run throughout the day, particularly frequently in the suburbs, and connect with the Metro.

Night trams, operating on a reduced number of routes, arrive at intervals of 30 minutes between 12.30am and 4.30am, as do night buses. The numbers and schedules of night trams (numbers 51 to 58) are visible at most tram stops; the same is true of night buses at bus stops (numbers 501 to 512).

Taxis

After midnight taxis are the most convenient form of transport if you want to get anywhere in a hurry and don't want to bother with the night trams or night buses. You'll find a number of taxi stands in obvious places in the city centre as well as in front of larger hotels.

Prague's taxi drivers have earned a bad reputation for overcharging visitors to the city. Though the situation is improving, a few precautions are still necessary. To avoid problems, always make sure the driver has the meter turned on. There is no need to negotiate a price: rates are now fully regulated, and listed on the door of every taxi. Some drivers, however, have been known to tamper with their meters in order to prey on tourists and late-night revellers. As a general rule, it's better to hail a moving cab than to take a standing one, especially near the major tourist sites and outside clubs.

Better still is to call for a radio cab. Three reputable firms with English-speaking dispatchers and reasonable rates are:
AAA, tel: 140 14,
Citytaxi, tel: 257 257 257, and
Profi Taxi, tel: 261 314 151.
AAA and Citytaxi also offer SMS and online booking (see www.aaataxi.cz or www.citytaxi.cz).

Taxi stands in the centre of Prague include:
Václavské náměstí (Wenceslas Square; almost anywhere in the square);
Národní třída (outside Tesco);
Obecní dům (Municipal House);
Hlavní nádraží (Wilsonova Station; follow the signs);
Staroměstské náměstí (Old Town Square, near the corner of Pařížská street);
Malostranské náměstí;
Hradčany;
Malostranská Metro station;
Karlovo náměstí (Charles Square).

Sightseeing Tours

Čedok agencies and the PIS *(see pages 233–4)* offer foreign-language-speaking tour guides to travel groups as well as to independent travellers, for both day excursions or trips lasting several days. They can also equip you with an interpreter or translator upon request. It is not unusual in Prague to hire a tour guide to

ACCOMMODATION

ACTIVITIES

A – Z

LANGUAGE

accompany you on foot through the city. The hourly rate for this service varies. Three-hour city tours called "Historic Prague" and "Jewish Prague" are conducted by numerous establishments which have kiosks dotting Václavské náměstí, Na přikopě and Staroměstské náměstí. Some are listed below:

Čedok
Na příkopě 18
Tel: 224 197 242
ww.cedok.cz

Cityrama
Štěpánská 21
Tel: 222 230 208
www.cityrama.cz

Martin Tour
Štěpánská 61
Tel: 224 212 473
www.martintour.cz

Prague Sightseeing Tours
Klimentská 52
Tel: 222 314 661
www.pstours.cz

Prague Walks
Týnská ulička 5
Tel: 603 271 911
www.praguewalks.com

English-language tours of Hradčany and headphone sets are organised by:
Informační středisko pražského hradu (information Centre of Prague Castle), III nadvori, Hradčany, Prague 1
Tel: 224 373 368
www.hrad.cz

Vltava Cruises

The frequency of cruises on the River Vltava depends on the weather, but there are plenty to choose from during the summer. Some ticket prices include a meal on board. An evening cruise under the Charles Bridge can be an unforgettable experience.

Information on cruises can be obtained from the quayside on the Rašín embankment at the Palacký Bridge (Palackého most) or on the Na Františku embankment at the Čechův Bridge (near the Hotel Intercontinental).

The following boat operators can also be contacted for times:

Evropská vodní doprava
Čechův most, nábrezí Na františku
Tel: 224 810 030
www.evd.cz

Pražská paroplavební společnost
Rašínovo nábřeží
Tel: 224 931 013
www.paroplavba.cz

První všeobecná člunovací společnost
Platérská 4
Tel: 603 819 947
www.prague-venice.cz

You can hire rowing boats and pedalos from small jetties on Slovanský ostrov.

Driving

Even for drivers who know Prague, the city can be a traffic nightmare. Large sections of Staré Město and Malá Strana have been completely closed to traffic. If you do manage to get through the maze of one-way streets and culs-de-sac to find yourself in the centre, at Václavské náměstí or the Powder Tower, you'll probably be turned away by the police (or may even get a ticket) unless you can prove you are resident at one of the hotels near by. It is therefore highly advisable to leave your car at home and explore the city either on foot or by public transport.

Car Hire

If you must rent a car in the Czech Republic you have to be at least 21 years of age and in possession of a valid driver's licence that has been in effect for at least a year. Credit cards are accepted as payment. For a good rate it is wise to shop around.

Czechocar (tel: 261 222 079; www.czechocar.cz), with its fleet of Škodas, offers reasonable terms. Another decent local operator is **Dvořák Rent a Car** (tel: 224 826 260; www.dvorak-rentacar.cz). The ubiquitous Škodas (manufactured by Volkswagen) have two major advantages:

Czech mechanics can repair them with ease, and they are not the most desirable booty for car thieves. It may also be possible to pick up a car in one town and deposit it in another.

Regulations

Drivers arriving in the Czech Republic by car must buy a road permit (800 Kč) for their vehicle at the border crossing, valid for the given calendar year, which is then displayed on their windscreen. By and large, the international traffic regulations apply here. The maximum speed limit within city boundaries is 50 kph (30 mph); on country roads 90 kph (55 mph); and on motorways 130 kph (80 mph). (The 800 Kč mentioned allows you to drive on those motorways for which a permit is required.) Exceeding the speed limit can result in a hefty fine. Driving after drinking even small amounts of alcohol is absolutely prohibited in the Czech Republic. Children under 12 years of age are not allowed to sit in the front seat, and the wearing of seat belts is compulsory at all times.

Parking

The policy is to keep the city centre as free of traffic as possible. To this end the centre has been divided into three zones: Zone A (Old Town), Zone B (Nové Město to the east of Václavské náměstí) and Zone C (to the west of Václavské náměstí). Within these zones parking spaces cost a nominal fee. Police and traffic wardens are extremely vigilant and clamped cars are a common sight. Vehicles that have been towed away are kept in Hostivař, Cernokostelecká, 15 km (9 miles) from the centre.

Breakdown

In case of breakdown tel: 112, or the police on tel: 158. Emergency non-stop towing services include: **ABA Emergency Repair**, tel: 1230; and the **Ústřední auto-motoklub**, tel: 1230.

A CCOMMODATION

SOME THINGS TO CONSIDER BEFORE YOU BOOK THE ROOM

Finding a Hotel

Finding a hotel room in Prague is getting easier all the time, but if you would like something cheap it's necessary to book well ahead, as most accommodation in the city is expensive and on a par with places like London and Paris. Due to the fact that hotel managements often have fixed contracts with foreign tour agencies, rooms can be reserved for travel groups quite far in advance of the intended trip. Therefore, individual travellers will usually be told that the hotel is fully booked. A possible alternative to this often frustrating search is to reserve a room through a travel agency or stay in one of the many affordable, pleasant *pensions* that have now emerged to accommodate the needs of more free-spirited travellers.

In the more expensive hotels facilities, decor and service conform to international standards. The bill can usually be paid in Czech crowns, western currencies or with major credit cards such as MasterCard, American Express or Visa.

ACCOMMODATION LISTINGS

HRADČANY

Hotel Hoffmeister
Pod bruskou 7
Tel: 251 017 111
www.hoffmeister.cz
On the corner of Chotkova as it winds up past the castle, the Hoffmeister is in a very

PRICE CATEGORIES

Price categories are for a double room, usually including breakfast:
€ = under €100
€€ = €100–€200
€€€ = more than €200

convenient location. Not as attractive as some Prague hotels from the outside, but with rooms and facilities that are luxurious. Comfortable and tasteful, and with an excellent spa and restaurant, the prices are surprisingly good compared to some other Prague five-stars.
€€€

Hotel Savoy
Keplerova 6
Tel: 224 302 430
www.hotel-savoy.cz

The Savoy offers luxury rooms, admittedly well done, of the kind found in many cities across the world. Perhaps it is this international familiarity that attracts the celebs, or, possibly the stunning views across the Strahov Monastery and Petřín Hill from the Savoy and Presidential suites' balconies. **€€€**

Hotel Questenberk
Úvoz 15
Tel: 220 407 600
www.questenberk.cz

With its tall Baroque façade, this converted 17th-century palace initially looks like a church. Inside, the renovation has retained enough of the original fabric to make it an atmospheric place to stay. The rather minimalist rooms do have antique furniture and all have marble bathrooms attached. **€€€**

U raka
Černínská 10
Tel: 220 511 100
www.romantikhotel-uraka.cz
Set in one of the only wooden houses left in Prague, and dating back to the mid-18th century,

this complex is now a lovely hotel. The spotless rooms are beautifully laid out, and there is a delightful garden for the use of guests. One of the more expensive places to stay, but quiet and romantic. **€€€**

Zlatá hvězda
Nerudova 48
Tel: 257 532 867
www.hotelgoldenstar.com
Perched looking down Nerudova and up to the

castle, the 'Golden Star' has one of the best views of any hotel in the city. Dating back to 1372, the building's interior has been preserved and restored, and this careful approach has been carried over into the rooms, with their period furniture and modern bathrooms. **€€–€€€**

U krále karla
Nerudova/Úvoz 4

Tel: 257 533 594
www.romantichotels.cz
This baroque building (it took its present form in 1639) is in a quiet and convenient location at the top of the hill, looking out over Petřín Hill and the Strahov. The rooms lean a little more towards Central European kitsch than some, but many people will enjoy the stained-glass windows. **€€**

MALÁ STRANA

Hotel Aria
Tržiště 9
Tel: 225 334 111
www.ariahotel.net
Expensive but chic, this new addition to Malá Strana plays heavily on its music theme. From Mozart to Dizzy Gillespie, each floor and room is dedicated to a particular music or musician. The fittings and fixtures are classy, as is the in-house music library. **€€€**

Residence Nosticova
Nosticova 1
Tel: 257 312 513
www.nosticova.com
If you have the money, this could be a delightful place to stay. Set above the excellent Alchymist restaurant, the fairytale apartments are beautifully furnished (one even has a grand piano), and all have an attached bathroom and kitchen. There are large reductions for stays during low season. **€€€**

Biskupský dům
Dražického náměstí 6
Tel: 257 532 320
www.hotelbishopshouse.com
Just off Mostecká, the "Bishop's House" is a

19th-century building close to the Charles Bridge. The plain rooms are clean and comfortable, and quiet given the hotel's proximity to one of the city's main tourist thoroughfares. **€€–€€€**

Dům u velké boty
Vlašská 30
Tel: 257 532 088
www.dumuvelkeboty.cz
Opposite the German Embassy, this small hotel is in a superb location. The building dates from the early-17th century, and care has been taken to ensure that the interior and furniture maintain the historic feel. Lovely comfy beds, spotless bathrooms and friendly owners all go towards making this one of the best places to stay in the city. **€€**

Hotel Neruda
Nerudova 44
Tel: 257 535 557
www.hotelneruda-praha.cz
A stone's-throw away from the castle, this building dating from 1348 now has a minimalist modern interior. You are paying for

the location as much as anything, but the rooms are clean and comfortable, and there is a pleasant café space where you can sit and sip hot chocolate. **€€€**

U červeného lva
Nerudova 41
Tel: 257 533 832
www.hotelredlion.com
A historic hotel set in a Renaissance house, previously the home of the Baroque painter Petr Brandl. The rooms have wooden floors and beautifully painted ceilings; their views aren't bad either. Under the hotel is a 14th-century cellar, now a bar. **€€€**

Pension Dientzenhofer
Nosticova 2
Tel: 257 311 319
www.dientzenhofer.cz
Set in the 16th century home of the famous Dientzenhofer family of architects, this is an interesting, secluded place to stay. The simple rooms all have attached bathrooms and are good value for the location. **€–€€**

U modrého klíče
Letenská 14
Tel: 257 534 361

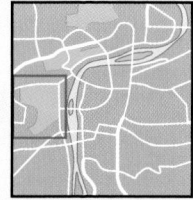
www.bluekey.cz
Just off the Lesser Quarter Square is a large Baroque building – "The Blue Key" – now a hotel. The plain rooms are large and clean, and the location is convenient, if you don't mind the trams rattling past. A number of the rooms have a small cooker and fridge. **€€**

U páva
U lužického semináře 32
Tel: 257 533 360
www.romantichotels.cz
In a quiet location close to the Charles Bridge and not far from Kampa Island, this hotel has the same owners as U krále karla, and consequently has the same somewhat charming lean towards kitsch. The rooms have a nicely opulent feel to them, some with views of the castle. **€€**

STARÉ MĚSTO

Hotel Josef
Rybná 20
Tel: 221 700 111
www.hoteljosef.com
A sleek designer-hotel near the Jewish Quarter. The interior, designed by Eva Jiricna, has stone-and-glass bathrooms attached to minimalist rooms with DVD and CD players. None of this is cheap (up to around €350), but it does make a change from the often heritage-heavy accommodation available elsewhere in the city. €€€

Hotel Paříž
Obecního domu 1
Tel: 222 195 195
www.hotel-pariz.cz
More luxury in this squeaky-clean Art Nouveau building from 1904. Unfortunately the rooms have been rather over-restored and the original furniture replaced with bland modern pieces that make a nod towards the original style. The Restaurant Sarah Bernhardt has fared rather better and retains its sparkling interior and wooden fittings. €€€

Residence Řetězová
Řetězová 9
Tel: 222 221 800
www.residenceretezova.com
This converted palace, just off Karlova, has nine large and comfortable apartments. Some are more luxurious than others, but all have a well-equipped kitchen and decent bathroom, and the location is excellent. €€–€€€

Apostolic Residence
Saroměsteké náměstí 26
Tel: 221 632 222
www.prague-residence.cz
Locations in the Old Town don't come much better than this tiny hotel. The charming rooms, with their wooden beams and period furniture, may be a little more noisy than some – on the square and above a restaurant – but they do have a view of Astronomical Clock. €€

U tří bubnů
U radnice 10/14
Tel: 224 214 855
www.utribubnu.cz
The "House at the Three Drums" can be found opposite Kafka's

house, in the Old Town. In this small, newly converted residence, you can choose between a room with an original painted wooden ceiling, one where the attached bathroom has a glass roof, or the two-storey attic apartment. €€

Hotel Černý slon
Týnská 1
Tel: 222 321 521
www.hotelcernyslon.cz
A lovely 14th-century building on the UNESCO protected list, very close to Old Town Square. The simple rooms – those in the attic have wooden beams – are excellent value, and the price includes breakfast. €–€€

Pension Unitas
Bartolomějská 9
Tel: 224 221 802
www.unitas.cz
There is a surprisingly homey feel to this cheap and clean hostel, considering it was used as the prison where Václav Havel was held during the 1970s (call ahead to reserve his room). The old cells have bunk beds

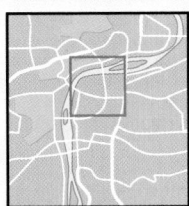

and there are a few rooms with twin beds. Excellent value considering its central location and the inclusive buffet breakfast. €

Travellers' Hostels
Dlouhá 33
Tel: 224 826 662
www.travellers.cz
This chain of hostels has half a dozen centrally located outlets, all clean and all very good value. The main branch is at Dlouhá 33, open all year; the others are open during the summer only. €

PRICE CATEGORIES

Price categories are for a double room, usually including breakfast:
€ = under €100
€€ = €100–€200
€€€ = more than €200

NOVÉ MĚSTO

Carlo IV
Senovážne náměstí 13
Tel: 224 593 111
www.boscolohotels.it
A very grand 19th-century building painstakingly converted into a luxury hotel. The interior designers have let their imaginations run riot with sumptuous rooms, a chic restaurant and a fabulous spa and swimming pool. It can also

be fabulously expensive, but perhaps worth it for this very continental version of stylish comfort. €€€

Hotel Palace
Panská 12
Tel: 224 093 111
www.palacehotel.cz
A Secessionist landmark, built in 1909 as a luxury hotel. It still performs this function today, though now it is

only the façade that retains its Art Nouveau appearance. The interior was gutted in the 1980s to make way for comfortable, if a little impersonal, modern rooms. However, this apparent act of vandalism is offset by the luxury and excellent service. €€€

Hotel Elite
Ostrovní 32

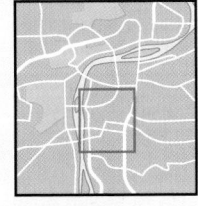

Tel: 224 932 250
www.hotelelite.cz
Not many hotels in the New Town have a suite

protected by the municipality, but the Elite has, due to its impressive 17th-century painted ceiling. The other rooms have also been tastefully preserved, with wooden floors, period furniture and an uncluttered feel. There is a pleasant courtyard bar and café for the summer, and the Ultramarin restaurant. €€–€€€

BELOW: the Art-Nouveau Hotel Paříž.

Hotel Axa
Na poříčí 40
Tel: 224 812 580
www.hotelaxa.com
An long-established hotel in a modern building close to náměstí Republicky, the Axa has simple but clean and comfortable rooms at good prices considering its location. Its proudest features are the fitness centre and pool. €€

Hotel Opera
Těšnov 13
Tel: 222 315 609
www.hotel-opera.cz
The inside of this 19th-century hotel does not quite match up to the impressive exterior. However, the rooms have recently been renovated and are pleasant and comfortable. Its central location and reasonable cost add considerably to its attractions. €€

Pension Museum
Mezibranská 15
Tel: 296 325 186
www.pension-museum.cz
This *pension* is in a convenient location just off Wenceslas Square. Well kept with a pleasant garden, the rooms are modern and clean with wooden floors. The large and airy accommodation is ideal for people with families, and the reasonable price includes a hearty buffet breakfast. €–€€

Penzion u šuterů
Palackého 4
Tel: 224 948 235
www.usuteru.cz
Great value, if simple, rooms very close to Wenceslas Square. Part of the building dates back to 1383, and the Gothic vaulting can still be seen in the cellar. Now with a Baroque façade, the hotel is in a great location and has a decent restaurant attached. €

Penzion u svatého Jana
Vyšehradská 28
Tel: 224 911 789
www.usvjana.cz
Right next door to the Church of St John on the Rock, this newly opened hotel is set in the church's Neo-Baroque administrative annexe. The rooms are fairly bare but clean, and the building is grand and in a quiet location. €

ELSEWHERE

Hotel Praha
Sušická 20, Dejvice
Tel: 224 343 305
www.htlpraha.cz
Out towards the airport, this Stalinist concrete monstrosity has managed to turn its previous incarnation as a place exclusively for apparatchiks to its advantage; there is a certain chic to its modernist bulk, large rooms and built-in security measures. Aside from these, there are garden terraces and excellent service. €€€

Hotel Adalbert
Břevnovský klášter,
Markétská 1, Břevnov
Tel: 220 406 180
www.intercatering.cz
This hotel is in an excellent and beautifully quiet location inside the Břevnov monastery; convenient for both the city centre (by tram) and airport (by bus). The 18th-century building is very attractive and the comfortable rooms are excellent value. €–€€

Pension 15
Vlkova 15, Žižkov
Tel: 222 719 768
www.pensions-pension-15.prague.st
Spotless if slightly spartan rooms with shared bathrooms and apartments at very good prices. Well run and modern, this is an excellent budget option

not far from the tram stops on Seifertova. €

Pension Paťanka
Paťanka 4, Dejvice
Tel: 224 314 309
www.patanka.cz
A bit out of the way, near the Hotel International, but quiet and well run, this *pension* has simple, comfortable rooms with en-suite bathrooms. The prices are very reasonable and include breakfast. €

Pension Vyšehrad
Krokova 6, Vyšehrad
Tel: 241 408 455
www.pension-vysehrad.cz
A quiet, friendly, family-run *pension* with impressive views and a very attractive garden. There

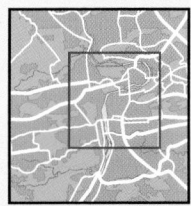

are only four simple but comfortable rooms, and a small dining room with a patio. €

PRICE CATEGORIES

Price categories are for a double room, usually including breakfast:
€ = under €100
€€ = €100–€200
€€€ = more than €200

ACTIVITIES

THE ARTS, NIGHTLIFE AND SHOPPING

THE ARTS

Buying Tickets

To get tickets it is best to go directly to the box office in order to get the lowest price (and for many places you can book tickets directly on-line), since ticket agencies mark up prices significantly or charge a commission. You can also buy tickets, at a highly marked-up premium, through tourist agencies. However, if you do need to go to a ticket agency, you could try one of the following:

Bohemia Ticket
Malé náměstí 13
Tel: 224 227 832
www.bohemiaticket.cz
PIS (Prague Information Service)
Staroměstská radnice
Tel: 12 444
www.pis.cz
Ticketpro
pasáž Lucerna, Štepánská 61
Tel: 296 329 999
www.ticketpro.cz
Ticket Art
Politických věznů 9
Tel: 222 897 264
http://vstupenky.ticket-art.cz
    The main box office for the **National Theatre** venues is situated in the glass buildings off Národní třída at Ostrovní 1 (open

daily 10am–6pm; tel: 224 901 448; www.narodni-divadlo.cz). There is a second box office at the Estates Theatre *(see below)*.

Classical Music and Dance

Opera

The quality of opera performances in Prague is quite high. Most opera is sung in its original language with digital surtitles in Czech. (Performances in Czech, of works by Dvořák and Smetana for example, do not have subtitles in foreign languages, however.) All three of Prague's major opera venues have beautiful auditoriums, each one different; they are:
Státní Opera Praha (Prague State Opera)
Wilsonova 4
Tel: 224 227 266
www.opera.cz
Metro: Muzeum
Nightly productions, usually of a very high standard. The repertory provides a mix of 19th century opera (Bizet, Verdi, Puccini) and more daring contemporary works. The box office is on the northern side of the opera house (open Mon–Fri 10am–5.30pm, Sat–Sun 10am–midday, 1–5.30pm).
Národní divadlo (National Theatre)

Národní třída 2
www.narodni-divadlo.cz
Metro: Národní třída
Trams: 17, 18, 21 and 22
Opera, ballet and theatre by the National Theatre ensembles.
Stavovské divadlo (Estates Theatre)
Ovocný trh 6
www.narodni-divadlo.cz
Metro: Můstek
Opera, dance and theatre; the première of Mozart's opera *Don Giovanni* was held here in 1787, conducted by Mozart himself. His operas are still regularly staged here. Part of the National Theatre network.

Ballet

The National Theatre Ballet frequently performs ballet classics such as *Swan Lake* and *Coppélia*, but has been branching out in more adventurous directions in recent years by including choreographies by George Balanchine and Jiří Kylián. The usual venues for National Theatre Ballet performances are:
National Theatre (Národní divadlo)
Národní třída 2
Tel: 224 901 448
Estates Theatre (Stavovské divadlo)
Ovocný trh 6
Tel: 224 215 001

TRANSPORT

ACCOMMODATION

ACTIVITIES

A – Z

LANGUAGE

The Ballet Company of the Prague State Opera is a recently-formed, medium-sized company, incorporating the **Prague Chamber Ballet**. Their performances have been receiving excellent notices in the local press. The venue for most performances is:
Státní Opera Praha (Prague State Opera)
Wilsonova 4
Tel: 224 227 266
www.opera.cz
Metro: Muzeum
The **Duncan Centre** (Branická 41, Prague 4; tel: 244 461 342; http://cjj.ecn.cz; trams 3, 16, 17 and 21), named after Isadora Duncan, is a popular centre for the teaching and performance of modern dance, and often hosts visiting foreign artists.

Concerts

Concerts of classical music, mainly chamber ensembles, with an emphasis on Mozart, Vivaldi, Dvořák and Smetana, are held in many churches and historic buildings. Aimed solely at pulling in the tourists, the standard is not always high and the repertory is very predictable. However, there

BELOW: buskers on the bridge.

are some exceptional venues, putting on some of the best concerts to be heard anywhere.
The **Česká filharmonie** (Czech Philharmonic) are one of the world's great orchestras and seeing one of their concerts at the Rudolfinum under their principal conductor Zdeněk Mácal is a real event. Their main concert series, which attracts many famous guest conductors and soloists, runs from October to May.
Czech Philharmonic
Rudolfinum, Alšovo nábřeží 12/náměstí Jana Palacha
Tel: 227 059 352
www.ceskafilharmonie.cz
Metro: Staroměstská
The other major resident orchestra is the **Symfonický orchestr hl.m. Prahy FOK** (also known by the less convoluted title of the Prague Symphony Orchestra). Less well-known than the Czech Philharmonic but still highly competent, they put on concerts in the splendid Obecní dům from September to June. Their principal conductor is Serge Baudo.
Prague Symphony Orchestra
Obecní dům, náměstí Republiky 5
Tel: 222 002 336
www.fok.cz
Metro: náměstí Republiky
A third orchestra, the **Symfonický orchestr Českého rozhlasu** (Prague Radio Symphony Orchestra; www2.rozhlas.cz/socr), is also resident in the city. Although primarily a recording ensemble for Czech Radio they put on a fine concert series in the Rudolfinum between October and March under their principal conductor Vladimír Válek. They are an outstanding orchestra, often including contemporary works in their programmes.
One of the most high profile chamber ensembles is the **Suk Chamber Orchestra**, named after the famous violinist and composer and founded in 1974 (www.suk-ch-o.cz). They tend to concentrate on the core Czech Classical and Romantic repertory.
Two orchestras established

since 1989 and starting to make an international name for themselves are the **Pražská komorní filharmonie** (Prague Philharmonia; www.pkf.cz), who put on an interesting mix of concerts at various locations in Prague (see their website for details), and the **Český národní symfonický orchestr** (Czech National Symphony Orchestra; www.cnso.cz).
The premier contemporary music ensemble is the **Agon Orchestra**, founded in the early 1980s to showcase the music of young Czech composers. They have a strong international profile, performing Czech and foreign works, and have appeared at festivals such as the Wien Modern (www.geocities.com/agon.orchestra).

Jazz Clubs

Prague has a select but lively jazz scene, with a number of decent clubs which at times attract respected foreign artists. However, there are several excellent local players who can be seen nightly at the venues below:
AghaRTA jazz centrum
Železná 16
Tel: 222 211 275
www.agharta.cz
Open daily 6pm–1am
Since its move to more spacious accommodation in the autumn of 2004 this has become a more comfortable, if more formal, venue. This is a good place to catch top local musicians, and they organise an on-going jazz festival, attracting classy foreign bands.
Jazz club U staré paní
Michalská 9
Tel: 224 228 090
www.jazzinprague.com
Open daily 7pm–2am
A home for jazz fans, this 100-seat club draws in some of the best musicians from the Czech Republic and abroad. They also run a "Jazzboat" on the river (see the website for details).
Jazz Club Železná
Mecca, U průhonu 3
Tel: 283 870 522

www.jazzclub.cz or www.mecca.cz
A long-standing club that has now moved from its Old Town location to join up with the Mecca nightclub in Holešovice. Chic and cool, the music tends to veer between funk, latin and world music.

Reduta
Národní třída 20
Tel: 224 933 487
www.redutajazzclub.cz
A dark and increasingly shabby perennial with a tourist crowd. The same jazz groups can be seen elsewhere in Prague, but this is where former US President Bill Clinton played on his saxophone when visiting in 1994.

U Malého Glena
Karmelitská 23
Tel: 257 531 717
www.malyglen.cz
Open daily 8pm–12.30am
Intimate (read tiny) basement that is home to some of the finest jazz in Prague. Good acoustics and a decent bar add to the attractions.

Ungelt Jazz & Blues Club
Týn 2
Tel: 224 895 748
www.jazzblues.cz
Open daily 8pm–midnight
A youngish club with lots of funk and blues, aimed more at visitors than locals, with a cosy stone interior and a casual, informal crowd.

Rock and Pop Venues

The places below, while generally given over to parties along the lines of "80s Night" (apart from the excellent Palác Akropolis), also host live music. Keep an eye on their websites, or check with a ticket agent such as Ticketpro.

Lucerna Music Bar
Vodičkova 36
Tel: 224 217 108
www.musicbar.cz
A big, shabby space off Wenceslas Square which pulls in locals and tourists for a varied programme of rock, pop and blues. Concerts by major performers on European tours are a draw throughout the year.

Palác Akropolis
Kubelíkova 27
Tel: 296 330 911
www.palacakropolis.cz
This converted theatre in Žižkov is a relaxed venue for high-quality music of all kinds, especially Gypsy tunes and world-music acts. It also has a decent DJ bar, as well as a passable café and restauarant.

Roxy
Dlouhá 33
Tel: 222 711 039
www.roxy.cz
A legendary Prague venue with smoky, above-average concerts – when it is not taken over by DJs (see page 225) – that include lasers and psychedelic lighting.

Festivals

A visit to Prague could be planned to coincide with one of the many festivals that take place during the year. The best time from September to June. Here is a selection of only a few annual highlights; however, you can almost bank on at least one festival taking place whenever you visit the city. For a full listing see www.pis.cz

January
OPERA – **Musical Theatre Festival** (www.divadlo.cz/jhd) A city-wide festival of musical theatre, including performances from youth theatres.

Prague Winter Festival
(www.praguewinterfestival.com) A commercial venture building on the success of the spring and autumn festivals, though not up to the standards of the other two.

January–February
12 Days of European Film
(www.eurofilmfest.cz) A festival split between the cities of Prague and Brno with diverse offerings from the European film industry.

March
Prague Writer's Festival
(www.pwf.pragonet.cz) This spring meeting of the minds draws some of the top scribes in the world. Past events were hosted by Nadine Gordimer, Salman

Rushdie and Gore Vidal, just to name a few.

March–April
Febio Fest (www.febiofest.cz) The largest international film festival in Central Europe.

April
One World (www.oneworld.cz) A film festival of documentaries focussing on human rights.

April
Khamoro (www.khamoro.cz) An annual festival of Roma culture with music and seminars.

May
Four Days (www.ctyridny.cz) An international festival of experimental theatre, as well as dance and music.

May–June
Prague Spring (www.festival.cz) This fabulous international music festival includes concerts at the Rudolfinum, Obecní dům and St. Vitus's Cathedral.

World Festival of Puppet Art
(www.puppetart.com) An enormous programme of live puppetry.

June
Prague Fringe Festival
(www.praguefringe.com) A cultural exchange on a massive scale, in which performing artists from dozens of countries meet in Prague to render everything from puppetry to classical theatre and musical cabaret.

Tanec Praha (www.tanecpha.cz) A wonderfully diverse celebration of modern dance.

September–October
Prague Autumn (www.prague autumn.cz) A young international music festival, not yet on a par with Prague Spring, but with some impressive visiting performers.

November–May
AghaRTA Prague Jazz Festival
(www.agharta.cz) A bit of a misnomer, since this "festival" is actually a series of high-quality concerts, usually one per month, from autumn to spring. Concerts are usually held at Lucerna Music Bar. Performers in recent years have included the Pat Metheny Group and saxophonist Joshua Redman.

TRANSPORT

ACCOMMODATION

ACTIVITIES

A – Z

LANGUAGE

Theatre

Theatre in Prague has a long and venerable tradition – as you would expect in the capital of a country which, in 1989, chose a playwright as its first post-Communist president.

Just over two hundred years earlier, in 1785, the Czech population of Prague had lobbied their rulers for the right to put on plays in their own language in the newly built Nostitz Theatre (today the Estates Theatre). And in 1881, when the brand new National Theatre burned down shortly after completion, sufficient public subscriptions were raised within a matter of weeks by the theatre-loving citizens to ensure that it was rebuilt again only two years later.

That same spirit is still very much alive today. Open any newspaper or listings magazine, read the posters plastered all over the city, and you will realise that the citizens of Prague think that theatre is still important. In an average week you might find productions of *Hamlet*, *Cabaret* and *The Inspector General*, together with a wide selection of original Czech plays, a revival of *Fiddler on the Roof* and perhaps a unique performance of Mozart's *Don Giovanni*, set to recorded music in the original Italian and "performed" by elaborately costumed puppets.

And all that is without including the numerous fringe and alternative venues, or the two other theatrical forms for which Prague is perhaps best-known, in addition to puppetry: mime and a speciality, "Black Light".

Black Light Theatre

Czech mime has a long and popular tradition, while Black Light is a sophisticated concept, first introduced in 1958 at the World Exhibition in Brussels. Since then it has gone from strength to strength. During the performances films and slides are projected on to multiple screens while actors, dressed completely in black to render them invisible, perform on stage, accompanied by a clever play of coloured lights. A certain amount of acrobatic skill is also often required of the actors.

Puppet theatre

Puppet theatre in Prague is surprisingly popular with adults as well as children, and, like mime and Black Light shows, it often appeals to tourists, as language is not a problem. The most popular traditional show uses Josef Skupka's time-honoured characters of Spejbl and Hurvínek, and there are avant-garde, highly original performances as well, notably those directed by Petr Nikl. The Praguers' love of puppets is also clearly evident in the many brightly coloured dolls available for sale throughout the city.

Theatre in Prague, as in many other cities in the world, is experiencing funding problems and the city's theatres must now scramble for private sponsorship. Still, it remains vibrant and exciting, with something to offer audiences of all kinds.

Divadlo Alfred ve dvoře
Františka Křížka 36
Tel: 233 376 997
www.alfredvedvore.cz
Mime theatre that does not pander to tourist tastes. The experimental, edgy acts are some of the best in Prague.

Divadlo Archa
Na Poříčí 26
Tel: 221 716 111
www.archatheatre.cz
Theatre with emphasis on the avant-garde. Archa hosts groups from Prague and abroad, including performances by the Agon Orchestra.

Divadlo Na zábradlí
Anenské náměstí 5
Tel: 222 868 868
www.nazabradli.cz
Famous as the theatre where Václav Havel worked; his plays are still performed here from time to time.

Divadlo Ponec
Husitská 24a

Tel: 222 721 531
www.divadloponec.cz
Primarily a contemporary dance venue, but also noted for its experimental mime productions.

Laterna magika – Nová scéna
Národní třída 4
Tel: 224 931 482
www.laterna.cz
Elaborate sets using different media make the Laterna one of the best black light theatres in Prague. Popular among tourists.

Národní divadlo marionet
Žatecká 1
Tel: 224 819 322
www.mozart.cz
The National Marionette Theatre puts on puppetry performances for all ages, with a long-running production of *Don Giovanni*.

Cinema

During the 1960s, Czech film achieved world renown, with excellent films such as Miloš Forman's *Loves of a Blonde* and the Academy-Award-winning *Closely Observed Trains*. As elsewhere, with notable exceptions particularly the excellent Kino Aero, Prague cinemas are now filled with standard Hollywood fare, usually played in English with Czech subtitles. Box offices indicate dubbed films by posting a small sign which reads "*České znění*". Posters at the cinemas, as well as their websites, are the best sources of information.

The following is a list of cinemas that show more daring English-language and foreign productions and cinema classics:

Kino Aero
Biskupcova 31
Tel: 271 771 349
www.kinoaero.cz

Evald
Národní třída 28
Tel: 221 105 225
www.cinemart.cz

MAT Studio
Karlovo náměstí 19
Tel: 224 915 765
www.mat.cz

NIGHTLIFE

Prague is no Paris or Berlin, but it is endeavouring to hold its own against smaller European capital cities as far as nightlife is concerned. Bars and clubs compete with casinos and sleazy pick-up joints to beckon those in search of adventure, and live jazz in particular is usually of a very high standard (see page 222). Late-night cafes such as the Globe (see page 158) may appeal to those not keen on loud music and dancing.

Generally, it's a good idea to avoid the places in the Wenceslas Square area, which tend to attract either mobs of teenage tourists, who don't know what else to do, or the dirty mac brigade; most locals won't go near such places. The better clubs are sprinkled all over the city, and there is no one best area for nightlife. The website www.techno.cz has up-to-date listings and information on the latest places to check out. The listings below are all reliable and are currently some of the best places in Prague.

Celnice
V celnice 4
Tel: 224 212 240
www.celnice.com
Open Sun–Thur 11am–2am,
Fri–Sat 11am–4am
Underneath the New Town restaurant and bar of the same name, this is currently one of Prague's best places for a night out. Very popular, with a well-dressed crowd.

Mecca
U průhonu 3
Tel: 283 870 522
www.mecca.cz
Open Fri–Sat 10pm–6am
Large and flash, the Mecca attracts top local DJs and packs club-goers in for its party nights. Now with jazz nights courtesy of Jazz Club Železná.

Radost FX
Bělehradská 120
Tel: 603 181 500
www.radostfx.cz
Open Thur–Sat 10pm–5am
Still the king of dance clubs, with a good crowd and top local and international DJs playing lots of House and R'n'B. The restaurant is one of the best vegetarian places in town.

Roxy
Dlouhá 33
Tel: 224 826 296
www.roxy.cz
Open daily from 7pm, parties start at 10pm
One of the best spaces in town, with an eclectic mix of top foreign DJs and contemporary art shows. There are also screenings of experimental cinema.

Ultramarin
Ostrovní 32
Tel: 224 932 249
www.ultramarin.cz
Open daily 10pm–4am
A chic stone-lined cellar that attracts a fashionable older crowd. Upstairs is a decent restaurant serving modern Asian and Pacific rim dishes.

Gay and Lesbian Venues

Favoured venues change fast and frequently, but the following are currently reliable in what is still a relatively new scene for Prague, and the patrons there can at least direct you to the latest dance clubs. Prague is generally very safe – though not necessarily out and proud – for gays and lesbians, and most people will encounter few problems. HIV rates of infection are not as high as the UK, though growing, but, as elsewhere, protection is a must. Also note that most gay clubs are hangouts for prostitutes and you will probably be approached. An excellent site for up-to-date information can be found at http://prague.gayguide.net The main lesbian site (all in Czech) is www.lesba.cz

Bar 21
Římská 21
Tel: 724 254 048
Open daily 4pm–4am
A mixed lesbian and gay cellar bar. Laid-back with a nice ambience; a good place for a quiet evening.

Club Termix
Třebízského 4a
Tel: 222 710 462
www.club-termix.cz
Open daily 8pm–5am
A classy mixed gay and lesbian club with good DJs and a long drinks list. There is also a dark room in which to get to know each other better.

Gejzee..r
Vínohradská 40
Tel: 222 516 036
www.gejzeer.cz
Open Thurs 8pm–4am, Fri–Sat 9pm–6am
A large and fun gay club, with all the essentials: two dance floors, chill-out spaces and a dark room "labyrinth". The well-designed space is also used for fashion shows.

Street Café
Blanická 28
Tel: 222 013 116
Open Mon–Thur 9am–11pm,
Fri–Sat 9am–4am, Sun 1–10pm
Previously MaLer, and still a popular venue for Prague's lesbians. A friendly, fun atmosphere, and a good place for breakfast.

Tingl Tangl
Karolíny Světlé 12
Tel: 224 238 278
www.tingltangl.com
Open Mon–Sat 8pm–5am
A gay, lesbian and straight bar and garden restaurant with a club downstairs. A drag cabaret is held on Wed, Fri and Sat.

SHOPPING

What to Buy

Prague is still not, and probably never will be, a shopper's paradise on the level of London, Paris or Milan. However, things have certainly improved and shiny new shopping centres, full of international chains, now ring the city centre; and a sizable number of international designers have set up shop along the posher avenues. Service has also markedly improved since the days of grumpy state-employed assistants who seemed to resent your presence in their establishment.

There are a number of locally produced items which are worth looking out for. You will not be able to avoid **Bohemian glass and china**, held in high esteem throughout the world due to their quality and fair price. New items from major manufacurers are still excellent, but now it's almost impossible to find a good deal in antique shops. Antique dealers have become wise to the foreign market for their wares and have altered their prices accordingly.

If you're looking for something typically Bohemian to take home as a gift, a Prague ham is a nice idea, but despite the fact that butcher's shops are numerous in the capital, authentic Prague ham is quite hard to find nowadays. It may prove less troublesome to get a bottle of the herbal liqueur **Becherovka** or some **Slivovice**. Fruity wines from Bohemia and Moravia will also be appreciated. **Wooden toys and puppets** make excellent gift items for children.

Street vendors – concentrated in Hradčany and on the Charles Bridge – sell handmade goods, such as marionettes and costume jewellery, as well as items of dubious use and value, such as refrigerator magnets depicting famous Prague sights. High quality **arts and crafts** are harder to find. However, local **fashions** by Prague designers are often interesting and well-made.

Classical music **CDs**, especially those of Czech music from Supraphon, are cheaper than in the UK. The performances, by superb Czech ensembles and musicians, are always good and often thrilling. Also look out for recordings by local jazz and experimental rock musicians.

Opening Times

Most shops are open 10am–6pm, although those in the centre, catering largely to the tourist trade, often remain open late almost year round.

On Saturdays most shops outside the centre of Prague close at noon or 1pm; shops in the centre, especially the larger department stores, may retain weekday hours on Saturday and Sunday as well.

Shopping Areas

Generally the best shopping is to be found in Staré and Nové Město, although some of the outlying districts now have huge shopping centres. The main commercial streets of central Prague with dependably long hours all year round are Václavské náměstí (Wenceslas Square) and Na příkopě. If you are looking for expensive international fashion then head for Pařížská, which runs off Old Town Square. Some small streets in the Old Town, such as V Kolkovně, Dušní, Týnská and Panská, have a number of exciting and unusual boutiques. The Týn Courtyard near the Old Town Square also has numerous little shops which are worth exploring. The main branches are given for the shops listed below, check their websites for other branches.

Department Stores and Shopping Centres

The department stores with the largest selection of goods, including gifts, fabric, clothes, shoes, perfume, groceries, travel accessories, stationery, electrical goods and books, are:
Kotva
náměstí Republiky 8
Tesco
Národní třída 26
The supermarket in the basement at Tesco is very popular.

There of the best, and largest, shopping centres are:

Palác Flóra
Vinohradská 149
www.palacflora.cz
Nový Smíchov Centrum
Plzeňská 8
Slovanský Dům
Na příkopě 22
www.slovanskydum.cz

Bohemian Crafts

Manufaktura
Melantrichova 17
Tel: 221 632 480
www.manufaktura.biz
A chain of stores specialising in local crafts, including wooden toys, hand-dyed fabric, ceramics, and beautifully painted eggs. The chain has eight locations, all situated along the main tourist routes.

Bookshops

Anagram Books
Týn 4
Tel: 224 895 737
www.anagram.cz
Serious literature; from philosophy to criticism, obscure titles to art history texts. You will mainly find new books, but there is also a limited collection of quality second-hand titles.
Big Ben Bookshop
Malá štupartská 5
Tel: 224 826 565
www.bigbenbookshop.com
Recent and classic paperbacks in English, with strong drama, poetry and central European history sections. English-language newspapers and magazines, and a selection of maps and guides.
Fraktály
Betlémské náměstí 5a
Tel: 222 222 186
www.fraktaly.cz
A superb small bookshop specialising in art, design and architecture. A good place to pick in-depth books on the Czech Republic.
The Globe Bookstore and Coffeehouse
Pštrossova 7
Tel: 224 934 203
www.globebookstore.cz

The new location of this classic expat book store is geared more towards an upwardly mobile local crowd. Readings by local and international authors are sometimes held in the café. Cheap Internet terminals but prices for the invariably dog-eared used books are rather high.

Shakespeare and Sons
Krymská 12
Tel: 271 740 839
www.shakes.cz
An earthy, old-style bookshop with polished wood tables and loads of natural light. Sells both new and used English-language books, and hosts regular poetry readings. The café is one of the nicest in Vršovice.

Fashion and Beauty

Though you will find few international-label bargains, young Czech designers offer high quality for surprisingly reasonable prices.

Botanicus
Michalská 2
Tel: 224 212 977
www.botanicus.cz
Locally-produced organic beauty products and essential oils.

Boutique Klára Nademlýnská
Dlouhá 3
Tel: 224 188 769
www.klaranademlynska.cz
Klára Nademlýnská's fashionable and sexy hand-made clothing.

Le Bohême
Štupartská 7
Tel: 224 837 379
Casual but classic pieces designed by Renáta Vokáčová, with lovely linen dresses on display during the summer.

Model Praha
Václavské náměstí 28
Tel: 224 216 805
www.modelpraha.cz
Hat designers for anything from fashion shoots to theatrical costumes.

Mýrnyx týrnýx
Saská ulička
Tel: 224 923 270
www.myrnyxtyrnyx.cz
Prague's quirkiest and most interesting secondhand clothes shop.

Nostalgie
Jakubská 8
Elegant, classic clothes designed by Marie Fleischmannová and made in good quality, natural fabrics.

Pavla & Olga
Vlašská 13
Tel: 728 939 872
Fashion one-offs, in interesting and unusual designs by local talent Pavla Michálková.

Glass

There is a huge amount of glass and crystal on display throughout the city, not all of it of high quality. The shops below are, if not the cheapest, all reputable and have interesting designs. Almost all of these places will also deal with the care and shipping of your new items, for a fee.

Arzenal
Valentinská 11
Tel: 224 814 099
www.arzenal.cz
Modern designs by Bořek Šípek.

Crystalex
Malé náměstí 6
Tel: 224 228 459
www.crystalex.cz
The factory store of a leading Bohemian manufacturer.

Erpet
Staroměstské náměstí 27
Tel: 224 229 755
www.erpet.cz
A wide range of top notch crystal.

Moser
Na příkopě 12
Tel: 224 211 293
www.moser.cz
The elegantly appointed flagship store of the best, most expensive, Czech glassware.

Modernist Replicas

Kubista
Dům u černé Matky Boží,
Ovocný trh 19
Tel: 224 236 378
www.kubista.cz
Wonderful reproductions of Czech Cubist works, as

well as some originals for sale.

Modernista
Konviktská 5
Tel: 222 220 113
www.modernista.cz
Taking the concept further with, as well as Cubist pieces, works by Adolf Loos and Functionalist designers.

Music

Bontonland (formerly Supraphon)
Jungmannova 20
Tel: 224 948 718
The first place to look for that classical disc.

Bontonland Megastore
Václavské náměstí 1
Tel: 224 473 080
www.bontonland.cz
The largest selection of music in Prague, including the biggest local groups. Booths allow you to listen before you buy.

Wine

Cellarius
Štěpánská 61
Tel: 224 210 979
www.cellarius.cz
A wine merchant with a good selection of Moravian wines.

BELOW: in Manufaktura.

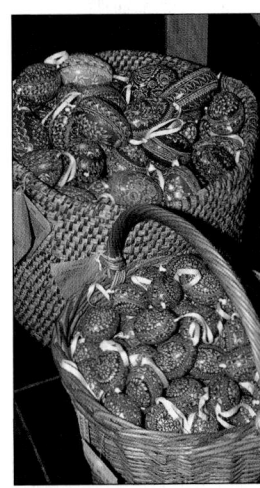

A - Z

A HANDY SUMMARY OF PRACTICAL INFORMATION, ARRANGED ALPHABETICALLY

A ddresses

Addresses in Prague are given with the street name first, usually omitting words such as *ulice* (street). You may also see two numbers for the same address – a quirk of, historically, two different numbering systems – generally it is enough (as used in this book) to use the lower of the two numbers.

B usiness Hours

Most grocery shops are open weekdays 7am–6pm, with speciality stores opening from 10am–6pm, although those in the centre catering to the tourist trade often remain open late year-round. Smaller shops may close their doors for a couple of hours during lunchtime. On Saturdays most shops outside the centre close at noon or 1pm, but shops in the centre, especially the large department stores, may retain weekday hours on Saturday and Sunday as well. The main commercial streets of Prague with dependably long hours year round are Wenceslas Square and Na příkopě.

C limate

Thanks to its protected position in a valley, Prague's climate is, for Central Europe, particularly mild. The average annual temperature is around 9°C (48°F). Summer averages are around: June 17°C (62°F), July 19°C (66°F); winter averages around: December

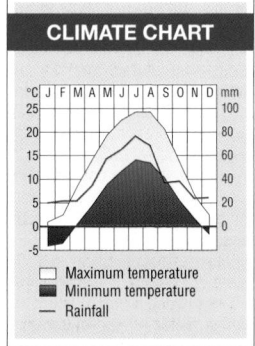

CLIMATE CHART

□ Maximum temperature
■ Minimum temperature
— Rainfall

ber 2°C (36°F), February 0°C (32°F). The average annual precipitation is 487 mm (19 inches). The least rain falls in February and the most in July.

Being situated between hills means air can become trapped in the city, making winter smog more likely. A report by the Organisation for Economic Cooperation and Development (OECD) revealed that, the amount of nitrogen oxide in Prague is well above the EU and OECD average; a rapid increase in traffic levels in Prague since the 1989 revolution has exacerbated a pollution problem. Air pollution overall in the Czech Republic, however, has decreased by 50 percent since the 1980s, but there is still a long way to go. Stricter controls imposed by EU entry are already starting to have an effect.

Customs

Czech customs proceedures have been greatly relaxed following accession to the EU. For non-EU nationals few changes are likely to have been made to existing visa arrangements but it would be wise to check with a Czech embassy or consulate before travelling.

Import

All items of personal use may be taken into the country duty free; any electronic, photographic and filming equipment should be listed, together with serial numbers, and presented to customs for confirmation. The list must be declared again upon departure. All items of personal use taken into the country must also be taken out.

At present you are allowed the following items for your own consumption (goods restricted to persons 18 years of age or older): 200 cigarettes, 50 cigars or 250 grams of tobacco, 2 litres of wine, 5 litres of beer, 1 litre of spirits. Foreign visitors are permitted to take gifts into the country with a total value not exceeding 6,000 Kč (approx. US$180).

if you want to bring a pet dog or cat with you through customs, you must be prepared to show a certificate of inoculation that is between three days and three weeks old.

Export

Non-commercial items (i.e. not intended for resale) of unlimited value can be exported from the Czech Republic without an export permit. Valuable historic objects may not be exported. To export antiques and rare cultural objects more than 50 years old, visitors need to get a special permit which can be very difficult to obtain.

Visas and Passports

There are no restrictions on EU citizens visitng the Czech Republic. For citizens of the United States, only a valid passport is required for stays of up to 90 days. Citizens of Canada, Australia and New Zealand must obtain a special visa before visiting the country, which can be arranged at Czech consulates throughout the world. Visitors to the Czech Republic are required to have a passport valid for at least 3 months after their planned departure from the country.

Czech Embassies

Australia
38 Culgoa Circuit, O'Malley
Canberra ACT 2606
Tel: (61) 2 62 90 13 86
Canada
251 Cooper Street
Ottawa, Ontario K2P 0G2
Tel: (1) 613 562 38 75
United Kingdom
26 Kensington Palace Gardens
London W8 4QY
Tel: (44) 20 7243 1115
United States
3900 Spring Freedom St. NW
Washington DC
Tel: (1) 202 274 9100

D isabled Travellers

Prague's public transport was not designed with disabled people in mind. Most Metro stations and all trams and buses involve climbing and descending what can be very steep steps. People in wheelchairs who wish to use public transport must be carried bodily on and off trams and buses, and pavement curbs do not often have ramps. But in general Praguers take a courteous view toward people with disabilities, and will make efforts to assist them.

E lectricity

AC 220 volts. Two-pin plugs or adaptors are needed for British appliances.

Embassies and Consulates

Australia
Klimentská 10
Prague 1
Tel: 296 578 350
Canada
Muchova 6
Prague 6
Tel: 272 101 800
www.canada.cz
Ireland
Tržiště 13
Prague 1
Tel: 257 530 061
New Zealand
Dykova 19
Prague 1
Tel: 222 514 672
South Africa
Ruská 65

EMERGENCY NUMBERS

General emergency: tel: 112
Ambulance: tel: 155
Fire Brigade: tel: 150
Police: tel: 158
Emergency road service:
tel: 1230, 1240
Lost Property:
tel: 224 235 085
Lost or stolen credit cards:
● **American Express:**
  tel: 222 800 222
● **Visa, Mastercard:**
  tel: 272 771 111
● **Diner's Club:**
  tel: 267 197 450

TRANSPORT

ACCOMMODATION

ACTIVITIES

A – Z

LANGUAGE

Prague 10
Tel: 267 311 114
United Kingdom
Thunovská 14
Prague 1
Tel: 257 402 111
www.britain.cz
United States
Tržiště 15
Prague 1
Tel: 257 530 663
www.usembassy.cz

G ay & Lesbian Travellers

The Czech Republic adheres to a live-and-let-live attitude toward gays and lesbians. Public displays of affection, however, might attract stares in Prague *(see also page 225)*.

H ealth and Insurance

While medicines are becoming more easily available, it's always a good idea for visitors to bring along any medication that they require regularly. Before setting out, it is also advisable to take out international medical insurance. If you have to pay for treatment, make sure you get a receipt for money to be reimbursed, together with a certificate of the exchange rate at the time you pay.

No inoculations are required, and there are no diseases to be wary of. Tap water is drinkable, although most Praguers drink bottled water, and visitors may prefer to do the same.

Medical Treatment

Western visitors have a number of options for medical treatment. If you fall ill in Prague, your best bet is to head for:
Canadian Medical Care
Veleslavínská 1
Prague 6
Tel: 235 360 133
www.cmc.praha.cz
All the doctors speak good English. There is also a dentist, physiotherapist and psychotherapist on staff. Be sure you have private health insurance as the fees –

which otherwise must be paid in cash – are very high.

The other hospital for foreigners is the state-run:
Na Homolce Hospita
(Nemocnice Na Homolce)
Roentgenova 2
Prague 5
Tel: 257 272 146
www.homolka.cz
Staff physicians speak reasonable English as well as other foreign languages. It can be reached by the Metro station Anděl on the yellow line B, then bus 167 to the last stop. Fees should be paid in cash; you must then arrange your own reimbursement.

Other good hospitals for visitors include:
Medicover
Tylovo náměstí 3
Prague 2
Tel: 234 630 111
www.medicover.cz
Physicians speak English. Western health insurance accepted.
Health Centre Prague
Vodičkova 28–30
Prague 1
Tel: 603 433 833
www.doctor-prague.cz
Good services for foreign patients and a number of languages spoken.

For **dental emergencies** try the clinics above, or contact:
Dental Emergency
Palackého 5
Prague 1
Tel: 224 946 981

Opticians

There are many shops now in the centre of Prague offering optical services, and western contact lens solutions are readily available. Some of the best are:
Eiffel Optic
Celetná 38
Tel: 221 613 302
www.eiffeloptic.cz
Attractive selection of glasses and express service for glasses and contact lenses.
Grand Optical
Na příkopě 19
Tel: 224 238 371

www.grandoptical.cz
All services, with a huge selection of frames and lenses.

Both of these shops have numerous branches across town; check their websites for other locations.

Pharmacies

Chemists *(lekárna)* are open during normal business hours. In case of an emergency after hours, you'll find the address of the nearest chemists on emergency duty posted in the window. The following chemists have extended hours:
Prague 1
Palackého 5
Tel: 224 946 982
Prague 2
Belgická 37
Tel: 222 519 731
Prague 3
Koněvova 210
Tel: 284 860 651
Prague 4
Antala staška 80
Tel: 261 006 432
Soukalova 3355
Tel: 241 770 498
Prague 5
Štefánikova 6
Tel: 257 320 918 (24 hours)
Prague 6
Evropská 55
Tel: 220 611 775
Pod marjánkou 12
Tel: 220 514 473
Prague 7
Milady horákové 18
Tel: 233 375 599
Prague 8
Heydukova 10
Tel: 266 082 017 (24 hours)
Prague 9
Gen. Janouška 902
Tel: 281 914 072
Prague 10
V olšinách 41
Tel: 274 821 187

I nternet and e-mail

Internet cafes are popping up all over Prague, especially in the centre. Most charge by the hour for computer time and the fees are reasonable. At least some degree of English is usually spoken by the personnel. Some good internet cafes to try include:

Bohemia Bagel
Masná 2 and Újezd 16
www.bohemiabagel.cz

The Globe Bookstore and Coffeehouse
Pštrossova 6
www.globebookstore.cz
One of the best and cheapest.

Jáma
V jámě
www.jamapub.cz

Internet Café Spika
Dlážděná 4
www.netcafe.spika.cz

Media

Newspapers

Foreign newspapers can usually be found in hotels and kiosks, and in some of the major bookshops. There are two English-language papers in Prague: *The Prague Post* (www.praguepost.com), which reports on news, business and cultural events as well as reviewing restaurants, clubs and shows, and the bi-monthly *Prague Tribune* (www.prague-tribune.cz) focuses on business and executive lifestyles; *The New Presence* (www.new-presence.cz) runs articles on political and social affairs translated from its Czech sister

publication, *Nová Přítomnost.*

You can pick up programmes of events, restaurant guides and general information brochures, including information on cultural events, free of charge in tourist offices such as those run by the PIS (www.pis.cz).

Television and Radio

Radio is generally privatised after being exclusively state-owned pre-1989, and television is heading in that direction thanks to competition from the private TV station **NOVA**, which has garnered the lion's share of the viewing audience with Czech-dubbed versions of (mainly) American fare.

On the radio, the **BBC World Service** can be picked up on 101.1 FM intermittently throughout the day and evening (with frequent BBC programmes in Czech and Slovak), as can local news in English on **Radio Prague**, with which it shares the same frequency.

The two state-run television channels are **ČT1** and **ČT2**. The latter broadcasts English-language European news both at midday and in the evening, as well as occasional movies and documentaries in English with Czech subtitles. As well as **TV Nova**, **Prima** is another privately

owned station. Both show popular Western serials dubbed into Czech, as well as local programmes. Numerous satellite channels are also available, including CNN, HBO and Skynews.

Money

Currency

The unit of currency is the crown (koruna or Kč), which is divided into 100 hellers (haléř). There are 20, 50, 100, 200, 500, 1,000, 2,000 and 5,000 crown notes and 1, 2, 5, 10 and 20 crown coins as well as 50 heller coins. It is not difficult to change back your crowns into other major currencies at banks and exchange offices in Prague. Although in theory Czech currency is freely convertible in every country around the world, in practice it is not always easy, so visitors are strongly advised to make their conversions from crowns into other their own currency while they are still inside the Czech Republic.

£1 sterling is currently worth around 43 Kč; €1 around 30 Kč; and $1 US around 23 Kč.

Cheques and Credit Cards

Travellers cheques are accepted by banks and hotels. Credit cards are accepted by many but not all shops, restaurants and hotels. Always check in advance to avoid embarrassment; signs of accepted cards are displayed on the door. When changing money and cheques, be careful: sometimes what looks like an exceptionally good rate may be accompanied by an inordinately high commission; this is especially true at Chequepoint Change kiosks.

The Black Market

While it is possible to exchange money on the black market anywhere in Prague, it has no benefit since the rates on the street and in the banks are no longer different enough to warrant the has-

BELOW: the national flag.

sle. The practice is officially forbidden and offenders will be prosecuted. Do not be tempted by offers, particularly as you might also be cheated: there are many fake notes in circulation.

Banks, Exchange Bureaux and ATMs

In general most banks are open 8am–5pm Monday to Friday. Exchange bureaux are open from 8am until at least 7pm; some in the centre even remain open 24 hours a day. Most hotels will exchange money around the clock, but their rates are slightly higher than at a regular exchange bureau or bank.

To decide which outlet to use, enquire about the commission rate before you hand over your money as they can vary considerably. Czech banks along Na příkopě and Wenceslas Square offer lower commissions than private exchange outlets.

By far the most convenient way of getting money is from one of many ATMs that accept foreign cash and credit cards. They are generally open 24 hours, the charges (from your own bank) are often lower than those offered by exchange bureaux, and it is a lot less hassle.

Tipping

A service charge is included in bills issued by hotels and restaurants in Prague. A ten percent tip is a good idea unless the service is unsatisfactory. In pubs and cheaper establishments, it is customary to round up the bill by a few crowns.

Postal Services

The main Post Office, **Hlavní pošta**, is at:
Jindřišská 14
Prague 1
www.cpost.cz
Open 24 hours a day, it is situated in a street off Wenceslas Square, in the southwest corner. The other post offices (marked with distinctive orange signs say-

ing *pošta*) are open Mon–Fri 8am–6pm, and Sat 8am–noon; smaller branches are generally only open Mon–Fri 8am–5pm at the latest.

Postal Charges

Stamps can be bought in post offices or, if you're in luck, at newspaper kiosks. Enquire about current postal rates for letters and postcards once you're in the country, as they go up frequently. You'll find orange letter boxes just about everywhere you look.

Couriers

The international delivery services offer a fast and reliable, but also expensive, means of sending important documents and parcels abroad. Employees speak English, and can arrange for courier pick-ups.

DHL
Václavské náměstí 53
Tel: 800 103 000
www.dhl.cz

FedEx
Olbrachtova 1, Prague 4
Tel: 224 440 024
www.fedex.com

TNT
Na radosti 399, Prague 5
Tel: 257 083 333
www.tnt.com

UPS
K Letišti 57, Prague 6
Tel: 800 181 111
www.ups.com

Public Holidays

The dates of national holidays at present are as follows:
1 January: New Year's Day
Easter Monday: variable according to the Roman calendar
1 May: May Day
8 May: Day of Liberation from Fascism
5 July: Feast Day of SS Cyril and Methodius
6 July: Anniversary of the death of Jan Hus
28 October: Day of the origin of the independent Czechoslovakia
17 November: Day of Students' Struggle for Democracy, commemorating the Velvet Revolution
25–26 December: Christmas
Various Christian holidays, for example the Feast of Corpus Christi and the Assumption of the Virgin Mary, are celebrated in different regions but are not considered national holidays.

Racism

Though the Czechs are enlightened in many ways, they have yet

BELOW: post office signs are easy to spot.

ČESKÁ POŠTA
IČO 47114983/21

to shake their cultural racism against the *Roma* (Gypsies), often discriminating against them in employment and in schools. Travellers with *Roma* features (dark hair, olive skin) may occasionally find they have trouble being seated at restaurants or getting snubbed by shopkeepers. A few instances of violence also occur each year; although these are quite rare, tourists should nevertheless still be vigilant.

S ecurity and Crime

The violent crime rate in Prague is still lower than that of many Western European cities. However, since 1990 the incidence of offences such as robbery and fraud have increased dramatically; cases of visitors having their handbags or wallets snatched are increasingly common, as are car theft and robbery from cars. It's a good idea to deposit valuables in the hotel safe and, if possible, always park at a supervised car park. Stay alert to your surroundings, especially in crowds.

Particular hot spots for pickpocketing and other crimes against visitors include Old Town Square, Charles Bridge, any crowded areas at Prague Castle such as Golden Lane and St. Vitus's Cathedral, and Wenceslas Square. Jostling on the Metro and trams can be the work of pickpockets, particularly as you get on and off; trams to be especially careful on are Nos. 9 and 22, which cater to tourist routes.

In case of emergency, either consult your hotel reception or contact the police directly by dialling **158**. If you should have the misfortune to lose your personal documents or have them stolen, get in touch immediately with your embassy representative.

Smoking

Seemingly the only place free from tobacco smoke is on public transport, otherwise the Czechs light up just about anywhere.

T elecommunications

There are two different kinds of telephones in operation in the city (provided they are not out of order). The first kind only accepts 2-, 5- and 10-crown coins and is therefore only practical for making local calls. These phones do not return coins if the line is engaged or if no one answers your call.

Most telephones, though, accept only phonecards which are available in various denominations; these phones may have how-to-use information in English, but if not, simply insert the card where indicated, listen for a dial tone, and dial your number. Phonecards can be purchased in post offices or from newsagents.

Long-distance calls without a phonecard are very expensive, and bear in mind that hotels will charge a 20–30 percent commission. The 24-hour phone centre at Prague's main post office (Jindřišská 14, Prague 1) is located around the corner in Politických vězňů. You must leave a deposit with one of the invariably grumpy attendants before you may dial. A series of phone books to Czech and foreign cities are also available here.

International dialling code
00 420 (Czech Republic) + 2 (Prague)

International access codes
AT&T: 00 42 000 101
MCI: 00 42 000 112
Sprint: 00 42 087 187

National and International directory enquiries
tel: 1181

Most people will find that their own mobile phone will work in Prague (even if the charges will be much higher than using phonecards). However, for longer stays it is better and much cheaper to buy one of the easily available local pay-as-you-go SIM cards. The main companies are

Eurotel (www.eurotel.cz) and Oskar Mobil (www.oskarmobil.cz).

In most hotels you can both send and receive a fax. Faxes may also be sent from the main post office. In addition, almost all first-class hotels provide office services which include access to various computers and printers. Photocopying is widely available (look for signs marked Kopírování).

Time Zone

Dunring Oct–Mar Prague is one hour ahead of GMT; Apr–Sept 2 hours ahead of GMT.

Tourist Information

The Czech Centre (www.czech centres.cz) can provide a wealth of information about Prague and the Czech Republic.

In the UK
Czech Centre
13 Harley Street
London W1G 9QG
Tel: 020 7307 5180
In London also contact:
Czech Tourism
Morley House, 320 Regent Street
London W1B 3BG
Tel: 020 7631 0427
www.czechtourism.com

In the US
Czech Center
1109 Madison Avenue
New York, NY 10028
Tel: 212 288 0830

In Prague
Czech Centres Administration
Rytiřská 31, Prague 1
Tel: 221 610 252

The **Prague Information Service** (**PIS**) can provide much useful information, including city maps and and addresses. For those who can read Czech, there are the more detailed *Přehled kulturních pořadě v Praze*, and *Kultura v Praze* (available in English as *Culture in Prague*), which list events according to venue; both are sold at news kiosks.

TRANSPORT

ACCOMMODATION

ACTIVITIES

A – Z

LANGUAGE

Prague Information Service
Staroměstské naměstí
Tel: 12 444
www.pis.cz
Branches at: Na příkopě 20; the
main (Wilsonova) railway station;
and in the Malostranská
mostecká vez in Malá Strana.

Travel Agencies

ČEDOK, the former state-run
travel agency, now private,
arranges all types of accommodation, as well as complete
holidays to Prague and other
destinations within the Czech
Republic.

In the UK
Morley House, 314–22 Regent St
London, W1B 3BG
Tel: 020 7580 3778
www.cedok.co.uk

In Prague
Na příkopě 18
Tel: 224 197 632
Václavské náměstí 53
Tel: 221 965 243
Rytiřská 16
Tel: 224 224 461
www.cedok.cz

W ebsites

Buses
www.csadcl.cz
Bus timetables for the Czech
Republic.
Contemporary music in Prague
www.musica.cz
A great site for contemporary and
experimental music.
Czech Railways
www.cd.cz
Timetables and information for
the railway network.
Czech theatre
www.theatre.cz
Links to theatres, history and cur-
rent performances.
The National Gallery
www.ngprague.cz
The many branches of the
national art collection.
The National Museum
www.nm.cz
The same but for the museums.

Online dictionary
www.slovnik.cz
Will translate English into Czech
and vice versa.
Prague Information Service
www.pis.cz
A mine of information, from
addresses to opening times to
emergency contact numbers.
Prague Music News
www.sdmusic.cz
Up-to-date listings and information on musical events in Prague.
The Prague Post
www.praguepost.cz
The weekly English-language
newspaper, including a full
archive search.
Prague TV
www.prague.tv
News, reviews and a lots of background information.
Radio Prague
www.radio.cz
A similar service but from the
radio station.
Square Meal
www.squaremeal.cz
An online guide to Prague's
restaurants.

Weights and Mesures

The Czech Republic uses the
metric system.

BELOW: Czech out ČEDOK.

When to Go

The best times to visit Prague are
the spring and autumn, when the
weather is mild. May is delightful
and the mild autumn has very
stable weather. These are also
the seasons when Prague's
parks and gardens are seen to
their best advantage. Summer
months mean that the main
tourist areas, such as Golden
Lane at Prague Castle and the
streets off Old Town Square, can
be unbearably crowded. The main
tourist season begins before
Easter and extends through to
September, with another huge
increase in visitors over Christmas and New Year.

Women Travellers

Although feminism still has a long
way to go in the Czech Republic,
women travelling in Prague and
the Czech Republic should not
expect to encounter any particular
problems. If you are by yourself
late at night, however, the usual
rules of common sense apply.
Keep in mind that pubs in Prague
can be very male dominated envi-
ronments, and solo women will
probably not feel comfortable.

LANGUAGE

UNDERSTANDING CZECH

Language

Along with Russian, Czech belongs to the Slavonic group of languages. Its closest neighbour is Slovak, to which it has roughly the same relation as southern English to Lowland Scots; the languages are mutually intelligible despite many differences in pronunciation and vocabulary. This is not of course much help to English-speakers, who can all too easily be put off by the impenetrable vocabulary, a formidable array of accents and a complex grammar involving bewildering changes in the ending of words. And it's true that acquiring fluency in Czech takes about twice as long as reaching the same level of ability in languages such as French or German. Local people will not expect you to have mastered their language, but as

in every country, they will be pleased if you have made the effort to acquire a few basics. You will also find it a great help to be able to understand street signs and other directions. One plus point is that Czech, unlike English, is pronounced exactly as it looks. A few – very few – words in international use can be deciphered; examples include *tramvaj* (tramway or tram), *recepce* (hotel reception), and *auto* (car). Many people in the tourism industry know at least some English (and German), but you should not assume this; it is always polite to ask "Promiňte, mluvite anglicky?" *(Excuse me, do you speak English?).*

Pronunciation tips

The stress in a word is always on the first syllable.

Vowels:

Long vowels are indicated by an accent: á, é, í, ó, ú or ů and ý.
Ě like "ye" in "yes"
Ý long "e" as in "feet"
Au like "ow" in "now"
Ou like "ow"in "show"

L and r can be pronounced as half vowels as in Plzeň (almost like Pulzen) = Pilsen), krk (almost like kirk) = neck)

Consonants

C ts as in "its"
Č like "ch" in "church"
Ch like "ch" in "loch"
J like "y" in yes
R trilled or rolled
Ř (unique to Czech, and even difficult for some natives) a combination of a trilled r and sh, as in Dvořák
Š "sh"
Ž like "s" in pleasure

Basic communication

Good morning/how do you do? *Dobrý den*
Good evening *Dobrý večer*
Good night *Dobrou noc*
Hello *Ahoj*
Goodbye *Na shledanou*
Yes *Ano*
No *Ne*
Please/you're welcome *Prosím*

Thank you *Děkuji*
Excuse me *Promiňte*
I'm sorry *Je mi líto*
How are you? *Jak se máte?*
(This may be interpreted literally!)
Fine, thanks *Děkuji, dobře*
And you? *A vy?*
Cheers! (when drinking) *Na zdraví!*

Help! *Pomoc!*
I am looking for ... *Hledám ...*
What? *Co?*
Where? *Kde?*
Where is/are? *Kde je/jsou?*
When? *Kdy?*
How? *Jak?*
How much? *Kolik?*
How much does it cost? *Kolik to stojí?*

I want Chci
We want Chceme
I would like Chtěl bych (chtěla
bych if the speaker is female)
I don't know Nevím
I don't understand Nerozumím
Do you speak English/German?
Mluvíte anglicky/německy?
Slowly, please! Pomalu, prosím!
Here Tady
There Tam

Numbers

0	Nula
1	Jeden, jedna (feminine), jedno (neuter)
2	Dva, dvě (feminine, neuter)
3	Tři
4	Čtyři
5	Pět
6	Šest
7	Sedm
8	Osm
9	Devět
10	Deset
11	Jedenáct
12	Dvanáct
13	Třináct
14	Čtrnáct
15	Patnáct
16	Šestnáct
17	Sedmnáct
18	Osmnáct
19	Devatenáct
20	Dvacet
21	Dvacet jeden (or jednadvacet)
22	Dvacet dva (or dvaadvacet)
30	Třicet
40	Čtyřicet
50	Padesát
60	Šedesát
70	Sedmdesát
80	Osmdesát
90	Devadesát
100	Sto
200	Dvě stě
300	Tři sta
400	Čtyři sta
500	Pět set
600	Šest set
1,000	Tisíc
1,000,000	Milión
A pair/few	Pár
Half	Půl

Times and dates

Monday pondělí
Tuesday úterý
Wednesday středa
Thursday čvrtek
Friday pátek
Saturday sobota
Sunday neděle

January leden
February únor
March březen
April duben
May květen
June červen
July červenec
August srpen
September září
October říjen
November listopad
December prosinec

Day Den
Morning Ráno
Afternoon Odpoledne
Evening Večer
Night Noc
Yesterday Včera
Today Dnes
Tomorrow Zítra
Now Teď'
What is the time? Kolik je hodin?
One o'clock Jedna hodina
Two/three/four o'clock
Dvě/tři/čtyři hodiny
Five o'clock Pět hodin

Signs

Autobusové nádraží **Bus station**
Celnice **Customs**
Informace **Information**
Muži, páni **Gentlemen**
Nádraží **Railway station** (Hlavní nádraží **Main station**)
Nástupiště **Platform**
Občerstvení **Refreshments**
Odjezd/odchod **Departure**
Obsazeno **Occupied, engaged**
Otevřeno **Open**
Pokladna **Cash desk, booking office**
Pozor **Danger**
Příjezd/příchod **Arrival**
Sem **Pull**
Směnárna **Bureau de change**
Tam **Push**
Vstup/vchod **Entrance**

Výstup/východ **Exit**
Záchod **Lavatory** (or WC, pronounced "vay-tsay")
Zakázáno **Forbidden** (Kouření zakázáno **No smoking**)
Zastávka **Tram/Bus stop**
Zavřeno **Closed**
Ženy, dámy **Women, Ladies**

Travel

Airport Letiště
Boarding card Palubní lístek
Bus Autobus
Car Auto
Class: first/second class
První/druhá třída
Flight Let
Funicular Lanovka
Passport Pas
Seat reservation Místenka
Station (Metro) Stanice
Steamer Parník
Taxi Taxi
Ticket Jízdenka
(**Return ticket** zpáteční jízdenka), lístek
Train Vlak
Tram Tramvaj
Visa Visum
Waiting room Čekárna

How can I get to...? Jak se dostanu na...?
By bus Autobusem
By Metro Metrem
By taxi Taxíkem
By train Vlakem
By tram Tramvají
On foot Pěšky

Book of (Metro/tram/bus) tickets Blok jízdenek
Where is the nearest Metro station? Kde je nejbližší stanice Metra?
I want to go to ... Chci jet do ...
A ticket to ... please Prosím, jízdenku do ...
How far is ...? Jak daleko je ...?
How long does the journey take? Jak dlouho trvá cesta?
Which is the (Metro) station for ...? Která je stanice pro ...?
How often does the tram run to ...? Jak často jede tramvaj do ...?
Do I have to change? Musím přestoupit?

Where do I change? *Kde mám přestoupit?*
I'm getting off at the next (Metro) stop *Vystupuji příští stanici*
You must get off here *Musíte vystupit zde*

Recorded messages on the Metro:
Ukončete výstup a nástup! Dveře se zavírají! **Do not enter or leave the train! Doors closing!**
Příští stanice – Hradčanská **Next stop – Hradčany**

Recorded message on buses and trams:
Příští zastávka – Národní divadlo **Next stop – Národní divadlo**

Directions

Right/left *Napravo/nalevo*
First left/second right *První nalevo/druhá napravo*
Straight on *Stále rovně*
After the traffic lights *Za semaforem*
Is it near/far? *Je to blízko/daleko?*
It's five minutes walk *Je to pět minut pěšky*
100 metres *Sto metrů*
One kilometre *Jeden kilometr*
It's behind/opposite/in front of/above/below *Je to za/naproti/před/nad/pod*
North *Sever*
South *Jih*
East *Východ*
West *Západ*

Accommodation

Campsite *Kemping*
Hotel *Hotel*
Private accommodation *Pokoj v soukromí*
Youth hostel *Mládežnická ubytovna*
Flat/apartment *Byt*
Family house *Vila*
Full board *Plná penze*
Kitchen *Kuchyň*
Key *Klíč*
Reception *Recepce*
Lift *Výtah*
Bath *Koupelna*
Shower *Sprcha*

I've a reservation *Mám reservaci*
Your name? *Vaše jméno?*
Do you have a free single/double room? *Máte volný pokoj pro jednu osobu/pro dva?*
A room with twin beds *Pokoj s dvěma lůžky*
A quiet en suite room *Klidný pokoj s koupelnou*
What is the rate for one night/a week? *Jaká je cena na jednu noc/na týden?*
May I see the room? *Mohu se na ten pokoj podívat?*
Is there a room which has a view of the river/the garden? *Máte pokoj s výhledem na řeku/do zahrady?*
The room number is ... *Číslo pokoje je ...*
On the ground floor *V přízemí*
On the first/second/third floor *V prvním/druhém/třetím poschodí*
Is breakfast included? *Je to se snídaní?*
May I have these shirts washed? *Mohu si dát vyprat tyto košile?*
May I pay by credit card? *Mohu platit kartou?*
I will pay cash *Platím v hotovosti*
The bill *Účet*
There is a slight mistake *Zde je malá chyba*

Having a drink

Beer *Pivo*
Lager *Světlé pivo*
Dark beer *Černé pivo*
Draught beer *Točené pivo*
Red wine *Červené víno*
White wine *Bílé víno*
Bottle *Láhev*
Tea *Čaj*
Tea with milk *Čaj s mlékem*
Tea with lemon *Čaj s citrónem*
Coffee *Káva*
Milk *Mléko*
Cocoa *Čokoláda*
Sugar *Zukr*
Juice *Džus*
Lemonade *Limonáda*
Water *Voda*
Mineral water *Minerální voda/Minerálka*
Sparkling mineral water *Perlivá minerálka*

Dining

Breakfast *Snídaně*
Lunch *Oběd*
Dinner *Večeře*
Restaurant *Restaurace*
Pub *Hospoda/Hostinec/Pivnice*
Canteen/Dining room *Jídelna*
Waiter *Číšník*
Waitress *Číšnice/Servírka*
Table *Stůl*
Menu *Jídelní lístek*
Wine list *Nápojový lístek*
Knife *Nůž*
Fork *Vidlička*
Spoon *Lžíce*
Plate *Talíř*
Napkin *Ubrousek*
Glass *Sklenice*
Cup *Šálek*
Ashtray *Popelník*
Bill *Účet*

A table for two, please *Jsme dva*
May I see the menu? *Mohu dostat lístek?*
Do you have a vegetarian menu? *Máte vegetariánskou nabídku jídel?*
I would like... *Rád bych...* (man), *ráda bych...* (woman)
Waiter! *Pane vrchní!*
Is service included? *Je v tom zahrnuto spropitné?*

Around town

Town *Město*
Old Town *Staré město*
New Town *Nové město*
House/building *Dům*
Private house/detached house *Vila*
Apartment block (built from prefabricated panels) *Panelák*
Street *Ulice*
Pavement *Chodník*
Lane *Ulička*
Avenue *Třída*
Square *Náměstí*
Market/marketplace *Trh*
Covered arcade/mall *Pasáž*
Steps *Schody*
Bridge *Most*
River *Řeka*
Island *Ostrov*
Embankment *Nábřeží*
Garden/s *Zahrada/Sady*
Tower *Věž*

TRANSPORT

ACCOMMODATION

ACTIVITIES

A – Z

LANGUAGE

Church *Kostel*
Cathedral/large church *Katedrála/Chrám*
Chapel *Kaple*
Monastery *Klášter*
Synagogue *Synagoga*
Cemetery *Hřbitov*
Castle/stronghold *Hrad*
Castle/country house *Zámek*
Palace *Palác*
Gate *Brána*
Courtyard *Dvůr*
Town hall *Radnice*
Theatre *Divadlo*
Cinema *Kino*
Museum *Muzeum*
Gallery *Galerie*
Exhibition *Výstava*
Embassy *Velvyslanectví*
Hospital *Nemocnice*
Post office *Pošta*
Swimming pool *Koupaliště*

Shopping, banks, etc.

Where is the nearest ...? *Kde je nejbližší ...?*
Do you have ...? *Máte ...?*
Do you have anything cheaper/bigger/smaller? *Máte něco levnějšího/většího/menšího?*
I'll take it *Vezmu si to*
Anything else? *Ještě něco?*
May I have a bag? *Mohu dostat sáček?*
I am just looking *Jenom se dívám*
Cheap *Levný/á/é*
Expensive *Drahý/à/é*
Enough *To stačí*
Too much *Příliš moc*

Antiques *Starožitnosti*
Bakery *Pekařství*
Bookshop *Kníkupectví* or just *Knihy* ("books")
Chemist *Drogérie*
Delicatessen *Lahůdky*
Fashion *Móda*
Florist *Květinářství*
Grocery *Potraviny*
Newsagent *Noviny/Časopisy*
Patisserie *Cukrárna*
Pharmacy *Lékárna*
Sale *Výprodej*
Second-hand books *Antikvariát*
Shoe shop *Obuv*
Shop *Obchod*

Souvenir shop *Suvenýry*
Stationer *Papírnictví*
Supermarket *Samoobsluha*
Travel agent *Cestovní kancelář*

Bank *Banka*
Bureau de change *Směnárna*
I want to change ... *Chci vyměnit ...*
British pounds *Britské libry*
American dollars *Americké dolary*
Czech crown/Czech crowns *Česká koruna/České koruny*
What is the exchange rate? *Jaký je kurs?*
Travellers cheques *Cestovní šeky*
Cashpoint *Bankomat*

Post office *Pošta*
How much is a letter/postcard to ...? *Kolik stojí dopis/pohlednice do ...?*
Postage stamps *Známky*
Parcel *Balík*
Airmail *Letecká pošta*
Letterbox *Poštovní schránka*

Telephoning

Telephone box *Telefonní budka*
Telephone directory *Telefonní seznam*
Yellow pages *Zlaté stránky*
Number *Číslo*
Extension *Linka*

How do I make an outside call? *Je to vnitří linka?*
I want to make an international call *Chtěl bych volát do zahraničí*
Hello *Haló*
May I speak to *Rád bych mluvil s...(male)/Ráda bych mluvila s..(female)*
Who is calling? *Kdo volá?*
Hold the line *Moment, prosím*
The line is busy *Mluví* (lit: "they are speaking") or *je obsazeno* ("it is occupied")
Sorry, wrong number *Promiňte, špatné číslo*

Health and emergenices

Help! *Pomoc!*
I need a doctor *Potřebují doktor*
Ambulance *Sanitka*

Police *Policie*
Fire brigade *Hasičský sbor/Hasiči*
Can you help me? *Můžete mi pomoci?*
I have had an accident *Měl jsem nehodu*
I'm ill *Jsem nemocný/nemocná*
It hurts here *Bolí mě tady*
I have lost ... *Ztratil jsem ...*
Passport *Pas*
Bag, attaché case *Taška*
Handbag *Kabelka*
Wallet *Náprsní taška*

Countries, citizens (male and female), nationalities

America, American *Amerika, Američan/Američanka, americký/á/é*
Australia, Australian *Austrálie, Australan/Australanka, australský/á/é*
Canada, Canadian *Kanada, Kanad'an/Kanad'anka, kanadský/á/é*
Czech Republic, Czech *Česká Republika* or *Česko* (informal), *Čech/Češka, český/á/é*
England, Englishman/woman, English *Anglie, Angličan/Angličanka, anglický*
Great Britain, Briton, British *Velká Britanie, Brit/Britka, britský/á/é*
Ireland, Irishman/woman, Irish *Irsko, Ir/Irka, irský/á/é*
New Zealand, New Zealander, New Zealand *Nový Zéland, Novozéland'an/Novozéland'anka, novozélandský/á/é*
Scotland, Scotsman/woman, Scottish *Skotsko, Skot/Skotka, skotský/á/é*
Slovakia, Slovak *Slovensko, Slovák/Slovenka, slovenský/á/é*
United States *Spojené státy*
Wales, Welshman/woman, Welsh *Wales, Velšan/Velšanka, velšký/á/é*

I am English (male) *Jsem Angličan*
She is British *Je Britka*
He is American, she is Canadian *On je Američan, ona je Kanad'anka*

Menu reader

Breakfast and snacks
Chléb **Bread**
Džem **Jam**
Máslo **Butter**
Míchaná vejce **Scrambled eggs**
Vejce **Egg**
Vejce na měkko **Soft-boiled egg**
Vejce na tvrdo **Hard-boiled egg**
Vejce se šunkou **Ham and eggs**

Hors d'oeuvres (Studené předkrmy)
Soup **(Polévka)**
Bramborová polévka **Potato soup**
Čočková polévka **Lentil soup**
Dršťková polévka **Tripe soup**
Fazolová polévka **Bean soup**
Gulášová polévka **Goulash soup**
Hovězí polévka **Beef broth**
Hrachová polévka **Pea soup**
Rajská polévka **Tomato soup**
Slepičí vývar **Chicken broth**
Zelná polévka **Cabbage soup**
Zeleninová polévka **Vegetable soup**

Meat (Maso) and game (Zvěřina)
Grilovaný/á/é **Grilled**
Hřbet **Saddle**
Na smetaně **In a cream sauce**
Pečený/á/é **Roast/baked**
Plněný/á/é **Stuffed**
Ragú **Ragout**
Řízek **Steak** (of any kind of meat)
Sekaný/á/é **Minced**
Smažený/á/é **Fried**
Uzený/á/é **Smoked**
Vářený/á/é **Boiled**

Bažant **Pheasant**
Biftek **Steak**
Dančí hřbet **Saddle of venison**
Drůbež **Poultry**
Guláš **Goulash**
Holub **Pigeon**
Hovězí maso **Beef**
Husa **Goose**
Játra **Liver**
Jehněčí maso **Lamb**
Jelení maso **Venison**
Kachna **Duck**
Kančí maso **Boar**
Klobása **Sausage**
Klopsy **Meatballs**

Koroptev **Partridge**
Krocan **Turkey**
Kuře **Chicken**
Moravský vrabec **"Moravian sparrow"** (pork with caraway seeds)
Párek **Frankfurter**
Perlička **Guinea-fowl**
Roštěná **Sirloin**
Skopkové maso **Mutton**
Slanina **Bacon**
Slepice **Chicken**
Srnčí maso **Venison**
Svíčková pečeně na smetaně **Beef fillet in cream sauce**
Šunka **Ham**
Telecí maso **Veal**
Vepřové maso **Pork**
Vídeňský telecí řízek **Wiener schnitzel**

Fish (Ryba)
Humr **Lobster**
Kapr **Carp**
Losos **Salmon**
Pstruh **Trout**
Rybí file **Fillet of fish**
Sardelka **Anchovy**
Sardinka **Sardine**
Sleď **Herring**
Štika **Pike**
Treska **Cod**
Úhoř **Eel**

Fruit (Ovoce) and vegetables (Zelenina)
Brambory **Potatoes**
Brokolice **Broccoli**
Celer **Celery**
Chřest **Asparagus**
Cibule **Onions**
Citrón **Lemon**
Čočka **Lentils**
Fazole **Beans**
Hlávkový salát **Lettuce**
Houby **Mushrooms**
Hrách **Peas**
Hranolky **Chips**
Hrozny **Grapes**
Hruška **Pear**
Jablko **Apple**
Jahoda **Strawberry**
Kapusta **Curly kale**
Kompot **Stewed fruit**
Květák **Cauliflower**
Kyselé zelí **Sauerkraut**
Lečo **Mixture of peppers, tomato and onion**

Malina **Raspberry**
Meruňka **Apricot**
Mrkev **Carrot**
Okurka **Gherkin/cucumber**
Petržel **Parsley**
Pomeranč **Orange**
Pórek **Leek**
Rajské jablko **Tomato**
Rybíz **Currants**
Rýže **Rice**
Salát **Salad**
Špenát **Spinach**
Švestka **Plum**
Třešeň/třešně **Cherry/cherries**
Višně **Morello cherry**
Zelí **Cabbage** (white)

Side dishes (Přílohy), desserts (Moučník) and miscellaneous
Bramborák **Potato pancake**
Broskev **Peach**
Brynza **Sheep's cheese**
Buchty **Sweet dumplings**
Česnek **Garlic**
Čočka **Lentils**
Domácí **Home-made, local**
Dort **Cream cake**
Horký **Hot**
Hořčice **Mustard**
Houskové knedlíky **Bread dumplings**
Jablkový závin **Apple strudel**
Knedlík **Dumpling**
Koláč **Cake**
Krém **Cream**
Křen **Horseradish**
Majonéza **Mayonnaise**
Máslo **Butter**
Noky **Gnocchi**
Nudle **Noodles**
Obložený chlebíček **Open sandwich**
Ocet **Vinegar**
Olej **Oil**
Omáčka **Sauce**
Omeleta **Omelette**
Ořech **Nut**
Ovocné knedlíky **Fruit dumplings**
Palačinky **Pancakes**
Pepř **Pepper**
Povidla **Thick plum jam**
Rohlík **Roll**
Šlehačka **Whipped cream**
Sůl **Salt**
Švestkové knedlíky
Sýr **Cheese**
Tvaroh **Quark/curd cheese**
Zmrzlina **Ice cream**

FURTHER READING

History

Bohemia in History Mikuláš Teich (Ed.) (Cambridge 1998)
Scholarly essays on some of the decisive periods and events in the development of the Czech lands.

Cities of the Imagination – Prague Richard Burton (Signal Books 2003)
A "cultural and literary history" that gets beneath the skin of the city. Burton's discussions of key figures and events – from Jan Hus, alchemy and the Golem to Kafka, Hašek and the Velvet Revolution – are both insightful and thought-provoking.

The Coasts of Bohemia: a Czech History Derek Sayer (Princeton 1998)
Immensely detailed, affectionate deconstruction of how the Czech nation delved into its past in order to fabricate itself a modern identity, with Prague as one of its most potent symbols.

Czechs and Balances Benjamin Kuras (Baronet 1996)
London-based but Czech-born, journalist and playwright Kuras casts a satirical eye on the ups and downs of his country's evolution.

Gloria and Miseria – Prague During the Thirty Years War Michal Šroněk and Jaroslavá Hausenblasová (Gallery 1998)
Beautifully produced and lavishly illustrated, a large-format book giving a thorough account of the glories and miseries (mostly the latter) of the conflict sparked by the second defenestration of Prague.

The Killing of SS Obergruppenführer Reinhard Heydrich: 27 May 1942 Callum MacDonald (MacMillan 1989)

Appointed Acting *Reichsprotektor* of Nazi-occupied Bohemia-Moravia in late 1941, cold-blooded killer Heydrich was assassinated by Czechoslovak parachutists sent from Britain. This is the dramatic, definitive story of this event, its prehistory, and its terrible consequences, which included the destruction of the village of Lidice and the massacre or deportation of its inhabitants.

The Masaryks – The Making of Czechoslovakia Zbyněk Zeman (Tauris 1976)
Highlights the decisive historical role played by philosopher president Tomáš Garrigue Masaryk in the creation of the new country of Czechoslovakia out of the ashes of Austria-Hungary, and follows the career of his son Jan, bon viveur and Foreign Minister, whose life ended tragically in yet another of the defenestrations for which Prague is famous.

Prague in Black and Gold: the History of a City Peter Demetz (Penguin 1997)
Very readable thematic account by a returned exile evoking the events and personalities of Prague history from the city's legendary beginnings to the mid-20th century. Highly recommended.

Prague in the Shadow of the Swastika Callum MacDonald and Jan Kaplan (Melantrich 1995)
Evocation in text and rare black-and-white photography of everyday life under the Nazi heel in the "Protectorate of Bohemia-Moravia" between 1939 and 1945.

Prague: the Turbulent Century Jan Kaplan and Krystyna Nosarzevska (Könemann 1997)

Fascinating trawl through 20th century Prague, a coffee table monster profusely illustrated with material drawn from film-maker Kaplan's unique archive of photographs, magazines, illustrations and ephemera of all kinds. Text in three languages (English, French, German). See also:

Prague 1900–2000: A Hundred Years of the City of a Hundred Towers Jan Kaplan, Václav Ledwinka and Viktor Šlajchrt
Another cornucopia of material from the seemingly inexhaustible Kaplan archive.

We the People Timothy Garton Ash (Penguin 1990)
Eyewitness account of the thrilling events of late 1989. British journalist and academic Garton Ash was present in the smoke-filled Laterna Magika theatre as students and dissidents prepared the peaceful overthrow of Communism.

Art and Architecture

The Architecture of Prague and Bohemia Brian Knox (Faber 1962)
Scholarly but poetic exploration of its subject, based on the journeys undertaken by the author at a time when Czechoslovkia was virtually closed to visitors from the West.

The Architecture of New Prague 1895–1945 Rostislav Švácha (MIT 1997)
This weighty tome gives the most thorough account of the major contribution made by Czech architects to the evolution of architectural Modernism.

Czech Art Deco 1918–1938 Various authors (Obecní dům 1998)
Lavishly illustrated catalogue of the landmark exhibition held in the Municipal House in 1998 of

Art Deco artefacts of all kinds, from porcelain and ceramics to furniture, architecture and the graphic arts.

Czech Modern Art 1900–1960
The National Gallery in Prague (1995)
Based on the collections splendidly housed in Prague's Trade Fair Palace, this is a useful introduction to the undeservedly little-known early-20th-century masters of Czech Modernism.

Kubistická Praha/Cubist Prague 1909–1925: a Guidebook
Michal Bregant, Lenka Bydžovská, Vojtěch Lahoda, Zdeněk Lukeš, Karel Srp and Rostislav Švácha (Odeon 1995)
Bilingual introduction to the extraordinary effusion of Cubist art in early-20th-century Prague and its unique influence on building design.

Plečnik: the Complete Works
Peter Krečič (Academy 1993)
The life and works of the Slovene architect, a precursor of architectural Postmodernism, who spent the central years of his life transforming Prague Castle into a fitting residence for the president of the democratic First Republic of Czechoslovakia, Tomáš Masaryk.

Prague – a Guide to the 19th and 20th Centuries Jiří Šourek and Zdeněk Lukeš (Artfoto 1997).
The most accessible introduction to Prague's rich heritage of 19th- and 20th-century building, with stunning colour photography and brief descriptive texts.

Prague – a Guide to Twentieth Century Architecture Ivan Margolius (Artemis 1994)
Architectural journalist Margolius packs an enormous amount of information about Prague's pioneering modern architecture into this handy volume, one of a renowned pocket-sized series of books on architecture and design.

Prague – Eleven Centuries of Architecture: Historical Guide
Jaroslava Staňková, Jiří Štursa and Svatopluk Voděra (PAV 1992)
Comprehensive introduction and guide to the city's buildings from the earliest days to the late 20th century, profusely illustrated with helpful line drawings.

Prague – Fin de Siècle Petr Wittlich (London 1992)
The most thorough account of the wonderful flowering of Art Nouveau/Secessionism that took place in Prague in the late 19th/early 20th century.

Prague – Twentieth Century Architecture Jiří Hrůza, Michal Kohout, Vladimír Šlapeta and Stephan Templ (Zlatý řez 2002)
An excellent guide, available locally – in a handy format for taking around the city – with detailed maps, cross-referenced to the buildings' descriptions and numerous photographs.

Rudolf II and Prague: the Court and the City Eliška Fučíková and others (Eds) (Thames & Hudson 1997)
Superlative 800-page publication, richly illustrated, which accompanied the large-scale exhibition devoted to court and city in the reign of this most mysterious monarch, patron of astronomers and alchemists as well as artists.

Literature

The Good Soldier Švejk and His Fortunes in the World War
Jaroslav Hašek, translated by Cecil Parrott (Penguin 1973)
While some prefer the prewar, anonymous translation into English of the adventures of Hašek's iconic anti-hero (one of Penguin's very first publications), this version by a former British ambassador is 100% complete, omitting none of the beery conscript's many expletives and less-than-savoury exploits. Parrott also wrote a biography of Hašek. Entitled **The Bad Bohemian** (Bodley Head 1978), it traces the dissolute trail followed by Švejk's alcoholic creator, anarchic jokester and founder of the spoof political movement entitled "The Party for Moderate Progress within the Bounds of the Law".

The Golem Gustav Meyrink (Dover Publications 1986)
Written in 1913, this version of the legend of Rabbi Loew's clay homunculus is the classic version of the occult tale.

I Served the King of England
Bohumil Hrabal (Chatto & Windus 1989)
Surreal experiences of another Prague anti-hero, a waiter who worked in the famous Hotel Paříž, then served, not the King of England, but his country's German occupiers. The author, the much-loved and wholly original Hrabal, is perhaps better known for his **Closely Observed Trains**, brilliantly filmed by Jiří Menzel.

The Joke Milan Kundera (Penguin 1984)
A marvellously funny look at the absurdities of life under Communism, this is an early novel by Kundera, who is probably the best-known Czech contemporary writer internationally, famous above all for **The Unbearable Lightness of Being** which was made into a successful film.

Kafka, Love and Courage, the Life of Milena Jesenská Mary Hockaday (Deutsch 1995)
Milena Jesenská was one of Kafka's lovers as well as the translator of his works from German into Czech. This account of her extraordinary life is set against the fascinating background of artistic and literary Prague in the early years of the 20th century, when the city's German and Jewish traditions were still very much alive.

Life with a Star Jiří Weil (Collins 1988)
A fictionalised account of this Jewish writer's horrific life in hiding during the Nazi occupation.

Prague: a Traveller's Literary Companion Paul Wilson (Ed.) (Signal Books 1995)
This carefully chosen selection of writings featuring the city is an excellent introduction to its literary heritage.

Prague Tales Jan Neruda (various editions).
Charming short stories from the

backstreets of the 19th century city by the "Dickens of Malá Strana".

The Spirit of Prague Ivan Klíma (Granta 1993)
Incarcerated as a teenager in the ghetto town of Terezín/Theresienstadt like thousands of other Czech Jews, Klíma became one of the most perceptive chroniclers of life under Communism. This collection of essays is a fascinating account of the many and varied influences on his development as a writer over more than five decades, and set his fictional works (such as **A Summer Affair** 1979, **My Merry Mornings** 1979, **Judge on Trial** 1986) firmly in their context.

Traveller's Literary Companion: Eastern & Central Europe James Naughton (Ed.) (In Print 1995)
Though shorter than the similar compendium by Paul Wilson, Naughton's chapter on the Czech Republic is equally useful, and includes choice extracts from the works of major writers.

The Trial Franz Kafka, translated by W. and E. Muir (Penguin 2004). Also in Penguin Modern Classics and translated by the Muirs are **The Castle** and **Description of a Struggle and Other Short Stories**. Kafka's creation of shadowy worlds in which individuals are helpless in the face of an unfathomable authority was eerily prophetic of the atmosphere of Prague when it was in the grip of the totalitarian rule of Nazis, then of Communists. Despite the enthusiasm of today's tourist industry for his image, the contemporary city seems to have little left of the sinister character so tellingly evoked in his novels and short stories.

Miscellaneous

Franz Kafka: a Biography Max Brod (Da Capo Press 1995)
A reprint of the classic account of Kafka's life by his lifelong friend and editor.

Magic Prague Angelo Maria Ripellino (Picador 1994)

More deftly than any other writer, Ripellino conjures up the esoteric ambience of the city in which strangeness was the norm, from the days of Rabbi Löw and Emperor Rudolf onwards.

The Night of Wenceslas Lionel Davidson (St Martin's Press 1996)
In Communist times, Prague made an excellent background for Cold War thrillers, of which this is perhaps the best, a wonderful evocation of a city in which absurdity is mingled with menace.

Prague Farewell Heda Margolius Kovaly (Gollancz 1988)
Having survived the Nazi concentration camps, the author then lost her husband in the Stalinist show trials of the early 1950s. A chilling account of life under Communism.

Remember Dubček: Dubček and Czechoslovakia 1918–1990 William Shawcross (Hogarth Press)
Authoritative biography of the Slovak politician whose hopes of giving Communism a "human face" were crushed in the Warsaw Pact invasion of August 1968, but who made an extraordinary comeback as Speaker of the Czechoslovak Parliament in 1989 before dying tragically in a mysterious car crash.

The Serpent and the Nightingale Cecil Parrott (Faber 1977)
A former British ambassador, responsible for the definitive translation of The Good Soldier Švejk into English, indulges in wry recollections of his period of office in Prague. A fascinating glimpse of diplomatic life under the rigours of Communism.

So Many Heroes Alan Levy (Permanent Press 1980)
Originally entitled Rowboat to Prague, this is a compelling account of the period leading up to the Prague Spring of 1968 and of the invasion which followed. Levy was subsequently expelled, but returned in triumph to Prague after the Velvet Revolution to found the weekly Prague Post.

Utz Bruce Chatwin (Vintage 1998)
As fascinated by the ambience of "Magic Prague" as Ripellino, Chatwin tells this extraordinary but fact-based tale of an obsessive porcelain collector living in Prague's Jewish Josefov.

Václav Havel – A Political Tragedy in Six Acts John Keane (Bloomsbury 1999)
Incisive and thorough biography of the writer-dissident turned president, which comes to the sad conclusion that Havel's post-Velvet Revolution career was to follow a downward spiral from the sublime to the ridiculous.

FEEDBACK

We do our best to ensure the information in our books is as accurate and up to date as possible. The books are updated on a regular basis, using local contacts who painstakingly add, amend and correct as required. However, some mistakes and omissions are inevitable, and we are ultimately reliant on our readers to put us in the picture. We would welcome your feedback on any details related to your experiences using the book "on the road". Maybe we recommended a hotel that you liked (or another that you did not), or maybe there are interesting new attractions, or facts and figures you have found out about the country itself. The more details you can give us (particularly with regard to addresses, e-mails and telephone numbers), the better. We will acknowledge all contributions, and we will offer an Insight Guide to the best letters received.

Please write to us at:
Insight Guides
PO Box 7910
London SE1 1WE
United Kingdom
Or send e-mail to:
insight@apaguide.co.uk

PRAGUE STREET ATLAS

The key map shows the area of Prague covered by the atlas section. An index of street names and places of interest shown on the maps can be found on the following pages. For each entry there is a page number and grid reference.

Map Legend

Motorway with Junction	✈✈	Airport		Motorway	Ⓜ	Metro
Motorway (under construction)	✝✝	Church (ruins)		Dual Carriageway	🚌	Bus Station
Dual Carriageway	✝	Monastery		Main Roads	❶	Tourist Information
Main Road	🏰🏚	Castle (ruins)			✉	Post Office
Secondary Road	⸫	Archaeological Site		Minor Roads	✝	Cathedral/Church
Minor road	∩	Cave			☾	Mosque
Track	★	Place of Interest		Footpath	✡	Synagogue
International Boundary	🏛	Mansion/Stately Home		Railway	⚊	Statue/Monument
Province/State Boundary	❄	Viewpoint		Pedestrian Area		Tower
National Park/Reserve	⚑	Beach		Important Building	⌁	Lighthouse
Ferry Route				Park		

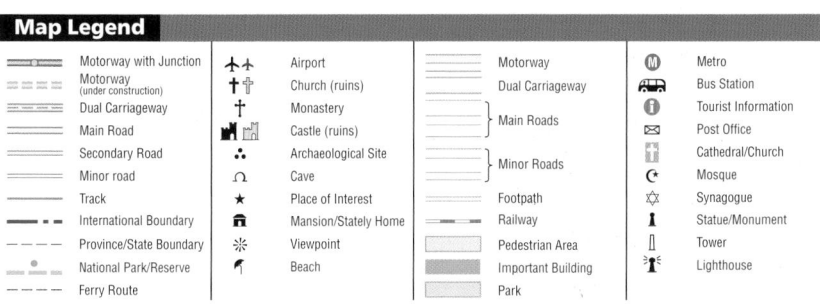

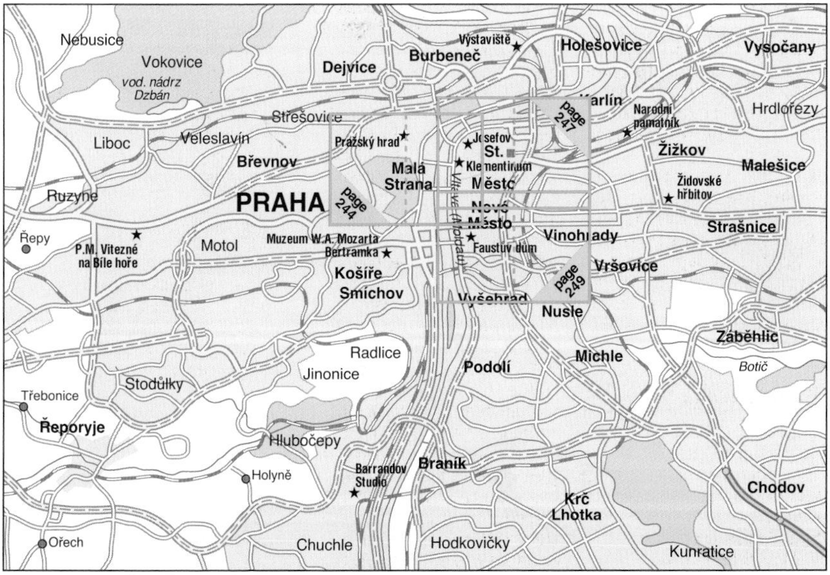

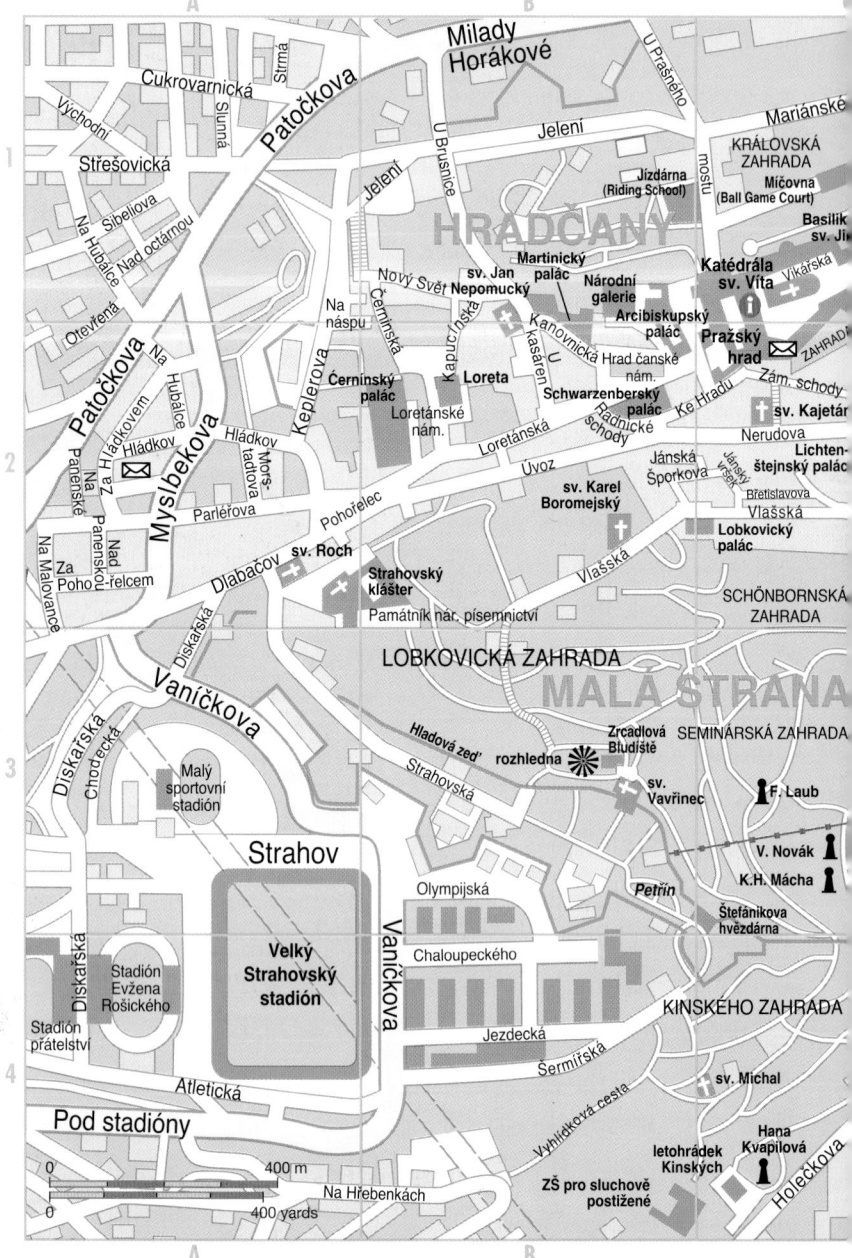

A   B

Cukrovarnická

Strmá

Patočkova

Milady Horákové

U Prašného mostu

Mariánské

Východní

Slunná

Jelení

KRÁLOVSKÁ ZAHRADA

Střešovická

Sibeliova

Na Hubálce

Nad octárnou

Jelení

U Brusnice

HRADČANY

Jízdárna (Riding School)

Míčovna (Ball Game Court)

Basilika sv. Ji

Otevřená

Na náspu

Nový Svět

Černínská

sv. Jan Nepomucký

Martinický palác

Národní galerie

Kanovnická

Kapucínska

Kasárni

Katédrála sv. Víta

Vikářská

Arcibiskupský palác

Pražský hrad

ZAHRAD

Patočkova

Na

Za Hládkovem

Hubálce

Hládkov

Myslbekova

Keplerova

Černínský palác

Loreta

Hrad čanské nám.

Schwarzenberský palác

Zám. schody

Ke Hradu

sv. Kajetár

Loretánské nám.

Loretánská

Radnické schody

Nerudova

Lichten-štejnský palác

Hládkov

Mors-tadtova

Úvoz

Jánská Šporkova

Jánský vršek

Břetislavova

Na Panenské

Parléřova

Pohořelec

sv. Karel Boromejský

Vlašská

Vlašská

Lobkovický palác

Na Panenské

Nad Panensko

Za Poho Ø-řelcem

Na Malovance

Diabačov

sv. Roch

Strahovský klášter

Památník nár. písemnictví

SCHÖNBORNSKÁ ZAHRADA

Diskařská

Vaníčkova

LOBKOVICKÁ ZAHRADA

MALÁ STRANA

Diskařská

Chodecká

Malý sportovní stadión

Hladová zeď' rozhledna

Strahovská

Zrcadlová Bludiště

sv. Vavřinec

SEMINÁŘSKÁ ZAHRADA

F. Laub

Strahov

Olympijská

Petřín

V. Novák

K.H. Mácha

Štefánikova hvězdárna

Diskařská

Stadión Evžena Rošického

Velký Strahovský stadión

Vaníčkova

Chaloupeckého

KINSKÉHO ZAHRADA

Stadión přátelství

Jezdecká

Šermířská

sv. Michal

Atletická

Vyhlídková cesta

letohrádek Kinských

Hana Kvapilová

Holečkova

Pod stadióny

0   400 m

0   400 yards

Na Hřebenkách

ZŠ pro sluchově postižené

A   B

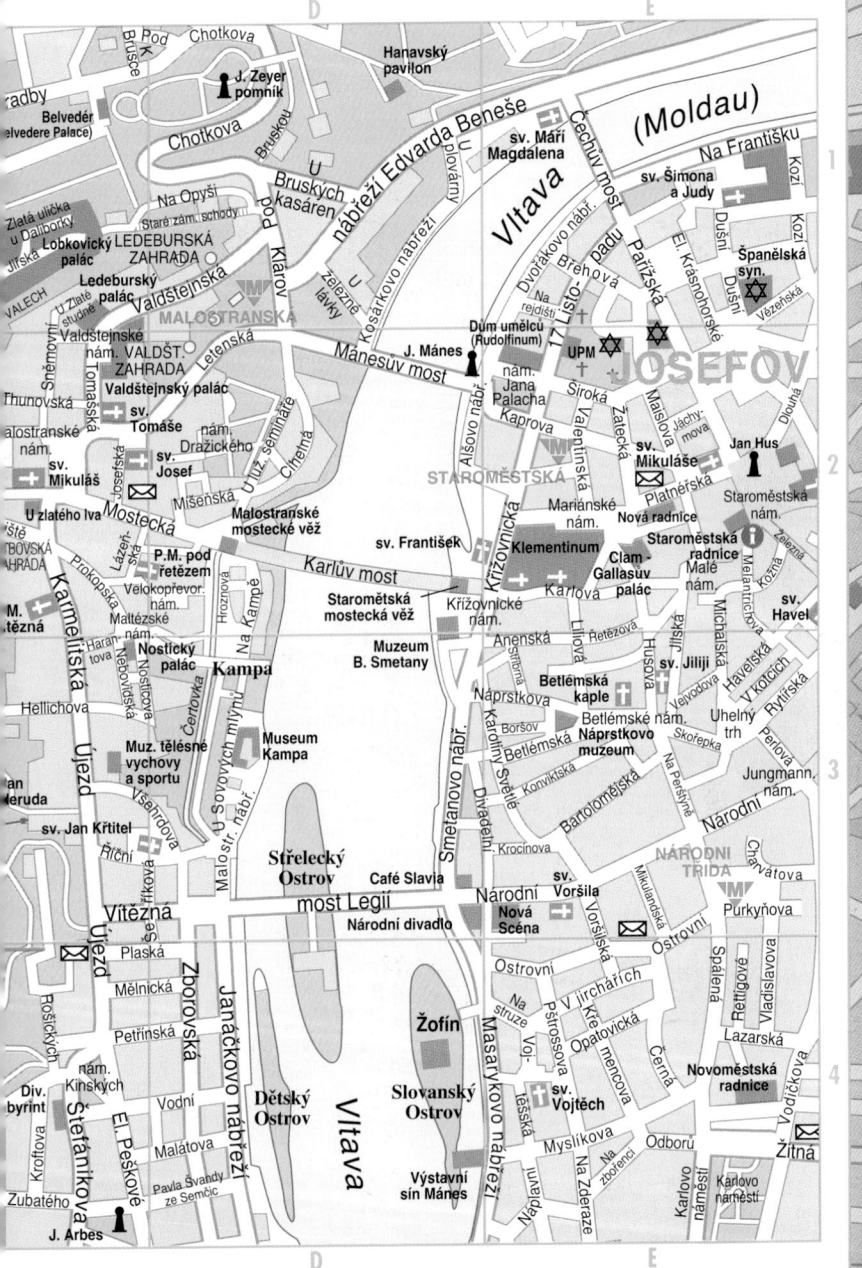

Pod Bruscu
Chotkova
K
Pod Bruscí
Hanavský
pavilon

radby
J. Zeyer
pomník

Belvedér
elvedere Palace)
Chotkova
Bruskou
U Bruských
kasáren
nábřeží Edvarda Beneše
U plovárny
sv. Maří
Magdaléna
Čechův most
(Moldau)
Na Františku
sv. Šimona
a Judy
Kozí

Zlatá ulička
u Daliborky
Jiřská
Na Opyši
Staré zám. schody
Pod Bruskou
Vltava
Dvořákovo nábř.
Břehová
Pařížská
El. Krásnohorské
Dušní
Dušní
Kozí
Vězeňská

VALECH
Lobkovický
palác
LEDEBURSKÁ
ZAHRADA
U Klárov
17. listo-
padu
Na
rejdišti
Španělská
syn.

U Zlaté
studně
Ledeburský
palác
Valdštejnská
železná
lávka
Košátkovo nábřeží
Dům umělců
(Rudolfinum)
UPM
JOSEFOV
Dlouhá

Šmýnou
Valdštejnské
nám.
MALOSTRANSKÁ
Letenská
Mánesův most
J. Mánes
nám.
Jana
Palacha
Široká
Maiselova
Jáchymova

Thunovská
Tomášská
VALDŠT.
ZAHRADA
Valdštejnský palác
sv.
Tomáše
nám.
Dražického
U luž. semináře
Chetná
Alšovo nábř.
Kaprova
STAROMĚSTSKÁ
Valentinská
Žatecká
sv.
Mikuláše
Platnéřská
Jan Hus
Staroměstské
nám.
Vězeňská

alostranské
nám.
sv.
Mikuláš
Josefská
sv.
Josef
Mišeňská
Malostranské
mostecké věž
sv. František
Mariánské
nám.
Nová radnice
Staroměstská
radnice
Malé
Melantrichova
Kožná
sv.
Havel

U zlatého lva
Mostecká
'ŠTĚ
'BOVSKÁ
AHRADA
Prokopská
Lázeň-
ská
P.M. pod
řetězem
Na Kampě
Karlův most
Křížovnická
Klementinum
Clam-
Gallasův
palác
nám.
Michalská
Jilská
Havelská
V kotcích
Rytířská

M.
těžná
Karmelitská
Nebovidská
Velkopřevor.
nám.
Velkopřevor-
ská
Hroznová
Staroměstská
mostecká věž
Křížovnické
nám.
Karlova
Liliová
Řetězová
sv. Jiljí
Vejvodova
Perlová

Hellichova
Nostický
palác
Kampa
Čertovka
Anenská
Smetana
Náprstkova
Betlémská
kaple
Husova
Jalovcová
Skořepka
Uhelný
trh
Jungmann.
nám.

an
eruda
Harant-
ova
Muz. tělesné
výchovy
a sportu
Museum
Kampa
U Sovových mlýnů
Malostr. nábř.
Náprstkova
Karoliny
Světlé
Boršov
Betlémská
Konviktská
Betlémské nám.
Náprstkovo
muzeum
Bartolomějská
Na Perštýně
Národní
nám.

sv. Jan Křtitel
Všehrdova
Smetanovo nábř.
Divadelní
Krocinova
NÁRODNÍ
TŘÍDA
Charvátova

Vítězná
Úlezd
Říční
Střelecký
Ostrov
most Legii
Café Slavia
Národní divadlo
Národní
Nová
Scéna
sv.
Voršila
Voršilská
Ostrovní
Purkyňova
Spálená

Plaská
Mělnická
Ostrovní
Na
struze
Voj-
V jirchářích
Pštrossova
Křemencova
Opatovická
Černá
Rettigové
Lazarská
Vladislavova

Petřínská
Zborovská
Janáčkovo nábřeží
Žofín
Masarykovo nábřeží
sv.
Vojtěch
Novoměstská
radnice
Vodičkova

Div.
labyrint
nám.
Kinských
Vodní
Malátová
Dětský
Ostrov
Slovanský
Ostrov
Mysliková
Na zbořenci
Odborů
Žitná

Zubatého
Štefánikova
El. Peškové
Pavla Švandy
ze Semíc
Vltava
Výstavní
síň Mánes
Na Zderaze
Karlovo
náměstí
Karlovo
náměstí

J. Arbes

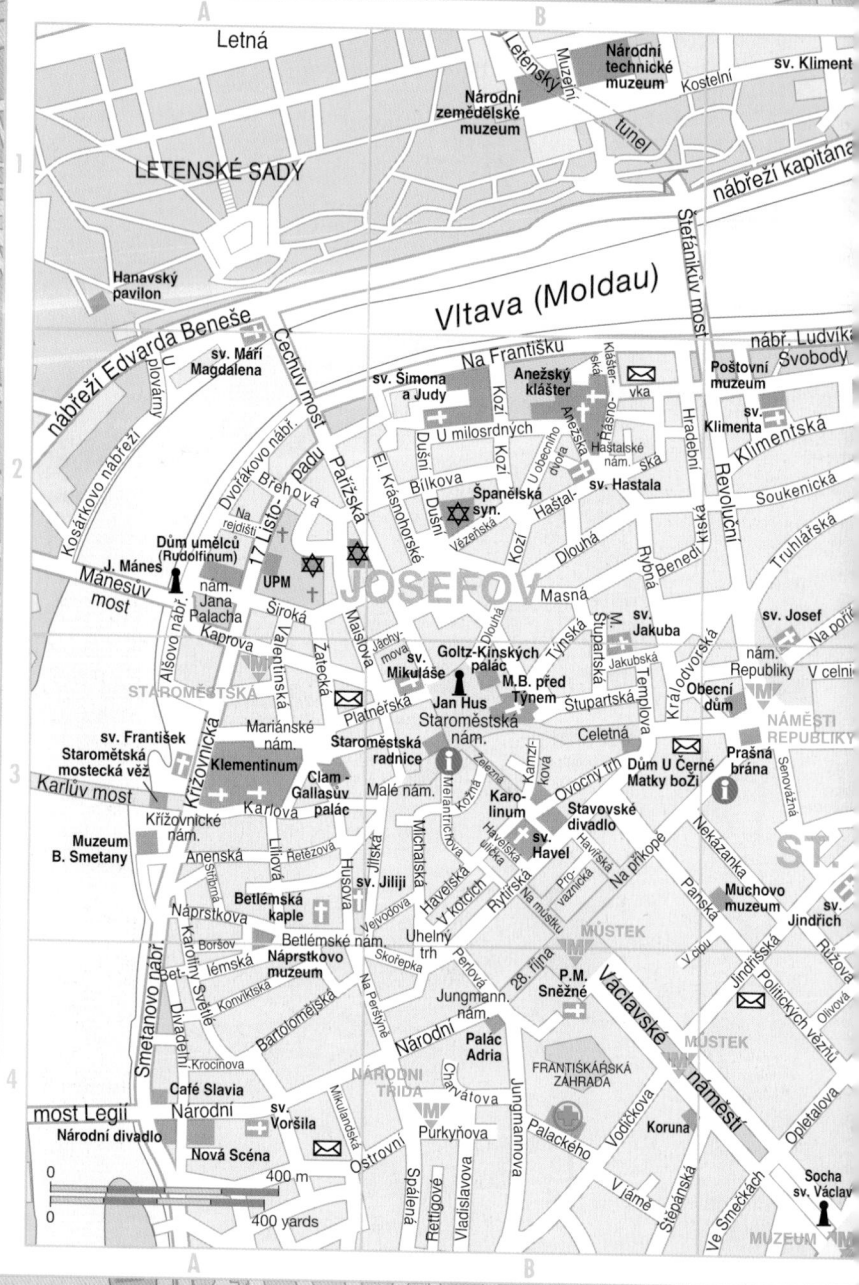

Letná

Letenský

Muzejní

Národní technické muzeum

sv. Kliment

Kostelní

Národní zemědělské muzeum

LETENSKÉ SADY

tunel

nábřeží kapitána

Štefánikův most

Hanavský pavilon

Vltava (Moldau)

nábřeží Edvarda Beneše

Na Františku

nábř. Ludvíka Svobody

sv. Máří Magdalena

Klášterská

Poštovní muzeum

Čechův most

Dvořákovo nábř.

sv. Šimona a Judy

Anežský klášter

vka

sv. Klimenta

Klimentská

Kozí

U milosrdných

Anežská

Haštalské nám.

Revoluční

Soukenická

Na rejdišti

17. Listo-padu

Břehová

Pařížská

E. Krásnohorské

Dušní

Kozí

U obecního dvora

Haštalská

sv. Hastala

Bílkova

Dušní

Španělská syn.

Kozí

Haštal-

Hradební

Truhlářská

Kozárkovo nábřeží

Dům umělců (Rudolfinum)

Vězeňská

Dlouhá

Rybná

Benedi

Na poříč

J. Mánes

Mánesův most

Alšovo nábř.

UPM

nám. Jana Palacha

Široká

JOSEFOV

Masná

sv. Jakuba

M. Řezníků

sv. Josef

Kaprova

Valentinská

Maiselova

Jáchy-mova

sv. Mikuláše

Goltz-Kinských palác

Týnská

Štupartská

Jakubská

Templová

nám. Republiky

V celni

STAROMĚSTSKÁ

Žatecka

Platnéřská

Jan Hus

M.B. před Týnem

Štupartská

Obecní dům

NÁMĚSTÍ REPUBLIKY

sv. František

Mariánské nám.

Staroměstská radnice

Staroměstské nám.

Celetná

Králodvorská

Prašná brána

ST.

Staroměstská mostecká věž

Křižovnická

Klementinum

Clam-Gallasův palác

Malé nám.

Melantrichova

Železná

Kamzí-ková

Karolinum

Ovocný trh

Dům U Černé Matky boží

Senovážna

Karlův most

Křížovnické nám.

Karlova

Husova

Jilská

Michalská

Havelská

Kožná

Stavovské divadlo

Na příkopě

Nekázanka

Panská

Muzeum B. Smetany

Anenská

Liliová

Retězová

Havelská

Na můstku

sv. Havel

Havířská

Na příkopě

Muchovo muzeum

sv. Jindřich

Betlémská kaple

Smetanovo nábř.

Skořepka

Náprstkova

Boršov

sv. Jiljí

Vejvodova

V kotcích

Rytířská

Provaznická

MŮSTEK

V cípu

Jindřišská

Růžová

Karoliny Světlé

Betlémská

Betlémské nám.

Náprstkovo muzeum

Konviktská

Uhelný trh

Perlová

28. října

Politických vězňů

Olivová

Na Perštýně

Jungmann. nám.

P.M. Sněžné

Václavské náměstí

Divadelní

Bartolomějská

Národní

Palác Adria

FRANTIŠKÁŘSKÁ ZAHRADA

MŮSTEK

Krocínova

Café Slavia

Národní

sv. Voršila

Charvátova

Jungmannova

Palackého

Koruna

Opletalova

most Legii

Národní divadlo

Nová Scéna

NÁRODNÍ TŘÍDA

Mikulandská

Purkyňova

Vodičkova

Štěpánská

Ve Smečkách

Socha sv. Václav

0   400 m

0   400 yards

Ostrovní

Spálená

Rettigové

Vladislavova

V jámě

MUZEUM

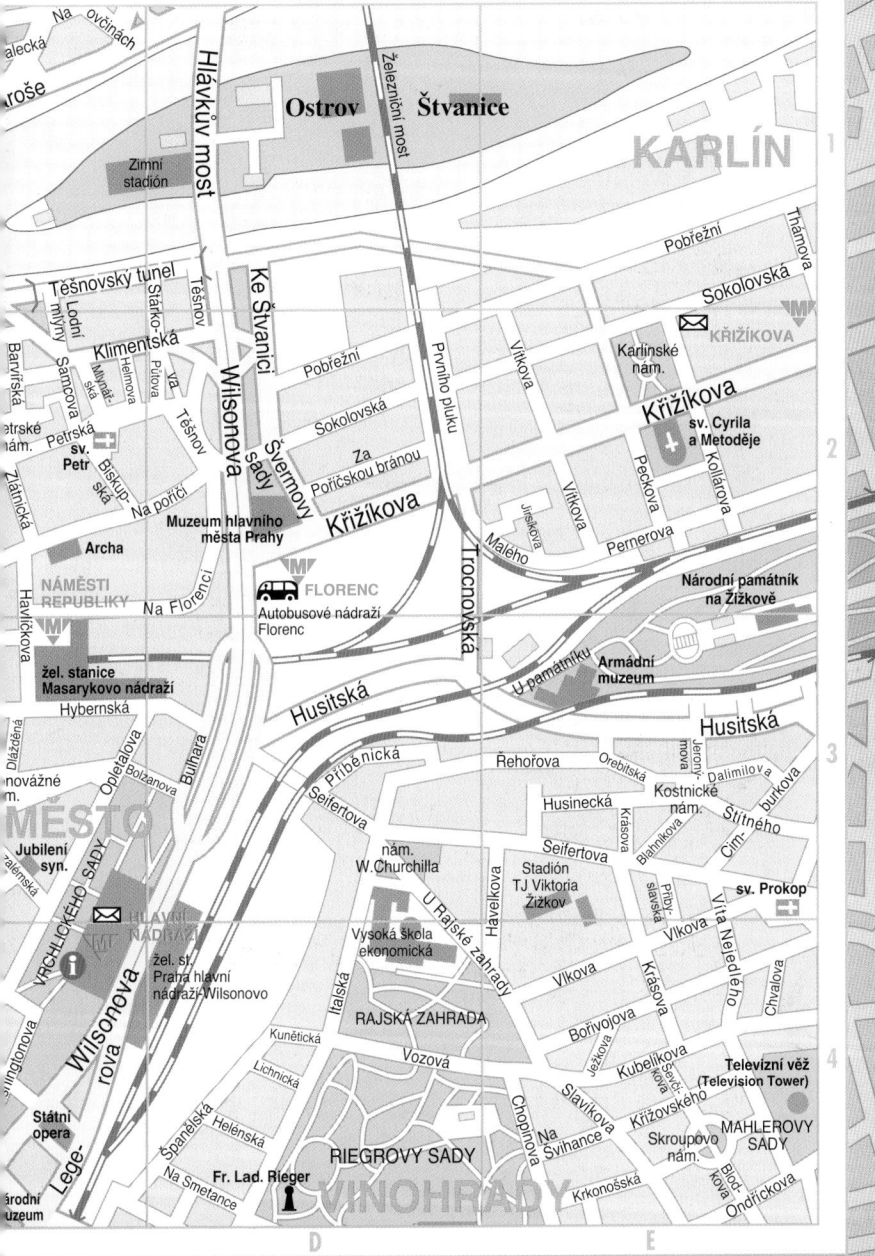

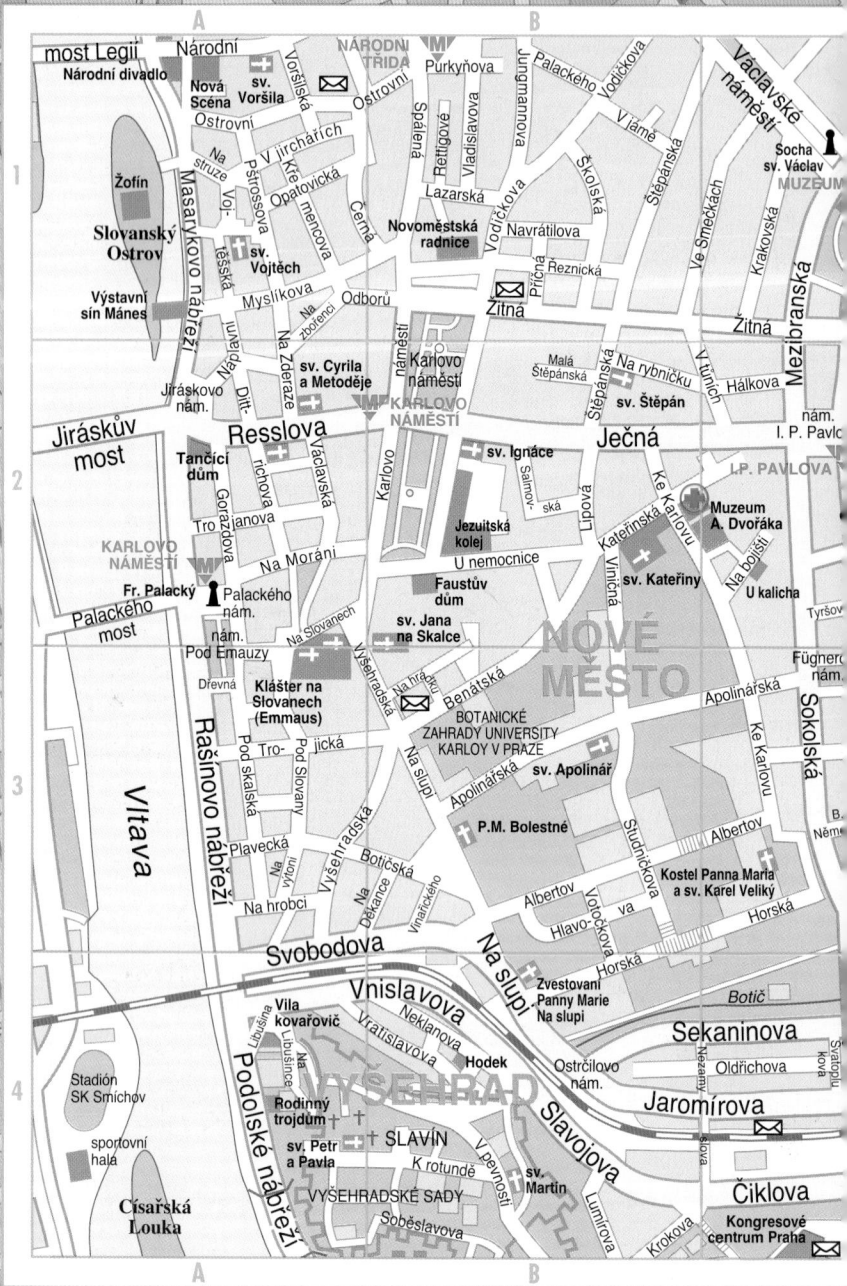

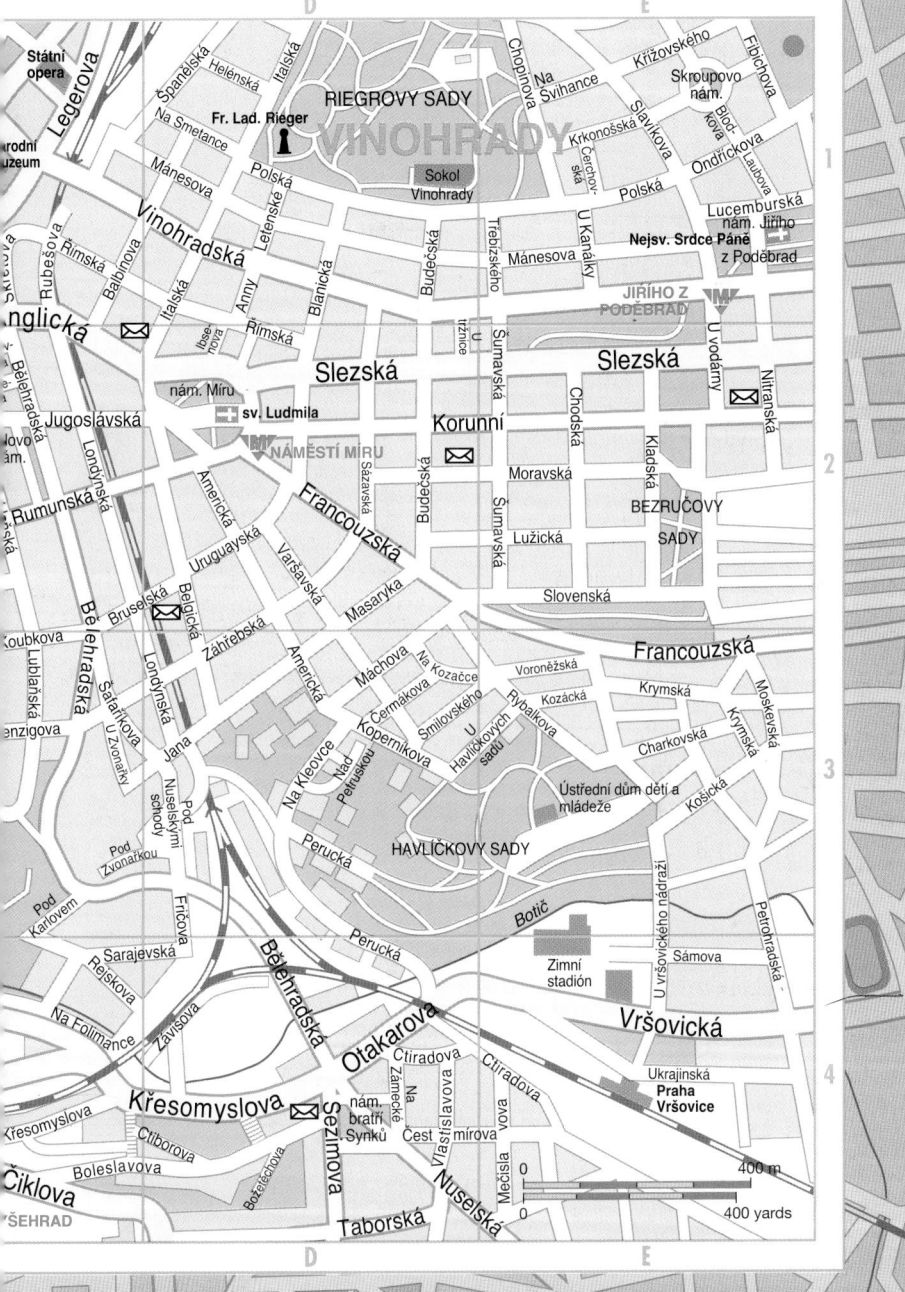

Státní opera

Legerova

rodní uzeum

Španělská Helénská Italská

Na Smetance

Fr. Lad. Rieger

RIEGROVY SADY

Chopinova

Na Švihance

Křížovského

Skroupovo nám.

Fibichova

VINOHRADY

Krkonošská Slavíkova

Blodkova

Ondříčkova

Mánesova

Polská

Letenské

Sokol Vinohrady

Krkonošská Čechova-ská

Polská

Laubova

Vinohradská

Rubešova Balbínova

Řimská

Italská

Anny

Blanická

Budečská

Třebízského

Mánesova

U Kanálky

Lucemburská nám. Jiřího

Nejsv. Srdce Páně z Poděbrad

nglická

Ibsenova

Řimská

tržnice

Šumavská

JIŘÍHO Z PODĚBRAD

U vodárny

Slezská

Slezská

Slezská

nám. Míru

sv. Ludmila

Korunní

Chodská

Kladská

Nitranská

NÁMĚSTÍ MÍRU

Budečská

Sázavská

Moravská

Šumavská

BEZRUČOVY SADY

Bělehradská

Jugoslávská

lova ám.

Rumunská

Londýnská

Americká

Francouzská

Lužická

Slovenská

Uruguayská

Varšavská

Masaryka

Bruselská

Belgická

Zahřebská

Máchova

Na Kozačce

Voroněžská

Francouzská

Koubkova

Lublaňská

Londýnská

Americká

Čermákova

Smilovského

Kozácká

Rybalkova

Krymská

Moskevská

enzigova

Šafaříkova

U Zvonařky

Jana

Kopernikova

U Havlíčkových sadů

Charkovská

Krymská

Na Kleovce

Nad Petruskou

Ústřední dům dětí a mládeže

Košická

Pod Nuselskými schody

HAVLÍČKOVY SADY

Petrohradská

Pod Zvonařkou

Perucká

Botič

Pod Karlovem

Fričova

Perucká

Zimní stadión

Sámova

Sarajevská

Rejskova

Bělehradská

U vršovického nádraží

Na Folimance

Závišova

Otakarova

Ctiradova

Vršovická

Na Zámecké

Ctiradova

Ukrajinská

Praha Vršovice

Křesomyslova

Sezimova

nám. bratří Synků

Čest

mírova

vova

Mečisla

Křesomyslova

Ctiborova

Boleslavova

Boženíčkova

Vlastislavova

Nuselská

0   400 m

Čiklova

ŠEHRAD

Taborská

0   400 yards

STREET INDEX

ART & PHOTO CREDITS

GENERAL INDEX

Prague Transport System

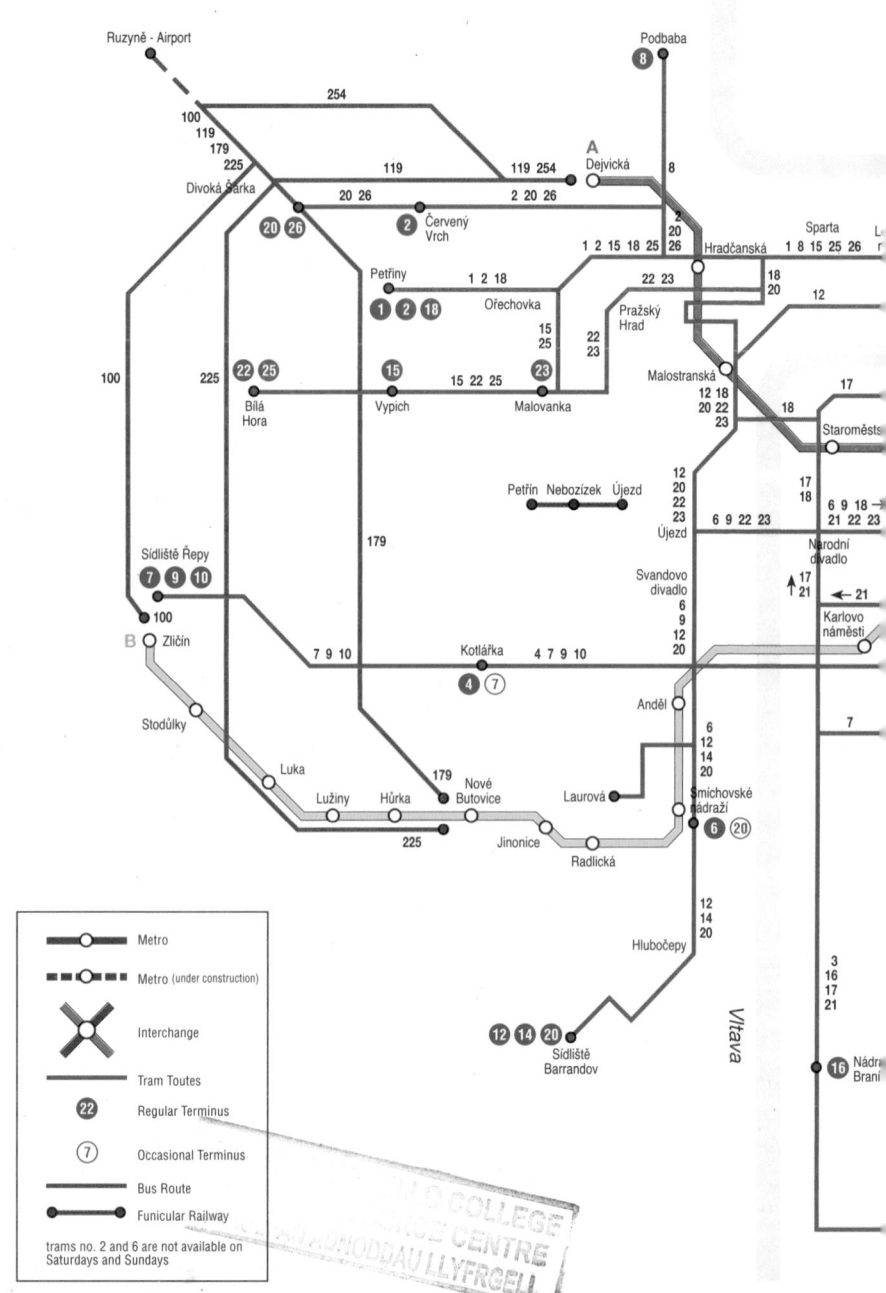